INTERNATIONAL VELVET

'To re-engage with the 1990s Welsh music scene via Neil Collins's excellent book has been a joy. It was such a formative time of my life and career having had the privilege of recording with many incredible artists. However, it was the friendships, the sense of camaraderie, the late-night discussions in Clwb Ifor Bach, or wandering home to Canton after experiencing another great new artist inspired by the Welsh musicians around them that brings back the most inspiring memories of that era.'
Greg Haver, producer and musician

'If you grew up in Wales in the '70s, rocked Bogiez nightclub in the '80s, fell apart in the '90s, then got back together in the noughties, then Neil Collins's *International Velvet* will take you on a wonderful romantic trip through your musical past. A fab read!'
Jay Pepper, Tigertailz

'Neil Collins has nailed it.
This is the history of a revolution that went right.'
Huw Williams, The Pooh Sticks

INTERNATIONAL VELVET

HOW WALES CONQUERED THE '90s CHARTS

Neil Collins
with a Foreword by Rhys Mwyn

Calon

2024

www.uwp.co.uk

British Library Cataloguing-in-Publication Data
A catalogue record for this book is available from the British Library.

ISBN: 978-1-91527-930-9

The right of Neil Collins to be identified as author of this work has been asserted in accordance with sections 77 and 79 of the Copyright, Designs and Patents Act 1988.

Cover artwork by Andy Ward
Typeset by Agnes Graves
Printed and bound in Great Britain by Bell & Bain Ltd, Glasgow

The publisher acknowledges the financial support of the Books Council of Wales.

For Mam and Dad

**To be born in Wales,
Not with a silver spoon in your mouth,
But, with music in your blood
And with poetry in your soul,
Is a privilege indeed.**

Brian Harris – 'In Passing' (1967)

CONTENTS

CONTENT NOTES

John Peel is mentioned frequently throughout this book. During his life and since his death in 2004, he has been the subject of sexual misconduct allegations (although he was never charged for any offences).

References to Peel throughout are in his capacity as a BBC Radio 1 DJ, who was very influential in raising the profile of Welsh bands and especially for his broadcasting of Welsh-language music to a UK audience.

The sexual offences of Lostprophets singer Ian Watkins are well documented elsewhere. A brief reference is made solely in terms of historical fact that the band topped the UK albums chart in 2006.

As this book is predominantly set in the '90s, venues are referred to as they were known then: Millennium Stadium and Cardiff International Arena (now known as Principality Stadium and Utilita Arena Cardiff respectively). The National Stadium (1984–97) is called by its more commonly used name, Cardiff Arms Park.

I have provided English translations of Welsh names where it will enhance the reader's understanding of this era. Please note that these translations come with a heavy dose of personal interpretation and Welsh-language speakers may bring their own meanings to these words.

FOREWORD

BY RHYS MWYN

Wales has always produced great bands, great artists, great singers, great songs. 'They Shoot Horses Don't They?', arguably one of the greatest songs of all time, was written and recorded by Rhondda band Racing Cars. Or take Badfinger, from Swansea, surely the epitome of a 'cult band'. And then we have The Alarm, Rhyl's finest, who went on to huge international success in the 1980s. At the time, it was just that most people had no idea they were Welsh. They do now!

By the 1970s, Welsh-speaking musicians and language campaigners had realised that forming rock bands singing (mostly exclusively) *yn Gymraeg* (in Welsh) was the key to reaching a new generation of 1960s-activism-inspired youth who were ready for Edward H. Dafis (although Meic Stevens always hedged his bets). Rock 'n' roll in their/ our own language. A soundtrack to the revolution. This is key to understanding what happens next.

Many people in many places on many occasions, must have pointed out that 'Welsh-language music' is not a genre. It's not even a thing. You can sing in the Welsh language and you can have music from Wales, which would be 'Welsh music'. The *Cymraeg* speakers are just as guilty: '*cerddoriaeth Gymraeg*' ('Welsh music') is just as nonsensical. It can only ever be '*Cymreig*' as in – 'of the place'. Finally, today, in 2024, it's more a case of 'we sing in Welsh – get with the programme'. I genuinely believe the majority (everywhere) have well and truly 'got over it'.

At the time of writing, bands like Adwaith and triple harpist Cerys Hafana use both English and *Cymraeg* (mainly the latter) and are making an impression way beyond Wales. New upstarts constantly shout and heckle from the sidelines. Soon there will be a new band or artist, a new buzz, and we'll all be talking, watching, listening, tuning in and cheering them on.

But this was not always the case. Sometime around 1992–3, the main bands singing in the Welsh language (who had all formed in the '80s) – I'm thinking specifically of Y Cyrff and Ffa Coffi Pawb – had reached the end of the road. Back and forth on the A470 provided no new adventures. The only prospects were repetition, another headline gig at the Eisteddfod and possibly the odd jaunt around Europe. Even at the occasional London gig we were jokingly referred to as futile or token gestures.

And so, they all split, or rather morphed into new bands. This is a crucial point in time as we welcome the Super Furry Animals and Catatonia, with experienced musicians from other bands such as U Thant, Crumblowers and Y Gwefrau making up the crack teams. Catatonia and the Furries would become the leading shining lights of this next stage. Gorky's Zygotic Mynci would be the new kids on the block, less obviously commercial, but bilingual from the off and destined to make an impression and be a cult band. Wales is rather good at producing 'cult bands'.

A simplified analysis would be that the Welsh-language bands of the '80s aspired to a John Peel Session on Radio 1. The '90s Welsh bands singing in Welsh, English or both languages aspired to *Top of the Pops*. The Welsh-language bands of the '80s had gathered around several rallying calls. Firstly, no singing in English! This was both political and due to the fact that composing in Welsh came naturally. Secondly, and very broadly, they had defined themselves as 'underground' and in open rebellion against the old traditional Welsh ways of doing things. Within a wider context this would be post-punk, anarcho-punk and in the tradition of independent labels. In other words, had Datblygu sung in English they may well have ended up on Rough Trade alongside Young Marble Giants.

Punk rock has to be acknowledged somewhere in this cultural mixing pot. Without punk rock there would have been no post-punk and Datblygu may never have happened. Punk had a huge effect culturally and especially so in Wales. It allowed us to rebel within a Welsh context. Let's argue that without punk rock, there's no Manic Street Preachers, but you would have had Stereophonics.

Interestingly, Anhrefn and Datblygu were to record several sessions for John Peel (Anhrefn recording the first-ever Welsh-language session for Radio 1). But, and again this is a key point, Peel always regarded Y Cyrff as being too commercial. And there is the clue, Y Cyrff frontman Mark Roberts went on to compose Top 10 hits with co-writer Cerys Matthews as a member of Catatonia.

The Alarm had an awakening in the late 1980s – Mike Peters started to learn the language and The Alarm started to wear their Welshness with pride. The Alarm were never to be included as part of Cool Cymru; that was for the new bands…

Newport and the south Wales valleys always had a strong rock tradition and produced fine bands, but it was the scene around TJ's in Newport in the early–mid-'90s that began to gain national attention. Manic Street Preachers and 60 Ft. Dolls probably struggled to find their Welsh voice initially, not singing in Welsh, not obviously 'Welsh' – or were they? They were brilliant bands though, with well-crafted songs and great choruses, plus they looked the way you wanted a band to look. Both these bands would have got to exactly where they did without Cool Cymru. From an academic/pop-theory point of view both the Manics and the Dolls offer great subject matter as to what constitutes Welshness, how their sense of place came through and how they came to terms with who they were.

I consider the Welsh pop landscape of today as one that has matured. The Welsh pop wars of the '70s, '80s and '90s were fought and won in a similar way to what happened with 'Madchester' or the trip-hop scene in Bristol or in Liverpool at Eric's (the music club) including Echo and the Bunnymen, The Mighty Wah and The Teardrop Explodes. We now know that we were – and *are* – cool! Maybe it took *NME*, or whoever came up with Cool Cymru, but I've always argued that Cool Cymru is far better than Uncool Cymru. Our battles in the 1980s just to get a Welsh-language Peel Session or appearances on *The Tube* or *The Old Grey Whistle Test* by bands singing in Welsh (Anhrefn/Datblygu/Yr Cyrff) were always battles against being 'uncool' to London eyes. Funnily enough, even during the '80s Pop Wars, the audiences never seemed that bothered about bands singing in Welsh – if the music was good, they could dance!

The Welsh bands associated with Cool Cymru of course hated the name and denied being part of any scene – predictably and rightly so, not wanting to be defined or limited creatively. Even TJ's and Newport got lumped with the moniker the 'new Seattle'. Apart from releasing Catatonia's first records and sorting out early gigs for them, along with some European dates for a proto-Super Furry Animals, I was never involved with Cool Cymru. My work continued in Wales at a grassroots level with bands like Big Leaves, and very much a mentality of 'let's make a few records and see what happens.' Later on, in the 2000s, that process continued, making early records with Gwenno. She went on to make Cornish cool – the logical conclusion.

Whether Cymru was Cool or not in the eyes of the media, whatever we all thought, whatever viewpoint we took, let's not be naïve – the bands all gained from the exposure and hype during 1996–2000. Whether they liked being defined, whether the slogan was naff, the record sales and bank balances seemed to be going in the right direction. This is what they had all wanted. Shut up and stop moaning. It goes with the territory. *Top of the Pops*. Selling out. Singing in English. This was only the ghosts of Andy Warhol, Andrew Loog Oldham or Malcolm McLaren spinning things from Llanddewi-Brefi. Just imagine if Cool Cymru had never happened...

Rhys Mwyn
January 2024

PREFACE

'Every day when I wake up, I thank the Lord I'm Welsh…'[1]

There's no song that epitomises 1990s Wales quite like Catatonia's 'International Velvet'. Yet at the start of the decade, such a lyric was inconceivable.

Back then, Cymru was anything but cool. Tom Jones, Shirley Bassey, Shakin' Stevens and Bonnie Tyler may have been mega-selling pop acts, but what did Wales have to offer the alternative music fan?

Within a few short years though, an explosion of bands including Manic Street Preachers, Super Furry Animals, Stereophonics, Gorky's Zygotic Mynci, 60 Ft. Dolls, Feeder and, of course, Catatonia erupted from this quaint land of harps and choirs. By its release in 1998, their album (also named) *International Velvet* not only topped the UK charts, but cast a jealous eye from across the world onto Wales.

No longer the butt of music press jokes, this new generation of Welsh talent were releasing No. 1 records and celebrating with huge gigs. Simultaneously, stars like Catherine Zeta-Jones, Rhys Ifans, Colin Jackson and Joe Calzaghe were becoming household names. This rise in Welsh celebrity coincided with an increasing pride and respect for *Cymraeg* following the Welsh Language Act 1993, which put Welsh on an equal footing to English.

Plus, Wales was now ready to begin governing itself. After the devastating defeats of the past, devolution was achieved with a 'Yes' vote at the 1997 referendum along with the creation of a National Assembly for Wales two years later. The chorus of 'International Velvet' typifies that seismic shift in the nation's confidence – a feel-good factor encapsulating music, culture, sport, language and politics.

The incredible success of Welsh music in the second half of the '90s was unprecedented, but it was the groundwork spanning previous ten years that made it all possible.

Bubbling away under the surface in the early '90s was an intriguing Welsh-language scene, which led to the formation of not only two of Britain's best bands of the era, but also two of the greatest Welsh acts of all time: Super Furry Animals and Catatonia.

Each group was lambasted for making the decision to go big and sing in English, but both defied their critics while still embracing their bilingualism. By the millennium, the Super Furries released *Mwng* – the biggest-selling Welsh-language album of all time – while Catatonia's song 'International Velvet' captured the best of both worlds.

Its verses are delivered in Welsh before the euphoric, English-language chorus tells the world how proud they are of their national identity. The transition was complete once crowds from across the border belted back the words with the same vigour. *The Guardian* wrote: 'It's hard to decide which is the more improbable – a hall full of Londoners claiming to be Welsh, or a Welsh band inspiring such loyalty.'[2]

What is often lost in translation is its irony. It's highly unlikely that Catatonia thanked the Lord they were Welsh on a daily basis, but now a band was happy with wearing its Welshness on its sleeve. As Cerys Matthews told the *Daily Record*:

> Hopefully, by now people realise that Wales is brimmed full of talent and we're great people with massive brains.[3]

Obviously, its chorus can be easily latched onto and enjoyed on a superficial level. Yet, it's so over the top, how can it be viewed as anything other than ironic? Addressing narrow-minded views of the Welsh, the song's opening line depicts stereotypes of a small, oppressed nation that has little to offer other than its skill for singing: '*Deffrwch Cymry cysglyd, Gwlad y Gân*' ('Wake up, sleepy Wales, Land of Song'). It then continues with more overtly ironic jabs at Welsh cultural clichés and its history as a defeated nation.

Therefore, the verses portray the decades of doubt Wales suffered, while Cerys's triumphant howl in the chorus embodies the rebirth of a country at last comfortable in its own skin. When asked by *Melody Maker* if the song could become the new Welsh national anthem, Mark Roberts replied: 'Probably not. The melody's too difficult to have them singing in the streets at closing time.'

In '*Blerwytirhwng?*' *The Place of Welsh Pop Music*, Sarah Hill said:

PREFACE

Catatonia intend to play in the mainstream culture, but on their own terms – they do not intend to conform to the British notion of what Welshness is, and their bilingualism is a statement of fact which needs no justification. That is 'English', but not quite.[4]

If 'International Velvet' wasn't the national anthem, it was certainly emblematic of a modernised, progressive Wales at the end of the twentieth century, and its influence resonated in three key performances in 1999.

At Port Talbot's Margam Park in late May, over 30,000 screaming fans boomed out the chorus as one with as much gusto as a massed Welsh choir. Cerys confessed she wept while singing it.

The Margam Park performance of the song illustrated how much it had connected with the public. Days before, though, there had been an overblown rendition that stripped away its irony and saw it delve into pantomime. On Wednesday, 26 May 1999, the Welsh Assembly was officially inaugurated with the Voices of a Nation concert. Top of the organisers' list were Catatonia to sing a certain song to celebrate the occasion. If only the band weren't so busy with preparations for their Home Internationals gigs in Llangollen.

Instead, they granted the BBC permission for a stellar cast to perform their anthem. Enter stage-left Tom Jones, Shakin' Stevens, Max Boyce, Bonnie Tyler, Charlotte Church and Mike Peters et al. belting it out to a confused live audience, who couldn't hear over fireworks. A song that was penned as a piss-take had achieved its aim. As one unimpressed journalist wrote: 'The live TV concert to celebrate the opening of the Welsh Assembly was an unmitigated disaster... "International Velvet" should've been a rousing all-star finale, but instead it was unbelievably embarrassing for Wales.'[5]

Regardless, 'International Velvet' was the perfect song to promote Wales on the world stage and it was everywhere from soundtracking sporting montages to being referenced by academics as personifying the transition in post-referendum optimism.

This buoyant mood was perpetuated by the Rugby World Cup, which was hosted in Wales in 1999. The state-of-the-art Millennium Stadium was the ideal new home for Graham Henry's exciting squad after a mid-decade period in the doldrums. Soon to be labelled 'The

Great Redeemer', Henry masterminded a 29–19 victory over South Africa to open the venue on 26 June 1999.

Three months later, Catatonia were requested to start the Rugby World Cup opening ceremony. Forget the Top 5 singles 'Mulder and Scully' and 'Road Rage'; it was 'International Velvet' – an album track – that the organisers wanted to be part of a diverse ceremony celebrating the nation's past, present and future. With a huge banner declaring *'Croeso i Gymru'* ('Welcome to Wales'), Cerys strutted onstage and unveiled a Welsh rugby shirt matched with sequins and sparkly eyeliner.

Introducing Catatonia, presenter Alan Wilkins said:

> This is a momentous day in sporting history as the magnificent new Millennium Stadium in Cardiff hosts the opening ceremony of the fourth Rugby World Cup...
>
> A new spirit in Wales, a new vibrancy, a new energy, a country acclaimed as the 'Land of Song'. The Welsh love to perform and no one more so than Catatonia, who kick us off with their massive hit, 'International Velvet'...Young, Welsh talent taking Wales into the new century.

With Manic Millennium providing an epic finale to the decade a couple of months later, the fascinating story of Wales in the '90s is a mind-blowing journey of growth and confidence that continues to inspire the country's vibrant music scene today.

Wales was a nation finally off its knees, and standing proudly.

If it was a movie plot, it would all seem so far-fetched. Thankfully, it was all true.

A MUSICAL BACKWATER

THE WELSH SCENE PRE-1990s

Wales – the Land of Song…

A resounding voice founded in folk songs and hymns that brought communities together for generations.

You only have to experience the national anthem on matchday to realise that 'Hen Wlad Fy Nhadau' ('Land of my Fathers') still stirs the same emotions as when it was written by Evan James and his son James in Pontypridd in 1856.

It even inspired the Welsh rugby team to a rare victory over the All Blacks in December 1905 at Cardiff Arms Park. As the New Zealand players performed the haka, the 47,000 in attendance burst into the anthem – the first time one had been sung before a sporting fixture. Eighty minutes later, the final whistle was blown on a 3–0 win.

Singing has long been a hugely popular pastime in Wales. During the early twentieth century, the Nonconformist tradition in Welsh chapels went through a revival and every coal mine in the valleys had its own male voice choir that competed at the Eisteddfod.

In the BBC documentary *Wales: Music Nation*, Huw Stephens said:

> Chapel singing is a vital part of Welsh music history. Not just because of how many people participated, but of how inclusive and democratic it all was.
>
> Men sang with women, rich with poor, old with young. This was music for everybody, and that's key to the music tradition of Wales.[6]

Singing in the south Wales valleys wasn't unusual, but there was one man who took it to the world – and it was so intrinsic to his life that he couldn't imagine hailing from anywhere else.

Tom Jones was a keen participant in the school choir where he was told off for drowning out his schoolmates singing 'Men of Harlech'. He said:

> The Sunday school teacher used to live next door to us, so I couldn't get out of going to chapel…It was great because we were singing gospel hymns. 'The Old Rugged Cross' was always a big favourite…
>
> Pavarotti said to me Wales is the only other country apart from Italy that feel it so passionately about singing. He sang at an Eisteddfod when he was young, and he felt it from the Welsh audience like he would've done if he was in Italy.[7]

On his way to becoming known as 'Jones the Voice', he honed his craft in local workingmen's clubs belting out covers like 'Great Balls of Fire'. Developed from a love of American soul music, his rich, bluesy baritone soon caught the attention of record labels.

In January 1965, Jones surged to No. 1 with only his second single. Despite the BBC initially refusing to broadcast 'It's Not Unusual' due to Jones's combination of open-collared shirts and tightly tailored trousers, the track gained traction on UK pirate radio.

Jones was also a huge hit stateside where he emulated The Beatles by appearing on *The Ed Sullivan Show*. Introducing one of his performances, Sullivan said: 'While every American kid starts playing baseball when he is about six, every Welsh youngster starts singing when he is about six.'

Another Welsh singer making waves on both sides of the pond was Shirley Bassey. In 1959, 'The Girl from Tiger Bay' became the first Welsh artist to have a chart-topping UK single with 'As I Love You'. Like Tom Jones with 'Thunderball', Bassey became world-famous after a trio of James Bond themes for *Goldfinger*, *Diamonds Are Forever* and *Moonraker*.

The extraordinary success of Dame Shirley Bassey and Sir Tom Jones continues to endure.

In 2020, Shirley Bassey became the first artist to chart an album in the UK Top 40 in seven consecutive decades with *I Owe It All to You*.

At the age of eighty in 2021, Tom Jones became the oldest male artist to have a UK No. 1 album with *Surrounded by Time*.

Likewise, Pontardawe-born singer Mary Hopkin had a No. 1 in 1968 with her debut single 'Those Were the Days'. Released via Apple Records, it sold over 1.5 million copies stateside and was produced by Paul McCartney. Ironically, it was only kept off the US No. 1 spot by 'Hey Jude'.

Also on Apple Records and benefitting from McCartney's mentoring were Swansea legends Badfinger (a nod to 'Bad Finger Boogie' – the working title for The Beatles' song 'With a Little Help from My Friends'). They issued their first single, 'Maybe Tomorrow', as The Iveys in 1968, and, under their more familiar Badfinger moniker, *Magic Christian Music* in 1970. It featured the McCartney-penned 'Come and Get It', which secured them a Top 10 hit in the UK and US.

Another transatlantic Top 10 hit followed with 'No Matter What' on their next album, *No Dice*, which also included 'Without You' – a breathtaking ballad that won Badfinger's Pete Ham and Tom Evans an Ivor Novello Award for Best Song Musically and Lyrically in 1972. It has since been covered by approximately 200 artists including Harry Nilsson and Mariah Carey, who reached No. 1 with their versions.

Although Badfinger sold over 14 million albums worldwide, including classics like *Straight Up*, their legacy is a heartbreaking 'what if' story that turned them from a 'Welsh Beatles' into one of the most tragic tales in rock 'n' roll. Left in dire financial circumstances due to unscrupulous management, Pete Ham and Tom Evans hanged themselves.

The 1960s were also significant for something that was hugely influential in Wales, and for music generally. In 1963, Welsh brothers Kingsley and Charles Ward founded the legendary Rockfield Studios in Monmouthshire, which became the world's first residential studio, hosting countless chart-topping acts like Queen, who worked on 'Bohemian Rhapsody' there. By 1970, Rockfield had its first chart-topping single, and fittingly it was by a Welshman, who had helped with the studio's creation. After Cardiff blues-rock band Love Sculpture split, Dave Edmunds reached the summit with a cover of Smiley Lewis's 'I Hear You Knocking'.

One of Rockfield's earliest recording artists were Amen Corner. The Cardiff group were the first all-Welsh group to achieve a No. 1 hit with '(If Paradise Is) Half as Nice' in 1969 (although Swansea-born Spencer Davis topped the charts twice in 1966 with his Brummie band). Led by the distinctive high vocals of Andy Fairweather Low and named after the weekly disc spin at Cardiff's Victoria Ballroom, the band burned brightly throughout a short career bursting with mod-pop gems.

Another rock legend who loved Rockfield was Robert Plant. After Led Zeppelin disbanded following John Bonham's death, Plant retreated to south-east Wales to record a couple of solo albums.

Although Led Zeppelin never recorded at Rockfield, they are inextricably linked with Wales via an eighteenth-century cottage near Machynlleth called Bron-Yr-Aur. Not only did their write much of their classic third and fourth albums there, but it also lent its name to their tunes 'Bron-Yr-Aur' and 'Bron-Y-Aur-Stomp'.

As Beatlemania took over the world throughout the 1960s, first-language Welsh youngsters were yearning for something they could claim as their own.

At the dawn of the decade, something was starting to change in concert halls across rural Wales, and this feeling was catalysed by a famous speech in February 1962.

A BBC Radio broadcast by poet, playwright and academic Saunders Lewis titled *Tynged yr Iaith* ('The Fate of the Language') discussed the future of the Welsh language, which risked dying out.

Lewis pulled no punches criticising the complacency of Welsh speakers in allowing a private bill sponsored by the Liverpool Corporation to drown the Welsh-speaking village of Capel Celyn in the Afon Tryweryn valley. The subsequent flooding of the community in 1965 created a reservoir, Llyn Celyn, which supplied Liverpool with water for industry. Tryweryn became a symbol of shame for the growing resistance movement.

A MUSICAL BACKWATER

Months after Lewis's speech, Cymdeithas yr Iaith Gymraeg ('the Welsh Language Society') was formed as a direct action pressure group. It campaigned for Welsh people's rights to use the Welsh language in every aspect of their lives, while demanding equal and official status.

Welsh-language voices of rebellion became commonplace in music. Co-written with Dafydd Iwan and Meic Stevens, Huw Jones issued a protest song in the aftermath of Tryweryn that vented the fury of a generation.

Bolstered by Heather Jones's ethereal backing vocals, 'Dŵr' (meaning 'Water') became the first single released on Sain ('Sound') in October 1969 – the label co-founded by Dafydd Iwan, Huw Jones and Brian Morgan Edwards.

As civil rights protests raged in the States, unrest simmered on home soil. While Woodstock emphasised peace and love, those feelings weren't reciprocated when an Englishman became the Prince of Wales at Caernarfon Castle in July 1969. Cymdeithas also embarked on a campaign of painting over English road signs. Some activists were sent to jail, including Dafydd Iwan, who was imprisoned four times.

Other Welsh musicians just wanted to revel in the exciting American sounds coming through their radios. Five scruffy Aberystwyth University students called Y Blew (meaning 'The Hair') mimicked Byrds-like jangly riffs and mixed them with Welsh-language covers of Cream and The Beatles.

It was, however, an original song that captured the imagination. Armed with a mission statement of 'We want people to scream in bad Welsh'[8] in 1967 Y Blew released their only single, 'Maes B'. One-hit wonders they may have been, but its influence as the first Welsh-language rock record was huge.

Named after the field at the Eisteddfod where the band played, Maes B is now the world's biggest contemporary Welsh-language music festival and the little brother of the National Eisteddfod.

Long-haired and decked in denim, the '70s generation strayed from traditional folk and harmony singing styles. Some of them caught the ear of Sain including Bethesda-based Brân ('Crow' or 'Raven'), who turned heads during their five-year existence by combining trippy prog-folk riffs with Celtic harp and flute.

Also on the label was the first Welsh-language supergroup. Edward H. Dafis was formed in 1973 when Dewi Morris and Hefin Elis of Y Tebot Piws ('The Purple Teapot') and Y Chwyldro ('The Revolution') joined forces. Named after Elis's pseudonym while writing a newspaper column for *Y Faner* ('The Flag'), they dominated the Welsh-language scene for the rest of the decade.

The beautifully understated folk arrangements of Endaf Emlyn shone through too. Raised in Pwllheli, his earliest musical experiences were at chapel, and he played violin in the National Youth Orchestra of Wales alongside John Cale and Sir Karl Jenkins. Emlyn debuted in 1972 with *Hiraeth* (a much-discussed, non-translatable Welsh term depicting an aching yearning and nostalgia for one's homeland). Its follow-up, *Salem*, has been described as the first Welsh concept album – influenced by childhood hymns and Sydney Curnow Vosper's painting of a Welsh chapel scene.

As Welsh-language music became increasingly politicised throughout the '70s, there was also more confidence to release satirical songs that ridiculed the status quo. Dubbed 'The Dylan of Pembrokeshire' and 'Y Brawd Hwdini' ('The Great Houdini'), Meic Stevens was originally spotted by (since disgraced BBC DJ) Jimmy Savile while performing at a Manchester folk club in 1965.

In 1969, he formed Bara Menyn ('Bread and Butter') with Heather Jones and her then boyfriend, Geraint Jarman. Their name was an ironic nod to the prospect of earning a living by singing in Welsh, while their debut single, 'Caru Cymru' ('Love Wales'), ridiculed the patriotic, mushy messages of their Welsh-language contemporaries.

Meanwhile, Jarman exhilarated multicultural audiences with a stunning fusion of rock and reggae that bridged the gap between Welsh-speaking communities and monoglot English-speaking people in Wales. With his band, Y Cynganeddwyr ('The Poets'), featuring Llwynypia-born, Hendrix-like guitarist Tich Gwilym, Jarman paved the way for a new generation of post-punk, post-Sain, Welsh-language artists heading into the '80s, who had a less self-conscious relationship with their Welsh identity.

While the '70s was synonymous with English-language rock music in Wales, relatively few bands broke through to the mainstream. One artist even moved to the other side of the world in search of stardom.

As a founding member of The Velvet Underground, alongside Lou Reed in New York, John Cale concocted an experimental and nihilistic sound with an avant-garde flourish that inspired the punk and New Wave scenes. After leaving the Velvets in 1968, he embarked on a diverse solo career including his 1973 masterpiece, *Paris 1919*.

With his extensive back catalogue encapsulating classical, drone and electronica to name just a few genres, a strong case can be made for the Carmarthenshire native being Wales's most influential musician ever. That's not to mention his many film scores and vast production work including Nico, Patti Smith, The Stooges, Squeeze and Happy Mondays.

Back home, a Cardiff heavy metal act soared to prominence. In complete contrast to their thundering sound, the band was named Budgie. Led by the remarkable vocal range of bassist Burke Shelley, the power trio melded Led Zeppelin blues with Black Sabbath riffs and Rush-like prog-rock.

Recorded at Rockfield, their classic 1973 third album, *Never Turn Your Back on a Friend*, started with a white-hot slab of speed metal called 'Breadfan', later covered by Metallica. Their respect within the metal genre was further demonstrated when they toured with Ozzy Osbourne. Plus, their legacy lives on with Iron Maiden, Soundgarden, Megadeth, Melvins, Queens of the Stone Age, Alice in Chains and Welsh rockers Florence Black all covering their songs.

Elsewhere, Man mixed American West Coast psychedelia with space rock. Renowned for their relentless touring and prolific output, the Merthyr Tydfil band released a record a year for much of the '70s, including *Rhinos, Winos and Lunatics* and *The Welsh Connection*, as well as a legendary live album from Penarth's Paget Rooms.

Equally unyielding with their touring schedule were south Wales collective Sassafras. Propagating harmony-infused rock 'n' roll, prog and country akin to Fleetwood Mac (whom they supported in the States), they held the record in the early '70s for the most gigs in one year with 332, beating Slade by one.

———

Welsh-language music began to crank louder in the '80s including the bluesy rough edges of poet and songwriter Steve Eaves. Yet, the emergence of bands like Plethyn and Bwchadanas proved there was still an appetite for Welsh folk music. Plus, Dafydd Iwan penned his most potent, political song, 'Yma o Hyd', in 1983.

Brimming with Welsh history, it was written in response to Wales's 1979 rejection of a devolved Welsh government, as well as Thatcherism and the impending miners' strike. Meaning 'Still Here', 'Yma o Hyd' resonates over forty years later. Spurred on by a YesCymru independence campaign, it topped the UK iTunes charts in January 2020, and again in June 2022 as the Welsh football team secured their first World Cup qualification since 1958.

Meanwhile, the '80s introduced experimental avant-garde and power-pop synth styles. As the fury of punk evolved into post-punk and New Wave, Welsh musicians were keen to put the battles cries of the folk revolutionaries behind them (despite The Alarm's rabble-rousing brand of acoustic rock, but more on them later).

Leading the charge was Cardigan quartet Ail Symudiad, who reeled off a thrilling blend of punk and New Wave in thrall to The Jam, Buzzcocks, The Specials and The Undertones. Formed in 1978 and centred around brothers Richard and Wyn Jones, they founded the label and studio Fflach, which provided a vital resource for countless Welsh musicians over the next four decades.

Likewise devising post-punk magic (in English) were Cardiff trio Young Marble Giants, who delivered the minimalist masterpiece *Colossal Youth* via Rough Trade. The album was a favourite of Kurt Cobain, whose wife, Courtney Love, covered 'Credit in the Straight World' with Hole.

On the same label were Scritti Politti, who morphed into one of the UK's biggest mainstream pop acts of the decade. A collective of art students and squatters founded at Leeds Polytechnic in 1977, the group was led by the Cardiff-born genius Green Gartside (nicknamed after the lush landscape of Wales). After issuing the cult classic *Songs to Remember* in 1982, Scritti Politti returned with their most successful album, *Cupid & Psyche 85*. Jazz legend Miles Davis recorded an instrumental cover version of Scritti's single 'Perfect Way' for his seminal 1986 album *Tutu*, and two years later played trumpet on their Top 20 hit 'Oh Patti (Don't Feel Sorry for Loverboy)'.

Chart-conquering pop artists don't come much more charismatic than Steve Strange. The Newbridge-born maestro fronted New Romantic pioneers Visage alongside Midge Ure, Rusty Egan and John McGeoch. Their self-titled 1980 debut and its follow-up, *The Anvil*, landed in the UK Top 20, while the spellbinding synth-pop single 'Fade to Grey' reached No. 1 in Germany and Switzerland.

No conversation about Welsh pop can escape mentioning the multi million-selling Shakin' Stevens and Bonnie Tyler. The music press may often have poked fun at their commercial fare, but you can't argue with their success. Evoking the sound of '50s rock 'n' roll, Shakin' Stevens was the biggest-selling UK singles artist of the '80s. 'This Ole House', 'Green Door' and 'Oh Julie' all reached No. 1 in 1981 alone. Produced by Dave Edmunds, Stevens's festive favourite, 'Merry Christmas Everyone', was delayed by a year so as not to clash with Band Aid. It paid off, with Shaky claiming Christmas No. 1 in 1985.

Another international phenomenon was the multi-platinum Bonnie Tyler. Born as Gaynor Hopkins in Skewen, she initially changed her stage name to Sherene Davis to avoid confusion with Mary Hopkin. Finding fame at a local singing competition in 1969 (coincidentally with a cover of 'Those Were the Days'), the raspy-voiced singer's rise was initially more of a slow-burn success.

'Lost in France' and 'It's a Heartache' were mere precursors to what lay ahead, especially her collaborations with renowned rock guru Jim Steinman. 'Holding Out for a Hero' is one of *the* great power ballads, while 1983 album *Faster than the Speed of Night* not only got to No. 1, but also spawned 'Total Eclipse of the Heart' – a single that has sold an incredible 6 million copies worldwide.

———

With such a lineage of music in both languages, how had Wales become viewed as a musical backwater by the early '90s?

There was so much more than just Harry Secombe, but that didn't make any difference to the English music press. In their eyes, Wales was an ancient land of choirs and cawl, daffodils and dragons, leeks and lava bread and shawls and stove hats; a place where sheep outnumbered people three to one.

'Wales was just viewed as a joke by the rest of Britain,' said Cerys Matthews in David Owens's *Cerys, Catatonia and the Rise of Welsh Pop*. 'To them it was all coal mines and mountains. We were second class...It was, "Oooh, you can't do that – you're Welsh."'[9]

Alternative acts that did break through, like Badfinger, Budgie, Amen Corner and The Alarm, were still anomalies across two decades, and outside of Wales, who actually cared that The Velvet Underground included a Welshman?

Record label reps were reluctant to travel across the Severn Bridge, and there were horror stories of Welsh bands driving over the border to send off their recordings with an English postmark.

Producer Greg Haver said: 'Being racist against the Welsh was still "acceptable" – every cliché and pun, every fucking headline...Record labels would go as far as Bristol...If an A & R guy came to Cardiff, we practically threw the bunting up.'[10]

Fellow producer Gorwel Owen added: 'I heard of English-language Welsh bands in north Wales who used to play on the idea they were from Liverpool.'[11]

The battle scars were visible into the '90s. Stereophonics sent out demos in whatever eye-catching packaging they could muster to prevent them being tossed into the rejection pile.

According to David Owens:

> To be a Welsh music icon pre-90s was to vault the twin pommel horses marked 'laughing' and 'stock.' Being Welsh then was none too dissimilar to committing some sort of heinous cultural crime...The Welsh were the butt of more jokes than the Irish and Scottish put together.[12]

But a fightback was mounting away from the English media's gaze, started by the Welsh-language bands of the '80s...

YEAR ZERO

INTRODUCING THE WELSH-LANGUAGE MUSIC REVOLUTION

'Datblygu have only one thing in common with other Welsh bands and that is their shared use of the language – nothing else. Datblygu's only message is a hope that you don't choke whilst dancing and coughing in the ruins.'

The above quote from David R. Edwards was used to promote Datblygu's 2020 album, *Cwm Gwagle* ('Void Valley'), but it's a statement that resonates throughout the group's career. In particular, it reflected their maverick frontman's unflinching individuality. What other musician would list John Peel, *Coronation Street*, Ian Curtis, Laurel and Hardy, *Eraserhead*, *Wings of Desire*, horse racing, The Fall and Bob Monkhouse as influences?

Yet, none of these inspirations came from Wales. In his autobiography, *Atgofion Hen Wanc* ('Memories of an Aging Wanker'), he said: 'I didn't like what was being expressed through the medium of Welsh – either in a book, literature in general, music, anything.'[13]

Described by *NME* as 'Kraftwerk with a hangover', Datblygu was formed in 1982 by Edwards and T. Wyn Davies at school in Cardigan. Colliding off-kilter, minimalist rhythms with Edwards's scathing, darkly funny lyrics, they were a mesmerising mix of poetry, philosophy and diatribe that often took aim at the outdated status quo in Wales.

Speaking to the *Welsh Music Podcast*, Elis James said:

> What was so thrilling about David R. Edwards was he didn't seem to like Wales, Welsh people or Welsh culture, but that was so brave because if, say, you're Mark E. Smith in a band in Manchester, that's a huge city. There are plenty of places to hide, and if you've burned all your bridges there, you can move to London or potentially America…Dave lived in Aberteifi!

He criticised TV producers for being narrow-minded, promoters for being unimaginative, audiences for treating gigs as social events rather than listening to the music. He had a big problem with the Welsh middle classes, and he had a go at Plaid Cymru...

He also criticised BBC Radio Cymru and S4C, who were the only people who would play him other than John Peel. If you criticise people in Welsh-language culture, it's so small that you're eventually going to bump into them in Tesco! But he walked it like he talked it.[14]

Away from his frustration with Welsh culture, Edwards's lyrics delved into the despair of Thatcherite Britain from his isolated, rural habitat, marginalised from the rest of Wales and ignored by central government. Ironically, the emergence of the Datblygu name (denoting development, progress, evolution and a separation from the past) coincided with a time of crushing social change. If the 1960s were a period of huge societal revolution, then it was the 1980s that introduced drastic change in Wales socially and with the Welsh language.

The final St David's Day of the 1970s had given the Welsh public a chance to vote for a Welsh assembly, but crushingly only one in four did so. The resounding 'No' result meant the chance for Wales to have more control of her destiny was lost for another generation.

Welsh mining communities soon experienced the full force of Thatcher's politics of recession and closure. Wales had been the heartland of the Industrial Revolution, thriving on coal, steel and slate, but now it was a hollow museum of its past. The '80s were bookended by half of the jobs in the Welsh steel industry being decimated and over twenty coal mines closing.

As Sarah Hill said in *'Blerwytirhwng?'*:

The failure of the devolution referendum in 1979 and the overall rightward progression of Anglo-American politics signalled a decisive shift in the sense of Welshness which had been nurtured over the preceding decades.

If Geraint Jarman's Welsh trilogy was a measure of this shift, illustrating as it does a gradual disintegration of the optimism of 'Hen Wlad Fy Nhadau', the music of Datblygu represents the extreme disillusionment of the generation which followed.[15]

The '80s got off to the worst possible start for Welsh-speaking communities as Thatcher's government reneged on its promise of a Welsh-medium TV channel. Soon after, MTV launched in August 1981 and ushered in the era of the music video. Without a platform, how could Welsh-language musicians hope to reach a television audience?

Step forward, Gwynfor Evans, the first Welsh MP in Westminster and leader of Plaid Cymru, who threatened to go on hunger strike unless a Welsh-language station was established. Consequently, Thatcher was forced into an embarrassing U-turn, and S4C began broadcasting on 1 November 1982.

———

Also forming in 1982 were Bangor punks, Anhrefn ('Disorder'). Energised by DIY and fanzine culture, the band included the ridiculously proactive Rhys Mwyn, who shared Datblygu's stance against outdated Welsh culture.

In his autobiography, *Cam o'r Tywyllwch* ('Stepping Out of the Darkness'), he wrote: 'Cymdeithas yr Iaith's slogan was "Everything in Welsh", and yet in the late '70s the Welsh rock groups, organisers and labels had succeeded in creating a small Welsh world that was totally irrelevant to most young people in Wales.'

Mwyn set up a meeting with David R. Edwards at the bandstand in Cardigan to discuss how they could ignite change. When bands like Y Cyrff from Llanrwst and Tynal Tywyll from Bethesda popped up, Mwyn also discussed the manifesto with them.

'When we met up with people like Dave Datblygu, Mark and Paul Cyrff, Ian Tynal Tywyll, we saw kindred spirits, fellow travellers,' said Mwyn to the *Welsh Music Podcast*. 'These were the revolutionaries. I always used to think of it like *The Magnificent Seven* where you're rounding these people up…None of us argued over the vision…We all spoke the same language.'[16]

A north Wales fraternity developed, which soon included Gorwel and Fiona Owen's electro/ambient outfit Plant Bach Ofnus in Anglesey and Bangor beatniks Fflaps.

Mwyn emphasised constant promoting of the scene via fanzines and word of mouth. Whoever found a gig would let their mates be the support. With the creation of Recordiau Anhrefn, Mwyn allowed

Datblygu, Y Cyrff, Fflaps and Llwybr Llaethog to have initial releases on his label before encouraging them to start their own.

Bullied, unconfident and covered in acne, Mwyn had been an unhappy teenager who hated school and the Urdd (a Welsh-medium youth activities organisation and festival). What did folk dancing and ancient tales of the *Mabinogion* mean to a disillusioned youngster, especially in an era of strikes and civil unrest?

Mwyn represents a generation of Welsh speakers born during the first decade of modern Welsh-language activism. As local industry jobs were lost, young people moved to Cardiff and surrounding areas, meaning that traditional Welsh practices like the Urdd and the Eisteddfod became less relevant and viewed with cynicism. Then Mwyn heard the Sex Pistols.

> When I saw the state of Johnny Rotten and Sid Vicious, they were covered in spots and I thought 'These people are in a band?!...Their skin is worse than mine!'
>
> I don't think I've ever heard such an anthem as 'God Save the Queen'...I identified with that nihilistic, bombastic, 'fuck you' statement...I was reborn, I was punk rock. I got really into Vivienne Westwood, Malcolm McLaren, Jamie Reid's artworks and the Situationists, but I couldn't find anything in Wales to identify with. It wasn't going to be Dafydd Iwan, Tom Jones, Shirley Bassey and Dave Edmunds...
>
> I remember my mum seeing Edward H. Dafis on the telly and saying, 'Come and have a look at this Welsh band,' and I looked at them and they just looked like farmers! It really was a case of everything in Wales is shit. It's always been shit...How can we create a new narrative?[17]

The fire was lit in Mwyn's belly when John Peel started broadcasting Welsh-language bands like Llygod Ffyrnig and Trwynau Coch at the height of punk in 1977.

> For all us lost souls, John Peel's show was crucial. You could argue that it saved our lives because whatever hell we went through in school, those two hours of Peel every night would make you feel so good for days.

> All of a sudden, it's sod the Sex Pistols and The Clash, we've got Geraint Jarman…These discoveries inform you, they inspire you, they direct you. It was like a road trip of discovery.[18]

In March 1985, Mwyn released a compilation via Recordiau Anhrefn that kickstarted the revolution. Recorded at Foel Studios, *Cam o'r Tywyllwch* brought together the very best Welsh-language bands of the mid-'80s with just 1,000 copies pressed. Inspired by the Crass label's *Bullshit Detector* collections, the album gathered three doses of fiery punk from Anhrefn, a couple of The-Smiths-meets-The-Byrds songs from Tynal Tywyll and two contributions from Y Cyrff in 'Lebanon' and 'Tic Toc'.

Elsewhere, an in-studio argument at the end of Elfyn Presli's 'Hangofyr' resulted in the first instance of the F-word on a Welsh-language record, while Machlud ('Sunset') featured a young Gruff Rhys. Head and shoulders above the rest though was Datblygu with 'Y Teimlad', which is one of the greatest songs ever written in the Welsh language.

The demo-like quality of the recording just added to the compilation's charm and authenticity. *Cam o'r Tywyllwch* may have made the bigger impact, but Mwyn thinks that its follow-up compilation, *Gadael yr Ugeinfed Ganrif* ('Leaving the Twentieth Century'), was superior as the bands had learned to play by then. Having already pestered the music press by phone, Mwyn ventured to London demanding they be heard: 'My belief in Datblygu, Y Cyrff and all these bands was so certain that I had no fear phoning these people up. I'm sure they must have thought, "It's that irritating little wanker from north Wales!"'[19]

Mwyn had no sense of embarrassment and relished taking on all comers. During a frosty interview on *The Old Grey Whistle Test*, Mwyn stared out host Andy Kershaw when he was asked to justify Anhrefn's decision to sing in their own language. Also, when the band released their debut album, they called it *Defaid, Skateboards a Wellies* – the first word meaning 'sheep' to pre-empt the inevitable anti-Welsh jokes.

On his day trip to London, Mwyn visited *NME*, *Sounds*, *Melody Maker*, *The Face*, *ZigZag*, Capital Radio and the BBC, armed with thirty compilations, and by the last train he was empty-handed.

Mwyn recalled:

You could just walk in with no appointments; it was insane. I'm going, 'Where's Mick Mercer? Where's Steven Wells?' And they would point to their desks. I would just say, 'We're from Wales. You need to listen to this.'

I went to the reception in the BBC and said, 'Is it possible to see John Peel?' and was told, 'He's in a wine bar around the corner.' So in I walked, and he's having a meal with a band called The Higsons. As I approached, he looked up and said, 'I hope you're not going to mug me.'

Two weeks passed and I was starting to think it wasn't happening, but I was driving and he played the Anhrefn song 'Rhywle yn Moscow' ('Somewhere in Moscow'). We'd been trying to get this underground scene happening in Wales, and then you're on John Peel to 3 million listeners…I remember sitting in the car thinking, 'Right then, you bastards, whatever happens from here, you can't stop this train!'

But then Peel kept playing it. Two days later, Datblygu are on. Three days later, Elfyn Presli are on. It was Year Zero – everything that has been done in Wales is now redundant. *This* is the new![20]

———

John Peel was so smitten with Datblygu's depiction of '*Sgymraeg*' (a scummy version of Welshness) that he gave the band five sessions between 1987 and 1993 and introduced their performance on *The Tube*.

With the introduction of multi-instrumentalist and soulmate Patricia Morgan in 1984, Datblygu's idiosyncratic blueprint was complete. While they frequently knocked heads with BBC Radio Cymru, their most prosperous local outlet was Geraint Jarman's iconic TV show, *Fideo 9*, which aired every Thursday at 9 p.m. from 1988–92. The concept was simple: S4C in conjunction with production company Criw Byw would not only give the floor to four Welsh-language bands each week, but would also pay them.

After four cassette-only releases via Casetiau Neon (run by Ultravox-like electro artist Malcolm Neon) in the early '80s and the *Hwgr-Grawth-Og* EP on Recordiau Anhrefn in 1984, Datblygu's debut coincided with the start of *Fideo 9*. With IVF becoming more commonplace and press stories circulating about multiple births, 'Wyau' ('Eggs') in 1988 offered a sharp social commentary.

Throughout, Edwards propagated an inimitable lyrical style melding American jazz poet Gil Scott-Heron with Morrissey and the madcap humour of Half Man Half Biscuit. On 'Dafydd Iwan yn y Glaw' ('Dafydd Iwan in the Rain'), he poked fun at a Welsh folk hero, but also sympathised with the weighty expectations on his shoulders and how revolutionary figures are re-evaluated over time.

Sarah Hill said:

> In the 1980s, the relationship between the younger generation of language activists and the generation which spawned the movement had become strained, and it was largely in the musical arena that the relationship between these two generations was contested.[21]

Elsewhere, 'Gwlad ar Fy Nghefn' ('Country on My Back') revolved around the problem of being a Welsh speaker with a love of words and language, who is simultaneously alienated from Welsh mainstream culture (sample lyric: 'Living in Wales is like watching paint dry').

Datblygu's masterpiece arrived with *Pyst* ('Posts') in 1990 and it came via another independent label in Gorwel Owen's Recordiau Ofn. Across fourteen tracks, Datblygu literally took the '*pyst*' out of Welsh-language rock opera, male voice choirs, folk festivals and pub poetry competitions (the fact the Eisteddfod judged poetry in contests was one of Edwards's lasting hates).

Sonically, *Pyst* is impressive too, with Gorwel Owen at the production desk. The hypnotic synths of 'Benjamin Bore' ('Morning Benjamin') provide the ideal opener, but it's immediately juxtaposed with the ominous strings of 'Mas a Lawr' ('Down and Out'), which emphasises the unpredictable nature of the album. While 'Am' offers perfect pop, 'Ugain I Un' is a country and western song touching on Edwards's love of betting on the horses, tinged with brutal sadness. When the horse fails a jump, it gets shot.

Wales Arts Review said:

> Datblygu songs often operate as vignettes or short stories on *Pyst* from the cattle markets of local discos ('Ms Bara Lawr' ['Ms Laverbread']), to driving in a long tailback to recycle whisky bottles while listening to experimental jazz on Radio 3 ('Nofel o'r Hofel ' ['Novel from the Hovel']).

Edwards, like the Welsh modernist writer Caradoc Evans, is at his best when focused on the grotesque, but he's never patronising to his subject in these songs. Datblygu always retain great feeling for the underdog, the exploited, tired, lonely and preyed upon.[22]

John Peel famously described Datblygu as 'the best incentive anyone could have for learning Welsh', and upon hearing *Pyst*, he said: 'If you've never bought a Welsh-language record in your life, buy this one.' One Sunday evening, Peel began his BBC Radio 1 broadcast by playing the first three tunes off *Pyst* in succession. *Fideo 9* also dedicated a half-hour programme to the band with a film called *ABCDatblygu* by Marc Evans featuring four videos of the album's songs.

The trilogy of classic Datblygu albums was completed with *Libertino* in 1993, and this time it was on Ankst, founded in 1988 by Aberystwyth University students Alun Llwyd and Gruffudd Jones. The duo loved bands like Y Cyrff, who they wanted to promote at a time when other labels were reissuing wartime Welsh tenors. Putting on gigs and publishing their own fanzine, they were anti-establishment in their cultural and political remit (Llwyd was imprisoned for his participation in Cymdeithas protests). Relocating to a damp, cramped Cardiff office with friend Emyr Glyn Williams, they used Enterprise Allowance Scheme support for cassette-only releases before progressing to 7" EPs and 12" singles.

A bold, twenty-track epic, *Libertino* contained arguably Datblygu's finest moment on 'Cân i Gymry' ('Song for Wales') – a razor-sharp evisceration of snobby Welsh middle-class conventions. It also skewered the Eisteddfod and referenced the ecstasy-fuelled rave scene on 'Maes E'. *Wales Arts Review* continued:

> Datblygu found itself in the middle of dance culture and it seemed natural that David R. Edwards would become an MC to Welsh-language culture. *Libertino* captures the energy and optimism of that time.
>
> Its collaborative nature featuring artists such as John Griffiths (Llwybr Llaethog), Fiona Owen (Plant Bach Ofnus/Eirin Peryglus) and Peredur ap Gwynedd (later of Pendulum) felt like a gesture to a broad community of like-minded Welsh artists…*Libertino* still feels like a shamanic guide to a new imagined Wales.[23]

In his foreword to David R. Edwards's autobiography, Emyr Glyn Williams said that signing Datblygu to Ankst in 1990 made the label feel like a 'completely bulletproof company'.[24] Edwards's band of 'non-conforming non-conformists' also made it obvious that there was more to music from Wales than rehashed Welsh versions of Anglo-American ideas:

> 'What we see when we look into the mirror of Datblygu is that it is the scum that rises to the top, not the cream… [Datblygu's] records offer an alternative reality that is as deep, emotional and rich as any artistic work that any Welsh artist has ever created.'[25]

———

It wasn't all about Welsh-language music in the early '90s. Introducing the 'world's wildest band', Tigertailz!

Before the Manics added a touch of glamour to the south Wales scene, there was an androgynous group using more hairspray than Hanoi Rocks. That gaping hole in the ozone layer was probably caused by the aerosols that gave their poodle perms more volume than a room full of ghetto blasters – and just like Spinal Tap, they were big in Japan!

Tigertailz were Wales's answer to Mötley Crüe. Originally known as Stagefright, they formed in 1983 when bassist Pepsi Tate and drummer Ian Welch pinned an ad at Spillers Records.

Located on The Hayes in Cardiff (before moving to the nearby Morgan Arcade in 2010), the world's oldest record shop was a treasure trove for collectors and essential for musicians on their journey to rock 'n' roll stardom. Guitarist Jay Pepper answered the call, and the backbone of the band was established.

As flamboyant front runners of the nascent UK glam-metal scene of the late '80s alongside Whitesnake, Def Leppard and The Cult, Tigertailz also rode the wave of American rock washing up on these shores. Akin to W.A.S.P. and L.A. Guns, Tigertailz may have transplanted the sleazy sound of the Sunset Strip to the rainy streets of Cardiff, but they were predominantly more influenced by British rock than glam.

Jay Pepper said:

We loved Black Sabbath, Judas Priest, Ozzy Osbourne, Status Quo, Rainbow, Slade, AC/DC, Led Zeppelin and the Sex Pistols. Yes, we liked Kiss, Van Halen, etc, but we were mainly fans of the classic British bands of the '70s and '80s.

But we got recognised because of our image…We wrote music that fitted that image and what the fans and record companies wanted to hear…I still much prefer listening to Judas Priest's *Unleashed in the East* or the Sex Pistols' *Never Mind the Bollocks* compared to most of the terrible glam music of the '80s and '90s.[26]

Initially meeting to jam in a local church hall, the trio mimicked the fretboard shredding of Randy Rhoads, Rick Parfitt and Angus Young. In a sign of things to come, a revolving door of musicians operated around them. Founding member Ian Welch was replaced by Ace Finchum of fellow metal act Crash KO, while the same band's Steevi Jaimz was recruited after seeing an ad in *Sounds*. The new singer didn't take long to announce himself.

'People in Wales just don't know what's happening on the current music scene,' Jaimz told the *South Wales Echo* in July 1986. 'Everyone's still into Free, and Led Zeppelin…Wales has been left ten years behind everyone else when it comes to music.'[27]

Produced at Loco Studios in Usk by in-house engineer and Welsh music cult hero Tim Lewis (aka Thighpaulsandra – later of Spiritualized), their self-released *Shoot to Kill* EP sold modestly but managed to prick the ears of major rock label Music for Nations – home to Metallica and Poison.

Produced by Steve James (son of *Carry On* star Sid James), their debut album, *Young and Crazy*, crash-landed in November 1987. Dripping with boyish exuberance, it's a record full of big guitars and even bigger choruses. Hell-raising frontman Steevi Jaimz's drunken spats with media and musicians soon wore thin though, and he was given his marching orders.

Nevertheless, Tigertailz returned with their rock masterpiece, *Bezerk*, in 1990 and preceded it with the single 'Livin' Without You' – a track previously featured on *Young and Crazy*, but rerecorded with new frontman Kim Hooker. Only a few years prior, Tigertailz had lost a Battle of the Bands competition to fellow Cardiff group Rankelson, but now they had overtaken them in the popularity stakes and hijacked Hooker.

'Pepsi wanted Kim in the band, even though he wasn't a singer and played bass in his previous band,' said Jay Pepper. 'So, we did a demo first with Kim singing and he really nailed it…I still think it's Kim's best performance from his time in Tigertailz.'[28]

Bezerk was preproduced in 1989 with Tim Lewis before being completed by heavy metal producer Chris Tsangarides. It spawned the singles 'Love Bomb Baby', 'Noise Level Critical' and 'Heaven' – a lighters-in-the-air piano ballad akin to Mötley Crüe's 'Home Sweet Home'.

'When *Bezerk* exploded it was like a big finger pointed at us from the sky and said, "It's your turn,"' said Hooker. 'And we made the most of every second from then on.'[29]

With 'Love Bomb Baby', they found their calling card in the form of an epic rock anthem full of infectious choruses that refused to budge from your head. Pepsi Tate said: 'That was like our statement of intent – completely over the top, catchy as hell and with a mega portion of 'Tailz-style topping!'[30]

Jay Pepper added:

All you ever want is for your songs to be recognised, so when *Bezerk* went into the UK Top 40, I thought we had achieved what we set out to achieve.

We had started a band, made demos, played up and down the country living in the back of a transit van. We paid our dues, and it paid off. I still think those songs sound great.[31]

Such was the clamour for *Bezerk* that a live video was spliced together from shows at St David's Hall and London Astoria.

But Tigertailz's time at the top was short-lived. Guns N' Roses killed off glam metal with their sprawling and unfocused *Use Your Illusion* albums in 1991 – the same year grunge went global.

Tigertailz's third album, *Wazbones*, eventually surfaced in 1995 despite being recorded three years earlier amid internal quarrelling and legal wranglings with the label. Not only had they missed the boat, but they had also frittered away over $200,000.

A 2008 retrospective by BBC Wales suggested it was time to re-evaluate the band's undervalued legacy: 'Tigertailz never did a Mötley Crüe and went grunge. They never did a Guns N' Roses and imploded. They stuck to their guns and were honest in their musical quest to bring glam, sleaze, pop and, yes, cheese to British hard rock.'[32]

That re-evaluation was given added poignancy following the tragic death from pancreatic cancer of Pepsi Tate aged forty-two. Born Huw Justin Smith in March 1965 as the son of Welsh actor Ray Smith, Tate was affectionately nicknamed 'The Boy'.

After receiving a terminal diagnosis, he managed to complete work with his bandmates on the *Thrill Pistol* album, which was dedicated to Tate and his family. He died less than a month after its release, shortly after marrying Welsh opera star Shân Cothi.

Tigertailz should be rightly remembered for *Bezerk* – their best work and a rock classic over thirty years later. The band still play it in full on anniversaries, and a companion album titled *Bezerk 2.0* was released in August 2006.

Kerrang urged us all to 'hail this rejuvenated band for the time-defying devils they are',[33] while BBC Wales added: '*Bezerk 2.0* sounds as if grunge and alt-rock never happened. Joyful in its rock ridiculousness, it's a fun, wig-out listen for those who feel no shame in playing air guitar.'[34]

…Anyone seen my hairspray?

———

While David R. Edwards's songwriting was about capturing the misery of Thatcherite Wales, Llwybr Llaethog's ethos extended into galaxies far beyond.

Painting vibrant textures from a cosmic palette of rap and reggae, dance and dub, electronica, hip-hop and punk, Llwybr Llaethog ('Milky Way') were experimental pioneers who delved into genres previously unexplored in their homeland, not least in Blaenau Ffestiniog.

The band was formed in London in 1984 by teenagers John Griffiths and Kevs Ford, who shared a love of reggae and punk. After several years touring northern Europe with ska band The Managing Directors, Griffiths had an epiphany while on holiday in New York. He fell in love with the Big Apple's hip-hop culture. from watching youths breakdancing at the Roxy nightclub to the fresh, exhilarating sounds of Kool DJ Red Alert. Griffiths returned home with a new musical vision.

Llwybr Llaethog married revolutionary hip-hop with left-wing politics and intelligent lyrics in Welsh. Proffering a bass-heavy, agit-rap style aligned with a sharp, satirical edge, the duo single-handedly invented the genre of Welsh-language hip-hop. 'In 1984 when we started, there was nothing even vaguely electronic,' said Griffiths. 'We had the first rap in Welsh.'[35] On their 1996 album, *Mad!*, they even ventured into Gaelic and Punjabi tongues.

In *'Blerwytirhwng?'*, Sarah Hill said:

> The 'mainstream' Welsh music of the 1980s continued largely on its straightforward rock trajectory (Derec Brown, Maffia Mr Huws), but the advent of smaller labels such as Fflach, Anhrefn and most notably Ankst expanded the palette of Welsh pop music to include new wave (Ail Symudiad, Malcolm Neon) as well as more experimental music (Llwybr Llaethog, Datblygu).
>
> These pockets of musical activity were centred around particular geographical regions of Wales (Bethesda, Cardigan), and the new independent labels of the 1980s were generally concerned with providing an alternative to the mainstream (Sain) fare.[36]

Arriving on Recordiau Anhrefn in 1986, Llwybr Llaethog breathed new life into a sedate scene thanks to hip-hop tropes like turntable scratching, audio sampling and cut-'n'-paste production. They may have shared little stylistically with their local contemporaries, but one thing they had in common with Datblygu was a hatred of Thatcher.

Their debut EP, *Dull Di-Drais* ('Non-Violent Method'), was strewn with leftist messages including scorn for 'The Iron Lady' and support for imprisoned, non-violent, direct-action Welsh-language activist Ffred Ffransis. His voice was sampled on the title track co-written with Rhys Mwyn and Nêst Thomas. If that didn't nail their political colours to the flag, the sleeve contained a bilingual Cymdeithas statement.

The band still drew criticism for their habit of recording outside their homeland. BBC Wales said: 'Many refused to take the act seriously, partly because of the pair's love for futurist gimmicks (one interview the pair did for Welsh TV was supposedly phoned in from outer space), and partly because of the group's physical dislocation from Wales. For a while, the pair recorded their music in a home studio based in a council flat in Peckham.'[37]

Regardless, Griffiths and Ford built on the reputation created by their impressive debut with its follow-up, *Tour de France*, which led to the first of four Peel Sessions in December 1987.

Expanded to a trio with bassist Ben Bentham, Llwybr Llaethog put out their debut album, *Da!*, in 1988, and it was more than just 'Good!'. Yet it's the 1990 follow-up, *Be?*, that's widely considered their best. BBC Wales described it as a 'mischievous skewering of dole-age culture that encompassed dub reggae and formative acid house', with Griffiths and Ford 'taking fragments of Welsh records and pasting them back into an anarchic whole'.[38] In particular, on 'Popeth ar y Record 'ma Wedi Cael ei Ddwyn' ('Everything on This Record Has Been Nicked'), they indulged (and mocked) their love of sampling.

With Ankst pushing the boundaries of contemporary Welsh music and delving into dance, they were the ideal base for an innovative 1991 collaboration between Llwybr Llaethog, Tŷ Gwydr and David R. Edwards titled *LL.LL. v. T.G. MC D.R.E.* In Tŷ Gwydr, Llwybr Llaethog found like-minded souls. Formed in 1989 by Mark Lugg and Gareth Potter from the debris of industrial funk pranksters Traddodiad Ofnus, Tŷ Gwydr vowed to get Wales dancing by infusing the energy of the club scene they were so immersed in.

The great collaborations didn't stop there. Ankst released the *Ap Elvis* compilation to celebrate its fifth birthday. Starting with Datblygu's update of 'Cân i Gymry', the collection included Beganifs, Fflaps, Steve Eaves and Ian Rush (a Mold indie band and not the legendary Liverpool striker).

The best was saved for last though as Llwybr Llaethog teamed up with anti-establishment poet Ifor ap Glyn for 'Fydd Y Chwyldro Ddim Ar Y Teledu, Gyfaill'. A techno-dub reinterpretation of Gil Scott-Heron's protest song 'The Revolution Will Not Be Televised', it examined Welsh-language media and emphasised that the revolution wouldn't be led by Wales's old guard: 'The revolution won't be shown on S4C…The music for the revolution won't be composed by Huw Chiswell…Or sung by Margaret Williams, Dennis O'Neill or Wyn Roberts…But it will be released on Ankst!'

Sarah Hill said:

> By bemoaning the omnipresence of middle-of-the-road artists on S4C and Radio Cymru, Ifor ap Glyn is stressing the importance of popular music to the formation of contemporary

political consciousness. That Ankst is named as the bastion of hope in an otherwise homogenous culture is itself important…

Ifor ap Glyn and Llwybr Llaethog are celebrating Ankst and its anti-establishment ethos in much the same way as contemporary rap labels served as an alternative to the mainstream.

[The fact] that rap had already infiltrated and changed the mainstream does not diminish the significance of the song to the development of Welsh pop. The cultural time-lag evident throughout the history of Welsh pop lessened largely due to the founding of Ankst.[39]

Yet, it was a Welsh band on a major American label that bridged the language divide and opened the doors to bilingualism…

BUILDING BRIDGES, NOT WALLS

VENTURING INTO BILINGUALISM

'I saw Welsh-language TV and there were some really impassioned speakers politically, but there were no subtitles and I felt that excluded people.'

Despite growing up in English-speaking Rhyl, Mike Peters felt 100 per cent Welsh. However, as a non-Welsh speaker, he was an outsider from his own culture. Feeling trapped by the traditions of Wales, that all changed for Peters after the creation of S4C in 1982. Speaking to the *Welsh Music Podcast* he said:

> We had a policy that whenever we played in Wales in the '80s, we had Welsh-language bands opening for The Alarm.
>
> I talked to them before the show and said, 'The audience are English-speaking Welsh people, like me. They don't necessarily understand what you're singing. Why don't you tell them what the songs are about in English before you play them in Welsh?' But they were like, 'No, that's selling out!'
>
> Language is supposed to be about communication, and should be a tool to explore other cultures. The Welsh language had a wall around it to protect itself. It's not about putting up barriers, so I was thinking, 'How can we make it more inclusive?' Bilingualism was the way forward.[40]

Bethesda band Maffia Mr Huws had been influential in opening the language divide throughout the first half of the '80s. Named after seeing 'Abercaseg Maffia' daubed in graffiti, they added the name of their Welsh teacher. Extending the reach of the language throughout Wales was vital to the group as they didn't want to be confined by geographical boundaries.

Therefore, they committed themselves to gigging relentlessly across the country, and often in places like the south Wales valleys where Welsh-language bands hadn't been seen before.

In his autobiography, Rhys Mwyn said:

> I sincerely believe that apart from the group Maffia Mr Huws and the buzz surrounding them in the early '80s, the Welsh pop world as we know it would be over.
>
> Some groups would've continued to sing in Welsh, but by playing over a hundred gigs a year during their heyday, Maffia kept the flame alive, and more than anyone else had the biggest influence on Anhrefn in realising that it was through singing all over the country – not by appearing on television twice a year – that you gained an audience.[41]

In 1987, Llwybr Llaethog and Anhrefn were invited to support The Alarm at St David's Hall, and Peters contacted the latter band for help with translating Alarm songs into Welsh. They came together at a Wardour Street studio with legendary David Bowie producer Tony Visconti, which eventually led to the first simultaneous release of an album in English and Welsh.

A different approach to broadening the language was needed, so *Change/Newid* was an apt title. Released in September 1989 and reaching No. 13, the album was the band's tribute to Wales and led to their biggest US hit in 'Sold Me Down the River'. Plus, 'A New South Wales' mixed the modern with the traditional by featuring the Morriston Orpheus Male Voice Choir and the Welsh Symphony Orchestra. Issued as a bilingual double A-side, it was the first-ever Welsh-language song to enter the UK Top 40.

By embracing bilingualism, The Alarm proved that it wasn't selling out the Welsh language. Instead, it was making it more accessible by allowing more people to understand the importance of protecting their own culture.

Peters had the album translated by four different people, who all returned differing results, but ultimately conveyed the same message. As a non-fluent Welsh speaker, Peters wanted his authentic, struggling grasp of the language to come across on the record.

When The Alarm returned to St David's Hall in 1989 for a Cymdeithas gig, the atmosphere was electric:

> We had Ffred Ffransis of Cymdeithas onstage with us at one point. I think it was the first time a lot of us from my generation felt like we could really embrace coming from Wales, and that we weren't a backwater nation…It was charged with a lot more awareness of being Welsh and being part of a country from north to south.
>
> That '89 gig was the spark, and unity happened in the '90s with the whole Cool Cymru thing…All of a sudden, those Welsh-language bands who had supported us, like Y Cyrff and Ffa Coffi Pawb, had become Catatonia and Super Furry Animals and they were singing in English and Welsh. That '89 concert was the beginning of that – it changed a lot of things.[42]

Change/Newid also featured the track 'No Frontiers/Dim Ffiniau', which was inspired by the changing political landscape across Wales and Europe, including the imminent fall of the Berlin Wall. Seeing himself as a 'midwife' to the ideas that pop into his head, Peters recalled to *Buzz* the story of being on tour with his hero, Bob Dylan. Seeing Dylan's real name of 'Robert Zimmerman' on the passport at immigration control normalised the star, and made Peters realise we're all equal as people. The melody for 'No Frontiers/Dim Ffiniau' burst into his mind: 'It's like the big man upstairs was sending some music down to planet Earth, it missed Bob Dylan and got me!'[43]

Dylan isn't their only mega star admirer. From Bruce Springsteen to Billy Corgan of Smashing Pumpkins and Billy Duffy of The Cult, they're all amongst The Alarm's legion of loyal followers. The Killers even covered 'Rain in the Summertime' at Cardiff Castle in June 2019 with Peters in attendance.

Bono once said, 'The Alarm and U2 were the bastard children of The Clash,'[44] and it's the Irish band that they've been most commonly compared with. In fact, The Alarm were initially dismissed as U2 copyists, with cynics labelling them 'U3'. (Coincidentally, U2's huge, guitar-led anthems are crafted by a man of Welsh parentage in The Edge

– aka David Howell Evans – a cousin of Catatonia's Aled Richards.)

For a man who would one day play Madison Square Garden, Mike Peters's music career started in modest surroundings at the Talardy Hotel in St Asaph. Performing with his schoolmates at his sister's birthday party in October 1975, he fronted Hairy Hippie.

After the revelation of seeing the Sex Pistols live the following year, Peters (under the alias 'Eddie Bop') turned to punk by forming The Toilets with future Alarm bandmate Nigel 'Twist' Buckle. The group's name quickly got flushed in favour of Quasimodo, who played note-for-note covers of The Who's *Live at Leeds* album.

As Thatcherism dawned, Peters's childhood friend, Eddie MacDonald, came onboard along with Dave Sharp. They mutated into a power-pop mod band called Seventeen and supported Dexys Midnight Runners, but (according to Peters) Kevin Rowland wasn't a fan: 'He came up to us after the second date and went, "Listen, you're a pile of rubbish. I don't want you on my tour."'[45]

Licking their wounds, the band repackaged themselves as Alarm Alarm – named after one of The Toilets' tunes. John Peel commented on BBC Radio 1 that with Duran Duran, Talk Talk and now Alarm Alarm, perhaps he should call himself 'John Peel John Peel'. The name was swiftly changed to The Alarm.

Their first gig was at Prestatyn's Royal Victoria Hotel in June 1981. Peters noticed the audience responding differently to them compared with how the previous bands on the bill were recieved, and that's not surprising armed with songs like 'Shout to the Devil' and 'Sixty-Eight Guns'. He said:

> The plan was then to move to London. I knew that if we were to stay in Wales, our energy would've imploded on us. We needed to find our feet and establish ourselves in the world. Getting a gig in London was really tough in 1981 and there wasn't a scene to plug into in Cardiff, so off we went to Manchester to make our single.[46]

Pressing a limited run of their debut single, 'Unsafe Building', via their own White Cross label, The Alarm were received with suspicion and derision. The London press was wary of Welshmen anyway, but especially ones dressed like cowboys with gravity-defying mullets as this early coverage from *Melody Maker* testified:

It's easy to see why this band attract contempt – the hilarious hairstyles and Jesse James meets Desperate Dan wardrobe, the unapologetic confidence of their 'stand' and crucially, their poaching and mixing of a bizarre amalgam of styles virtually invite ridicule.[47]

After unemployment riots across the country, The Alarm's music became less pop, more political. Armed with a clutch of predominantly acoustic, power-to-the-people anthems, they toured with The Beat, Stiff Little Fingers, The Jam and U2. 'When great music is made, there are usually great people behind it, and The Alarm are great people,' said Bono. U2's agent, Ian Wilson, soon became their manager, leading to a deal with IRS Records.

By the mid-'80s, The Alarm were already on their way to becoming superstars, with two classic albums under their belts. As David Owens said: '*Declaration* and *Strength*, had titles carved straight out of Orwell's Ministry of Propaganda. However, the music was not contrived – just brimming over with unstoppable enthusiasm.'[48]

Likewise, iconic shows like their Spirit of '86 gig in front of 26,000 fans at Los Angeles's University of California in April 1986 made them a global success. It was beamed around the world via MTV's historic first-ever live satellite broadcast in the USA, UK, Europe, Japan and Australia.

Peters told the *Toronto Sun*:

We actually had to order the satellite to come over in space and wait until it was literally overhead at 3 p.m. in Los Angeles, so we could beam it live around the world. Live Aid was only the year before, but it wasn't a live-around-the-world thing – Britain had to wait to see the American and Canadian events, so this was the first time you could see it simultaneously on MTV.[49]

The following year, The Alarm supported U2 again, but this time on home soil at a sold-out Cardiff Arms Park. Peters said:

When we came out and said, 'We're from Rhyl, north Wales,' the place just went mental and we blew the gig to bits!
    Luckily for U2, they had The Pretenders on after us because we owned Cardiff that day. I played a bit of the national anthem on

my harmonica before 'Blaze of Glory', and it was spine-tingling. That was another moment of awakening for our nation. We could actually come together and celebrate our unity whether we could speak the language or not.[50]

Heading into the new decade, The Alarm's fifth album, *Raw*, was again released bilingually as *Tân* in April 1991. Following a series of personal tragedies affecting the group, it was understandably a less focused work than *Change/Newid*, featuring the Dylan-esque beauties 'God Save Somebody' and 'Wonderful World', plus a cover of Neil Young's 'Rockin' in the Free World'. *Tân* also included a Welsh-language rendition of John Lennon's 1971 No. 2 hit, 'Happy Xmas (War Is Over)'.

Soon after, an exhausted Mike Peters called time on the first iteration of The Alarm, after ten years, with a shock announcement from the stage at Brixton Academy.

Fortunately, that didn't last, and The Alarm remain one of Wales's most beloved bands over forty years on from their humble beginnings. Thanks to the American tours with U2 and Bob Dylan, they're also the most popular Welsh group stateside today and continue to host their transatlantic annual fan festival, The Gathering.

———

'I got drum lessons in school because it got me out of French…'[51]

The last person fifteen-year-old and obsessive Clash fan Mark Roberts expected to bond with about punk was his geography teacher.

Yet, here he was at Ysgol Dyffryn Conwy waxing lyrical about Joe Strummer with Mr Schiavone – a man who usually talked contour lines and capital cities.

Although a competent pupil, Roberts's passion was music, and from the age of eleven, he dreamed of being in a band. Raised on a diet of ABBA and the *Grease* soundtrack, as a teen his tastes shifted into the latest New Wave singles and the indie jangle of The Smiths.

When Roberts realised he shared similar musical tastes with Tony Schiavone, they exchanged notes on The Clash and offered recommendations. Already a dab hand at hosting gigs locally and spreading word of mouth via his fanzine, *Llymych*, Schiavone soon became an unofficial manager of his pupil's band.

Roberts rounded up his mates, including bassist Barry Cawley and drummer Dylan Hughes with Emyr Davies initially on vocals. In between Welsh-language covers of The Clash, their early songs were sketchy manifestations of teenage angst.

'Thankfully some of it will never see the light of day,' laughed Roberts. 'There'll be some embarrassing stuff in there…Notebooks full of horrible lyrics…Rockets, bombs and gangsters!'[52]

Once they left education, the line-up was shaken up with Davies leaving the group and Roberts becoming the de facto frontman. Cawley switched to rhythm guitar, which allowed Roberts's mate, Paul Jones, to jump in on bass and begin one of the longest running partnerships in Welsh music.

Gathering momentum via a series of Cymdeithas gigs in north Wales and amassing a keen following at Llanrwst Community Centre, Y Cyrff's songs extolled post-punk bands more than their beloved Clash. David Owens said:

> They weren't about three chords, two-minute songs and an idea. They were luxuriously crafted, producing an ambitiously lush sound that twisted and contorted around Mark's dark and brooding guitar structures.
>
> It echoed early R.E.M., Echo and the Bunnymen and The Smiths, but Mark's songwriting was ambitious and the words powerful – not as political as some Welsh bands, but loaded with imagery of everyday life. With songs like 'Yr Haint' ('The Plague'), The Housemartins they certainly weren't.[53]

Despite their relative inexperience, Y Cyrff had a confidence that belied their years. After their first recorded work appeared on *Cam o'r Tywyllwch*, Y Cyrff issued their aforementioned first single, 'Yr Haint', on Recordiau Anhrefn. A sub-three-minute slice of Bunnymen brooding melancholia, Schiavone sold it at the tuck shop and even on a school trip to the Soviet Union. Y Cyrff followed Rhys Mwyn's advice to the letter by self-releasing their second single, 'Pum Munud' ('Five Minutes'), in 1986 on their own DNA label.

The band were now in demand with gigs across Wales including a show-stealing set at the Eisteddfod, and it wasn't long before S4C offered them a TV gig. That didn't sit well with the band though.

Rhys Mwyn said:

> Paul, Mark and I had a meeting to decide whether it was politically correct to do S4C. I said, 'I think you should do it as it's good exposure'. We all had that underground thing of 'Maybe we shouldn't be doing telly', which showed how DIY we were…It was a little bit Clash doing *Top of the Pops*, but if it brought the music to a wider audience, all the better.

This included venturing into playing English-speaking student unions in Wales. There was a backlash. Mwyn continued:

> My thinking was that anyone coming to a Welsh university should hear some Welsh culture. When Y Cyrff and Anhrefn started playing so-called English student union gigs in Wales, the Welsh nationalists were up in arms – 'You're playing in front of English people, you can't do that!'
>
> We said we would play in front of anyone, so there was a rift with the harder-line, narrow-minded nationalists who were upset, which is ridiculous.[54]

In the meantime, Schiavone sold out a limited run of a bootleg cassette containing Y Cyrff studio tracks and live cuts called *Dan y Cownter* ('Under the Counter'). With Y Cyrff fast becoming one of the most touted bands in Wales, Sain snapped them up and released the mini-album, *Y Testament Newydd* ('The New Testament').

David Owens added:

> The album comprised seven songs of ornate grandeur and stark lyricism. The religious title worked on several levels – the Welsh-language music scene was writing a new chapter in Welsh history. It was a new beginning and those Welsh-speaking kids who were following the bands had a radical new agenda to cling to.[55]

Y Cyrff were by far the most professional and musically proficient amongst this crop of emerging talent. The only other Welsh-language band to rival them was Jess. Hailing from Cardigan and led by Jim Morrison-esque frontman Brychan Llŷr, they delivered on their early promise with their 1990 classic, *Hyfryd i Fod y Fyw* ('Good to be Alive'), on Recordiau Fflach.

While a lot of their contemporaries were blissfully ramshackle and frittered away any earnings on booze after gigs, Y Cyrff had their own bank account. Not only were they making regular appearances on *Fideo 9*, including a show in Warsaw, but they also performed on *The Tube* and *The Old Grey Whistle Test*.

Speaking in Richard King's *Brittle with Relics: A History of Wales, 1962-97*, Rhys Mwyn said:

> The thing with Peel that people don't realise today is if you got played – or especially if you did a session – if you then went up to Sunderland or Birmingham, people knew your songs because they listened to John Peel.
>
> We did a gig in Harlow in Essex, which Attila the Stock-broker [punk poet] curated – it was Y Cyrff, Anhrefn and Datblygu, and it was full!
>
> Throughout the '80s and that period of Datblygu, Y Cyrff, Fflaps and Anhrefn recording Peel Sessions, we all felt strongly that it was important that we sang in Welsh on those sessions. I remember talking with Fflaps about this because they were from a more bilingual background, saying, 'Look, it's important because John Peel's picked up on the Welsh-language records that I've put out and that's what we're trying to do.'[56]

When drummer Dylan Hughes left to join Anhrefn shortly before the Polish gig, it should've caused panic. Instead, Y Cyrff quietly went about their business and replaced him with Mark Kendall, who had been taught to play drums by Roberts at school. The new line-up rounded off 1988 by supporting The Alarm at Colwyn Bay in front of 1,500 people.

The next year brought Y Cyrff's most well-known song, 'Cymru, Lloegr a Llanrwst' ('Wales, England and Llanrwst'), which became a huge anthem, especially in areas where the Welsh language had precedence. Opening with more Bunnymen-esque riffs before exploding into a euphoric chorus, it started their self-titled 1989 EP. The song's title is thought to have originated from a statement by

Llywelyn ap Gruffudd ('Llywelyn the Last' – one of the last Princes of Wales before Edward I's English rule) acknowledging the town as a Free Independent Borough in 1276.

Alun Llwyd, Emyr Glyn Williams and Gruffudd Jones at Ankst had been avid devotees of the band since the start, so who better to manage them? Signing with the label later in 1989, they released live recordings from Cardiff and Warsaw on the EP *Awdl o Anobaith* ('Ode to Despair'), which featured the barnstorming single 'Hwyl Fawr Heulwen' ('Goodbye Sunshine').

Most notably, Ankst were at the helm for Y Cyrff's long-awaited, full-length studio album, *Llawenydd Heb Ddiwedd* ('Endless Joy'), in 1991 after a seven-year wait. Swansea-born *NME* journalist Iestyn George was smitten:

> I was working for the BBC at the 1991 National Eisteddfod in Mold, and all I remember was playing that album over and over in my car. I thought it was as good as anything I'd ever heard.
>
> It was quite handy – Steve Lamacq was editing the 'On' section of *NME*, which features new bands, so it wasn't too difficult for me to get Y Cyrff in there. Although I think he said yes because I kept going on about them![57]

Y Cyrff could easily have released more albums like *Llawenydd Heb Ddiwedd*, but their songwriting flair was crying out for a wider audience. Despite critical acclaim and a triumphant St David's Day show with Anhrefn and Fflaps at London's Powerhaus, the band yearned for something bigger than their limited living in Wales.

Speaking to David Owens in August 1991, Paul Jones said:

> We're trying not to get stuck on the endless circle of playing Welsh clubs because you can get trapped in that situation.
>
> We make an effort to try and not play strictly Welsh-speaking places, and recently we've had some great nights with a mixed crowd of both Welsh and English speakers.[58]

Armed with a string of classic albums and his *Fideo 9* vehicle, Geraint Jarman was one of the most influential figures in the transition from '80s to '90s. Previously banned by Cymdeithas for singing in Welsh to English audiences, he knew about the restrictions placed on the language more than most:

> There's a feeling when you know the time is right. You could tell at that time something was going to happen. Not only with Y Cyrff. Musicians were collectively talking about it, but keeping their plans very quiet for fear of reprisals.[59]

Rhys Mwyn added:

> They learned their craft, but they all grew up and realised that they had gone as far as they could. I think people eventually realised that you could be big in Wales, but it doesn't keep the wolf from the door…Respect don't pay the bills.[60]

All roads led to Pontrhydfendigaid in Ceredigion, and more specifically, The Pavilion, where Y Cyrff played their final gig. On Saturday, 7 December 1991, the renaissance of Welsh-language music reached its pinnacle on a momentous day featuring over thirty artists including Ffa Coffi Pawb, Fflaps and Crumblowers. One of the biggest Cymdeithas fundraisers ever, it ran from midday to midnight and was a fitting finale for a scene that had outgrown itself.

Watching Y Cyrff's set that night was a young girl who harboured dreams of rock 'n' roll stardom herself. Who knew that she would be fronting Mark Roberts's new band within a year? Or that they would top the UK charts by the end of the decade.

———

'You don't really want me to pronounce it on radio,' Gruff Rhys once told Jonathan Ross.[61]

Translated into English, the band's name inoffensively means 'Everybody's Coffee Beans' – in Welsh, it sounds like 'Fuck Off Everybody'.

Confronting the stuffed shirts and hinting at a sense of mischief that would sustain throughout their career, Ffa Coffi Pawb set out as they meant to go on. Like Y Cyrff, Ffa Coffi Pawb can lay claim to being one of the most important bands in Welsh music history. Within this psychedelic pop quartet lay the lineage of not just one iconic Welsh band, but two. Frontman Gruff Rhys and drummer Daf Ieuan would go on to form Super Furry Animals, while guitarist Rhodri Puw later replaced John Lawrence in Gorky's Zygotic Mynci. Plus, bassist Dewi Emlyn became a tour manager for both bands.

Born in Haverfordwest in July 1970 before moving to north Wales, Gruff Rhys spent his teenage years drumming for local bands Machlud and Emily. In 1986, Rhys formed Ffa Coffi Pawb with his classmate Rhodri Puw at Ysgol Dyffryn Ogwen in Bethesda, while bonding over Anhrefn, Datblygu and Y Cyrff, plus Joy Division and The Jesus and Mary Chain.

Gruff made the transition from behind the hi-hats to behind the mic, and with it came a change of instrument. He had previously put his rudimentary six-string skills to the test dabbling on his brother's left-handed guitar. When his sibling left home though, Rhys only had access to a right-handed one. Rather than invert the nut and restring it, he taught himself to play the instrument upside down, so that the bass strings were on the bottom.

At least that's how he played it when he did actually use it. In a precursor to his future eccentricities with the Furries, Gruff could often be seen at gigs armed with a power drill, producing sparks and squeaks as he ploughed it into Rhodri Puw's guitar.

They also found a primitive way of multitracking at their makeshift studio. In Mr and Mrs Puw's living room, they laid down tracks onto cassette and then played them via the stereo. Then they would play along to the recording, while capturing both on another tape recorder. The end result was *Torrwyr Beddau Byd Eang Cyf* ('Worldwide Gravediggers Ltd'). Fifty copies were produced and sold in pubs around Bangor, but the pretty penny they now command far exceeds the original asking price.

Ffa Coffi Pawb were one of the main beneficiaries of Rhys Mwyn's 'Pop Positif' movement, and it was at one of its meetings that Gruff first met producer Gorwel Owen, to whom he sold a tape. They still collaborate regularly today.

After a shifting membership, Rhys and Rhodri settled on a line-up with Daf Ieuan and Dewi Emlyn. The four-piece began to work on their songcraft a bit more seriously from 1987 onwards, but they remained ragged. 'We were awful live because we didn't ever rehearse,' recalled Daf to BBC Wales. 'And we were always drunk. Phenomenally drunk.'[62]

Gruff added: 'We didn't have any equipment for the first four years. We'd borrow the equipment off the main band. It got to the point where we started to headline, and we were borrowing the support band's gear. I think it was well after royalties started coming through before we bought anything.'

Ffa Coffi Pawb's debut album, *Dalec Peilon* (along with a live tape split with Crumblowers at Cardiff's Square Club), coincided with the inception of S4C's *Fideo 9*.

'It was a great way of making money because it meant you didn't have to have summer jobs,' said Daf. 'Do a couple of TV gigs and you get a cheque for £800. I thought, "I'm not going to start working for £2 an hour if I can keep doing this."'

Produced by Gorwel Owen and released on the Bangor-based label Casetiau Huw, *Dalec Peilon* was the culmination of four madcap musical minds uniting. The blueprint for the Furries was evident from the start too. 'Valium' revolved around a local gent who smoked the drug – a mind-bending forerunner to the Furries' 'Smokin" – while later tunes like 'Ms Cornflakes '91' captured Gruff's knack for great song titles. One of their earliest and most peculiar recordings, 'Llosgi'n Nhy i Lawr' ('Burn the House Down'), was a forty-three-second snippet of anger following The Smiths cancelling a north Wales gig in 1986.

As experimentation became the norm in Welsh-language music, Ffa Coffi Pawb set about crafting a dozen straightforward pop tunes for the follow-up, *Clymhalio* ('Mutual Masturbation'). Released via Ankst in 1991, it featured the gorgeous, synth-infused 'Breichiau Hir' ('Long Arms'). Thinking they were making accessible music for a mainstream audience, the band were frustrated to find the old ways persisted.

'Our second album was explicitly pop to get what we thought was contemporary, melodic Welsh-language pop on Radio Cymru,' said Gruff. 'But Radio Cymru were still playing songs from the '70s.'[63]

Hei Vidal followed in January 1992, but their best work also turned out to be their last. Amongst the twelve-song collection were gems like 'Lluchia Dy Fflachlwch Drosda I', which demonstrated a growing maturity, while 'Sega Segur' and 'Arwynebol Melyn' wouldn't have sounded out of place on the Furries' debut *Llanfair... (In Space)* EP.

Like Y Cyrff, Ffa Coffi Pawb found it hard to reach a wider, new audience. Despite the switch to Ankst and being arguably the highest profile Welsh-language band, they made the difficult decision to split.

Gruff said:

> We were really good friends, so it was really tough. But it was impossible to keep any momentum. There seems to be a three-album limit on Welsh-language bands. After you've played in Tregaron ten times, you notice that people in Tregaron start getting sick of you.
>
> It was a really weird time. We were making a bit of money, playing loads of gigs in Wales, but we were still completely isolated from the rest of Britain. Anhrefn used to give us gigs. They had loads of international contacts, they helped us out as much as they could, but our music wasn't really in line with the anarcho-punk circuit. We played gigs in squats in Holland.[64]

Living up to their boozy reputation, the band were sometimes paid with alcohol, so they filled their boots – not just sinking many a pint, but many a barrel.

The group were never going to be content to be paid in beer tokens indefinitely, and with the demise of *Fideo 9*, Welsh-language bands lost a weekly national launch pad.

This all resulted in a civil war – you either supported this new generation's desire to reform under different guises with English songs, or you saw them as traitors to the Welsh language.

THE KINNOCK FACTOR

THE MANICS AND ANTI-WELSHNESS

'You imagine what it's like to have your head stuck inside a fucking lightbulb, then you tell me how I'm supposed to feel!'[65]

Still reeling from the harsh treatment he had received from the English media, Neil Kinnock was furious with Tony Blair's press secretary, Alastair Campbell, that New Labour were jumping into bed with *The Sun*.

After all, it had only been a few short years since the infamous front page on the eve of the 1992 general election that had effectively killed off his campaign. Alongside the light bulb containing his head was the headline: 'If Kinnock wins today, will the last person to leave Britain please turn out the lights?' Even more sickening was the tabloid's ownership of the Conservative victory the following morning: 'IT'S *THE SUN* WOT WON IT'.

Owned by Rupert Murdoch, *The Sun*'s 'lights' headline had previously been used by one his newspapers during the 1975 Australian federal election. Likewise, *The Sun* had been tireless in its mission to turn the British public against the Labour Party and decimate its leader. Much of the media gleefully jumped on the bandwagon. *Private Eye* ripped it out of Kinnock, while his *Spitting Image* puppet blithered on incessantly and at one point even broke into 10 Downing Street.

Plus, an epithet was attached to his name that has plagued him ever since. Combining its love for alliteration and targeting his verboseness, the media nicknamed him 'The Welsh Windbag' (a moniker that has also been variously affixed to Dylan Thomas, David Lloyd George, Anthony Hopkins, Tom Jones, Harry Secombe, Archbishop of Canterbury Rowan Williams and Craig Bellamy).

In Wales, Kinnock was a divisive figure, having been one of the main voices behind the 'No' campaign for devolution in 1979. He also didn't throw his full support behind the miners in the national strike of 1984. Away from his homeland, he was viewed with even more suspicion. Red-headed and emotional, Welsh and with a strong accent, Kinnock was really up against it in 1992 to convince Middle England he was the man to lead the country – especially after presiding over a landslide defeat in the 1987 general election.

As Mike Parker said in *Neighbours from Hell? English Attitudes to the Welsh*:

> I canvassed for the Labour Party in the 1992 election in some of Birmingham's more curtain-twitching suburbs, and lost count of how many people said, 'I'm not voting for that Welsh whinger/ windbag/wanker/waste of space,' before triumphantly slamming the door in my face.[66]

Just ten days away from the 1992 general election, Kinnock scored a disastrous own goal at a rally in Sheffield Arena. If only the Welsh flag hanging the wrong way around and a campaign video soundtracked by Simply Red had been the worst of it.

Opinion polls suggested a narrow Labour majority, and, overwhelmed by the reaction of the crowd, Kinnock became overly optimistic. As Alwyn W. Turner said in *A Classless Society: Britain in the 1990s*:

> [Kinnock] gave the impression of already celebrating a Labour victory combined with the winning of the Oscar for Best Actor and the taking of the world heavyweight title. It seemed to confirm all the negative elements of his public image.[67]

The Tories ended up claiming an unexpected, fourth consecutive term. Margaret Thatcher poured salt onto Kinnock's wounds by declaring John Major's unlikely victory as the 'end of socialism'.

In his resignation speech, Kinnock blamed the influence of newspapers in swaying the result and threatened to complain to the Press Complaints Commission. He referred to a piece written by Conservative former treasurer Alistair McAlpine, which lauded Kelvin MacKenzie, David English and Nicholas Lloyd (editors of *The Sun*, *Daily Mail* and *Daily Express*) as the 'heroes of the campaign'.

———

'Richey was paranoid about ever coming across as Welsh,' said Nicky Wire to *Melody Maker*. 'He always called it the Neil Kinnock Factor: "Turn out the lights."'[68]

In 1992, Manic Street Preachers were suffering similarly anti-Welsh treatment. While the country was merged in the 'Madchester', shoegaze and baggy scenes, this altogether different beast burst out of Blackwood.

A perfectly symmetrical quartet, the band's chiefs of propaganda were the androgynous glamour twins of Nicky Wire and Richey Edwards flouncing down the wings. Sandwiched in between was the band's masculine, musical middle propelled by drummer Sean Moore behind a snarling Rottweiler in frontman James Dean Bradfield.

While Bradfield and Moore felt a kinship for Kinnock, with his constituency office located a few doors away from their childhood home, it's safe to say that Richey Edwards wasn't a fan. 'Everything Kinnock stood for is everything my grandfather would've spat at. Labour were told by the right-wing press they had to move towards the centre, but they should have gone more extreme.'[69]

Richey may not have had much time for his fellow Welshman, but shouting from the rooftops about their national identity certainly wasn't part of the Manics' modus operandi in the early '90s. A mess of eyeliner and spray paint, they had to be almost laughably OTT to gain any traction in a music press that ignored anything Welsh. In Marc Burrows's anthology *Manic Street Preachers: Album by Album*, Rhian E. Jones said:

> The Manics' blend of escapist glam plus radical aesthetics – Situationism crossed with Adrian Street – was a fundamental component of their early years.
>
> Their style was deliberately provocative, ludicrous and defiant as a means of self-defence, and as a frantic attempt to evade the world with which they had grown up…You have to go big if you don't want to go home.[70]

Gathering ridicule and rave reviews in equal measure, it didn't really matter whether you liked the Manics in their early days – just as long as you were talking about them. When they released their first single proper on Heavenly Records in January 1991 ('the wildest sounding record this week by several universes' – *NME*[71]), 'Motown Junk' was the most talked about song ever to reach No. 94 (its line of 'I laughed when Lennon got shot' undoubtedly helped). Revisiting this thrilling mishmash of The Skids and Public Enemy in 2014, *NME* said: 'They were still stencilling their own T-shirts and playing to half-full pub back rooms, but this icon-skewering single showed that the Manics meant business.'[72]

Notoriety was more important initially than critical acclaim, but when 'You Love Us' came out in May 1991 (an inversion of the Rolling Stones' 'We Love You'), it simultaneously encouraged fans and goaded critics. No matter how much you tried to hate this band, you would inevitably fall in love with them one way or another.

One of their earliest devotees was Philip Hall at Hall or Nothing PR, who travelled to Blackwood with his brother Martin to watch them rehearse. Not even the sight of a bleeding and maniacally grinning Nicky Wire could deter him after the bassist had somehow smashed his guitar into his own face.

Once Philip came onboard as their manager, the Manics were *everywhere*, gracing covers and gobbling up column inches. He showed remarkable faith in this young band, outlaying considerable personal finance and letting them live with him and his new bride, Terri, in Shepherd's Bush. This was especially risky when the band were still a bit of a mess live and sections of the press saw them as a short-lived novelty act.

Once journalists encountered the Manics, though, they were immediately entranced. Here's how David Owens recalled his first meeting with them:

> 'Er, Dave, four aliens have just landed in reception for you...'
>
> The voice on the other end of the phone line sounded puzzled...This wasn't the sort of call I was expecting from the *South Wales Echo* security desk, and when I headed downstairs to investigate, I could see why. Terry, our affable 60-year-old front-office commissioner and unofficial look-out post, was eyeing my guests suspiciously...
>
> All four wore skin-tight white jeans and looked a dazzling

collision of mod, punk and casual chic. The effect was un-forgettable – just as if a spaceship had spilled its contents into the newspaper's offices…

They hadn't even released their *New Art Riot* EP (the follow-up to their debut single, 'Suicide Alley') and yet they were talking as if they were the greatest and most vital band that ever walked the planet.[73]

Their name was stunning too. When James Dean Bradfield journeyed to Cardiff in the late '80s to busk on The Hayes, a disgruntled homeless man uttered: 'Oh, here's the fucking manic street preacher again…'

Slaying sacred cows and their contemporaries, the Manics had a knack for a cutting quote ('We will always hate Slowdive more than we hate Adolf Hitler'[74]). They even took aim at their own Welsh identity. Richey reserved particular vitriol for his hometown: 'If you built a museum to represent Blackwood, all you could put in it would be shit. Rubble and shit…Blackwood was a museum living in the fucking past.'

This shouldn't be construed as hatred for their surroundings. As biographer Martin Power said: 'Blackwood gave birth to the Manic Street Preachers as much as their parents ever did.'[75] Nicky Wire later acknowledged that the location of their upbringing was a crucial element: 'I don't think we could've done it if we hadn't grown up in a shithole where the only way to escape was to create your own reality.'[76]

Much of that early rhetoric can be explained as four young, wildly ambitious individuals who wanted to break away from the constraints of Wales. Yet, that process wasn't without its frustrations. David Owens added:

Being Welsh of course, they were met with wholesale suspicion, but their blistering attack and defensive gang mentality meant the barbs and the criticisms of their Welshness and everything else just bounced off them…

Although fiercely patriotic, the Manics still told truisms about Welsh culture and the divides brought about by language. I remember Nicky Wire famously saying: 'You have to be wary of romanticism. Wales is a much more complex and divided place than some people think. It isn't this glowing ember of close-knit communities. There's animosity there too. Some north and west Walians resent us talking about Welshness because we can't speak Welsh.'[77]

In particular, Richey had very little time for the Welsh language, and criticised The Alarm releasing bilingual albums:

> We've never learned anything from other Welsh bands, just never to be remotely like them. It's really patronising the way they suddenly learn to speak the Welsh language when they'd written songs about the bright lights of the Mersey or Liverpool about two years before.
>
> And the Welsh language was never important to us at all. I mean, what's the point in resurrecting something that's completely dead? Dead culture doesn't interest us.[78]

The Manics are often viewed as the sacrificial lambs that took the blows to pave the way for other Welsh bands. Yet before them, The Alarm had to withstand a lot of anti-Welsh flak. It wasn't all just jokes about their spiky hair and U2-lite comparisons. Nicky Wire's first-ever gig was The Alarm at St David's Hall: 'They were too nice and too positive. But to give them their due, they had it ten times harder when they started, simply being Welsh.'[79]

With myriad influences from The Clash to New York Dolls, the early Manics didn't take inspiration from anything Welsh. Musically, there was very little to even suggest they were a Welsh band – it wasn't referenced in the lyrics or via Bradfield's singing accent. As Richey said: 'If I tried to write a Springsteen-esque lyric about Wales, it'd be: "I went to the Pontypool factory / Then drove up Caerphilly mountain / And drank tea from a plastic cup". You can't do it.'[80]

Simon Price elaborated:

> While it is not quite accurate to say that the Manics could only have come from south Wales, it is true to say that they could only have come from *somewhere* like south Wales – anywhere in chronic exile from the swing of things.
>
> Despite early song titles like 'England Is a Bitch', there was nothing specifically Welsh about their desire to rise up and

dance in the ruins of Buckingham Palace. Cymric nationalism, cottage-burning and 'Free Ffred Ffransis' graffiti were never part of their agenda.[81]

One of the Manics' earliest photoshoots was outside Buckingham Palace, and their fierce hatred of the monarchy has been a lasting motif. Most memorably, 'Repeat' featured continual use of the line 'Repeat after me, fuck queen and country'.

When the band were due to perform 'Love's Sweet Exile' on *The Word*, they switched to the eight-line haiku of 'Repeat' at the last second. They even had the balls to sing it in fiercely royalist Thailand. A terrified Nicky Wire hid for the rest of the trip after concluding the song with the words: 'Long live the King, may he reign in hell.' His stance still hasn't changed: 'I'd rather fucking stab my eyes out with a pencil than accept a MBE,' he told *Mojo* in 2021.[82]

Early on, the Manics had far more in common with American FM rock than their contemporaries like Ned's Atomic Dustbin and Carter the Unstoppable Sex Machine. Even then, they were gloriously out of time, in thrall to the dying embers of hair metal as grunge exploded. Slash-like soaring solos permeated their debut, *Generation Terrorists*, while Bradfield's sexual grunts and groans on 'Slash 'n' Burn' mimicked Axl Rose's on 'Rocket Queen'.

Despite its distinctly British themes, the ominous outro to 'Natwest–Barclays–Midlands–Lloyds' was seemingly taken straight from the piano denouement to 'Epic' by Faith No More. The Manics did foresee the financial crash on that song though. Plus, the burning European stars on the album's back cover not only questioned the naïve triumphalism that greeted the fall of the Berlin Wall, but also predicted the break-up of the European Union and Brexit.

While the alternative music scene was mired in stoic indie credibility, the Manics possessed an insane ambition. In 1990, Richey fired acid-tongued missives to the industry's movers and shakers without a flicker of irony: 'We want to be the biggest rock 'n' roll nightmare ever and we want to take the monarchy and the House of Lords with us. We'll do whatever is required and give you the biggest posthumous record sales.'[83]

In one of their earliest interviews, James Dean Bradfield spat: 'We'd rather be sensationalised than just be another *NME* band and get easy, critical respect…There's no glory in the life of legendary toilets of Britain, we'd just rather go straight to the big venues instead.'[84]

After just two singles on Heavenly, the Manics signed with Sony for a ten-album deal worth £250,000, and they had no qualms in being photographed shaking hands with the suits. Bradfield told *Raw*: 'We could never reach as many people as we wanted unless it was on a major. We were willing prostitutes.'[85]

Early notice was served to Sony that this wasn't just any band. Smashing together nihilism and narcissism, sex and socialism, the Manics celebrated their heroes with literary and cultural quotes accompanying each song in the sleeve notes. Yet their most subversive ideas came via the artwork itself. They quickly rejected the label's suggestion of a phallic nuclear cruise missile poking through red velvet theatre curtains with *Generation Terrorists* daubed across it.

Instead, Richey requested Andres Serrano's *Piss Christ* (a model Jesus suspended in blood and urine). Another proposal was for Bert Stern's infamous defaced photos of Marilyn Monroe. The Hollywood star hated her last-ever photo session so much that she scraped her nails across the pictures and threw paint over them.

Richey also liked Marc Quinn's *Self*, a cast of a human head made out of the artist's own blood. Inspired by the situationists, one idea was to have the sleeve made out of sandpaper so it would destroy all the other records in the rack. Another concept for the 'You Love Us' artwork was for it to feature Chris Eubank – a figure people loved to hate.

All these ideas were deemed too costly or controversial, and the final design was disappointingly bland in comparison. Tom Sheehan's shot of Richey's crucifix and bare chest could've come straight off the record sleeve of any American rock band.

The Manics' manifesto in 1992 was as ambitious as it was absurd: to offload over 16 million copies of their debut album, outsell Guns N' Roses' *Appetite for Destruction*, headline several nights at Wembley Stadium and then burn out in a blaze of glory (perhaps literally, given their claim of setting themselves on fire on *Top of the Pops*).

Their hyperbole had to be outrageous to overcome racism from the music press. The barrage of headlines included, 'Cymru Feel the Noize', 'LlanfairPG Calling', 'The Newport Dolls', 'Guns N' Daffodils', 'The Boyos Are Back in Town', 'This Is Spinal Taff', 'You Make Me Feel Mighty Rhyl' and 'It Takes an Advance of Millions to Hold Us Bach'…

While they may not seem that offensive in isolation, it was the sheer volume of jaded jibes that soon wore thin. It didn't even matter if they were accurate. As Nicky Wire said: 'Every single fucking Welsh cliché was used. Whether it was Taff or leek or daffodil…"You Sexy Merthyr Fuckers?" We're 10–20 miles away from Merthyr…"The Boys from Bangor?" Bangor is 300 fucking miles away from us! We're closer to London than Bangor!'[86]

Even when Welsh bands had 'proved' themselves by the mid-'90s, the puns persisted, and the Manics' battles with anti-Welshness continued throughout their career.

In 1996, an increasingly frustrated James Dean Bradfield called host Davina McCall racist on MTV's *Hanging Out*. Unintentional she may have been, but McCall's ham-fisted attempt at the language ('*Gogogoch*') brought to mind all the clunky clichés like '*yaki da*', '*popty-ping*' and '*hoffi coffi*' that non-Welsh speakers find hilarious.

When Anne Robinson put Welsh people into *Room 101* in 2001, Nicky Wire gave her short shrift at the Manics' Cardiff Coal Exchange gig. That same year, on their B-side 'Little Trolls', Wire penned a scathing riposte to *Sunday Times* columnist A. A. Gill who had branded the Welsh as 'loquacious, dissemblers, immoral liars, stunted, bigoted, dark, ugly, pugnacious little trolls'.[87]

With so much ridicule to contend with, the '4 REAL' incident shouldn't have been a surprise. After a gig at Norwich Arts Centre in May 1991, Steve Lamacq claimed that the Manics' attention-seeking tactics were doing all the talking at the expense of the songs. As they argued over the band's legitimacy, Richey produced a razor blade and carved '4 REAL' into his forearm.

Even when 'Motorcycle Emptiness' was released in June 1992 – the Manics' first sign of genuine greatness – journalists couldn't resist the low blows. In *Melody Maker*, Jon Wilde wrote: 'Self-amusing pastiche of the epic rock ballad, already covered by Max Boyce on his forthcoming album, *A Faint Whiff of the Barmaid's Apron*. My Auntie Doris tells me she still doesn't have a clue what they're on about. Still, it beats shovelling for coal.'[88]

After all the grandiosity, *Generation Terrorists* charted at a relatively low No. 13. But these songs were simply too good for a short shelf life. Far from being 'Born to End' as one song title suggested, the Manics were showing signs of longevity far beyond their one-album-wonder claims.

Away from obvious highlights like 'Motorcycle Emptiness', 'You Love Us' and 'Slash 'n' Burn', 'Little Baby Nothing' offered a perfectly formed lyric with an acoustic-rock backing akin to Bruce Springsteen's E Street Band. After the band's request for a duet with Kylie Minogue drew a blank, the Manics approached porn star Traci Lords, who delivered an incredible vocal (described by Bradfield as like a 'female Joey Ramone'). Lords fit the bill so much better too given the song's subject matter of a woman being sexually exploited by men.

Elsewhere, 'Stay Beautiful' broke one of producer Steve Brown's unwritten rules: that a song shouldn't have the word 'fuck' in the chorus. When he heard 'Why don't you just fuck off?' throughout, he thought the band were pulling his leg. He removed the profanity and increased the volume of the guitar riff underneath. The trick paid off, giving the band their first Top 40 hit.

Initially titled *Culture, Alienation, Boredom and Despair* (referencing the lyrics to 'Little Baby Nothing' and Richey's tattoo), the album weighed in at a whopping seventy-two minutes across eighteen tracks. Its excessive length makes it a flawed masterpiece, while its programmed drums have aged it worse than any other Manics record.

Reduced to twelve tracks, there's an absolute classic within, but you have to admire their preposterous courage in releasing a debut double album. Despite not referencing a single song, Barbara Ellen's *NME* review addressed all the usual concerns, while still giving it top marks:

Is it derivative? The answer has to be 'yes'. In this department, the Manics are to the creative life force what Ronnie Biggs was to British Rail…But who cares? *Generation Terrorists* is the most ambitious, scene-stealing debut album of the '90s…People who steer too close to the sun often get their wings melted. The great thing is the Manics dare to fly. So, ten out of ten and stuff the marking system.[89]

Irrespective of such high praise, the review was still accompanied by an illustration of a lady in traditional Welsh lady garb spray-painting the band's shirts. *Ych a fi!*

In their early days, the Manics and Stereophonics were just as likely to secure coverage in rock magazines as they were in the mainstream music weeklies.

From local bands reverberating pub windows to singalongs before last orders, the south Wales valleys have long been a bastion for heavy music. This was no different for the Manics and Phonics with their respective loves of Guns N' Roses and AC/DC, favourites in their native Sirhowy and Cynon valleys. James Dean Bradfield's riffs found admirers in *Raw* and *Metal Hammer*, while Kelly Jones's loud guitars on *Word Gets Around* made them regulars in *Kerrang*.

Speaking to *NME* in 1998, Kelly said: 'In Wales, you just play all the old stuff. You become fashionable when you have to, when you go to college or whatever, but you've always got that background...We had to listen to Led Zeppelin until our ears bled. That's what the valleys are like.'[90]

Stereophonics drummer Stuart Cable agreed: 'It was always our brothers' and sisters' record collections. Basically, you don't put nothing on except AC/DC, Led Zeppelin or Deep Purple. If you came back with an Adam and the Ants record, you'd probably get beaten up.'

Bassist Richard Jones added: 'You walk into a pub in the valleys and you'll only find music from the '60s, '70s and '90s on the jukebox. Nothing from the '80s.'

In an article for *Louder Than War* titled 'The Sound of the South Wales Valleys – How It Evolved', Michael Hicks wrote: 'There's a theory that heavy metal and rock thrives in areas of heavy industry because they are unpretentious, no-nonsense genres whose percussive, aggressive sound echoes the sounds of industry.

'There was once a large heavy metal scene in the south Wales valleys that echoed the times – loud guitars and simple melodies...The pubs of the valleys are very much the lifeblood of live music...

'These towns are sleepy on the weekdays and come to life on Friday and Saturday. People let go on the weekend. The music made and consumed here has a similar pace. The verses are quiet and slow (the working week), the choruses are loud and euphoric (the weekend).'[91]

Not much had changed a year later when the Manics returned with their second album, *Gold Against the Soul*. They became the latest recipients of the 'Welsh Windbag' label thanks to Keith Cameron in *Vox*, while in *Select*, Stuart Maconie said they were 'bach with a vengeance'.[92] Plus, *NME*'s review came under the headline 'Meek Leek Manifesto' and referred to them as 'Gwentboys'.[93]

This time, the accompanying artwork depicted colliery wheels, leeks, daffodils, and tattoos professing love for Mam, rugby and sheep. Looming large in the background was a Hollywood Hills-esque 'BLACKWOOD' sign. Ironically, the artwork was by Newport's own Jon Langford of art-punk collective The Mekons, but that didn't prevent a backlash.

Paul Edwards, of Abergavenny, raged in *NME*'s Angst letters page:

Racism comes in various guises, but then as open-minded, liberal journalists, you're no doubt aware of that. May I applaud *NME* on yet another brilliant display of double standards. Long may you continue to support and champion the underdog.[94]

NME let their 'self-confessed rugby-loving, beer-drinking Welshman', Iestyn George, respond. While he didn't try to justify the illustration, he emphasised the irony of it being by a 'Newport-born and bred artist', and compared it with the self-deprecating Welsh wit of Max Boyce and cartoonist Gren. George also wrote that 'judging by the swelling mailbag, at least *NME* can be proud of provoking a reaction from the most apathetic generation of Welsh people in living memory'.[95]

A concise and slick ten-track collection in response to their debut's bloated length, *Gold Against the Soul* is the ignored middle child between *Generation Terrorists* and *The Holy Bible*. It's top-heavy and has the clunkiness of 'Drug Drug Druggy' and a meandering final three tracks, but (along with *Lifeblood* in 2004) it's the Manics' most underappreciated and misunderstood album.

Nicky Wire may have labelled it 'empty stadium rock' and 'an attempt at selling out that didn't sell', but it's a far better record than his mockery suggests. Saturated with some of Bradfield's best vocal and guitar work, it includes two of their best singles in 'From Despair to Where' and 'La Tristesse Durera' (Scream to a Sigh), while 'Sleepflower' is still a fan favourite forever requested at gigs.

Considering all the flak they withstood, in the early days the Manics didn't even find much support in their homeland, where their big mouths, bravado and slagging off of Wales weren't well received. One review was indicative of this Welsh apathy for the band. In the Cardiff University newspaper, *Gair Rhydd*, Duncan Heavisides wrote: 'Manic Street Preachers have nothing of any worth or value to offer. Tonight proved that. In a few years, they'll be gone and no one will care.'[96]

James Dean Bradfield recalled one particularly hostile gig to *Uncut*:

> Projectiles were quite common at our gigs. There was a great deal of spitting. I remember being spat at one night and watching this arc of thick phlegm moving towards me and just not being able to close my mouth in time and thinking, "Yum, cider and black."
>
> We played Swansea's Singleton Park in the early '90s at one of those Heineken festivals. Cardiff City and Swansea City fans had a full-scale battle. After kicking seven shades out of each other, they turned their bloodlust upon us. Flagon bottles were flying at us from all directions. I think someone hit Nicky on the side of the head with a flagpole.[97]

Decked in a floral frock and headscarf, Wire was a particular target that August 1993 evening and was later admitted to hospital with a concussion. The bassist reacted by smashing his guitar into an amp, while Bradfield issued an ultimatum that the band would leave should another item be thrown. Seconds later a can landed at his feet, and the Manics were gone.

An organiser appeared onstage pleading for calm and prophetically warned that if another missile was thrown, the Manics would never play Swansea again.

With a couple of tunes jettisoned from their set, the band eventually returned. After an ironic finale of 'You Love Us', Richey Edwards took the brave decision to dive from a speaker stack into the front rows.

The Manics didn't return to Swansea for twelve years. As Alun Hamnett said in *Record Collector*: 'A minor detail omitted from that karaoke favourite is that the green, green grass of home is all too frequently littered with broken glass.'[98]

———

While the Manics set their sights on surpassing Guns N' Roses, The Darling Buds weighed up against another music heavyweight – Madonna.

Unlike the Blackwood boys' baiting of bands, this was an inadvertent clash. After all, why would you challenge the Queen of Pop in her imperious phase? Her last three albums, *Like a Virgin*, *True Blue* and *Like a Prayer*, had all stormed to No. 1.

Lining up her fifth album in October 1992 – a concept record of sultry songs with an accompanying explicit book imaginatively titled *Sex* – Madge was shocked to learn another artist had already 'nicked' its name.

A couple of weeks earlier, The Darling Buds had issued their third album, *Erotica*, with similar artwork. There would be no comparison in terms of success. The Newport band failed to dent the Top 40, while the 'Material Girl' reached No. 2 in the US and UK.

'How dare she,' laughed singer Andrea Lewis Jarvis in a 2020 interview with *Repeat* fanzine. 'The timing of that! Ours was packaged up ready to go and already called *Erotica*. We were really chuffed with it and then boom, the biggest artist in the whole bloody world "stole" it!'[99]

Erotica is still the Buds' last album to date, and although it combined the same instantly accessible pop hooks as its predecessors with a more mature songwriting style, it has been overlooked. Produced by the acclaimed Stephen Street (The Smiths, Blur), its lead single, 'Sure Thing', is one of the best things they ever recorded despite its lowly rank of No. 71. *Melody Maker* guest reviewers EMF were less convinced: 'This isn't really going to stick its head up, not with what's going on in music at the moment. It's not going to get anyone's attention.' Unbelievable!

Another of Erotica's singles, 'Long Day in the Universe', should've provided the band's breakthrough in America when it was featured in the Mike Myers dark romcom *So I Married an Axe Murderer*. But they were hindered by line-up changes and frustration with the record label. Shortly after the album was completed, Jimmy Hughes left and was replaced by future Feeder drummer Jon Lee, who only recorded a couple of B-sides before departing for Dennis McCarthy. Matt Gray of Soldier Dolls was added as a second guitarist, but signed to Sony, they found themselves marooned as a little fish in a big pond.

Speaking to the *South Wales Argus*, Andrea said:

> *Erotica* had a couple of singles that were doing really well on American college radio, and we were doing a lot of promotion over there…We wanted to stay on tour and record more material, but we were signed to Columbia Records UK so they were like our bank.
>
> They wanted the American side to pick up the bill for what we were doing because we were doing better out there, and there was a bit of a conflict.[100]

Missing their partners, friends and families while stuck in limbo, the Buds returned home from Los Angeles after ten months and called it a day.

It was a sad situation for an act who were one of the most promising guitar-pop bands in the UK, gracing magazine covers, recording radio sessions and creating a cult following with their rip-roaring live gigs complete with confetti cannons. Formed in 1986 when Andrea was just nineteen, the Buds mixed the catchy, simple sound of their beloved Beatles, Byrds, Blondie and Buzzcocks with The Smiths and post-punk acts like Bauhaus, Cocteau Twins and Echo and the Bunnymen.

Their name referenced both Shakespeare's 'Sonnet 18' ('Rough winds do shake the darling buds of May') and H. E. Bates's 1958 novella *The Darling Buds of May*, which spawned a '90s TV series starring Catherine Zeta-Jones. Despite a modest start with a drum machine, Andrea and Co. soon introduced the world to their brand of perfect pop (or should that be 'perfick' pop?).

Their debut single, 'If I Said', in February 1987 on their own Darling label was funded by lead guitarist 'Harley' Farr (nicknamed after the motorcycle as his real name, Geraint, wasn't cool enough). Using inheritance money left behind by his late nan and capitalising on recording at Loco Studios where he worked, Harley jacked in his engineering apprenticeship to pursue his dream.

Like Rhys Mwyn, he set off for London armed with music. 'If I Said' was so good that it ended up being reissued by Native Records and received airplay from their favourite DJs. Andrea said:

> Harley asked whether he could put them in John Peel's pigeon hole and Janice Long's. And then it went to *Melody Maker* and *NME* and *Sounds* and the same thing would happen. The cleaners were saying, 'Slot it in here, love…' It was brilliant luck…John Peel phoned us and said, 'There's been a lot of interest in your band,' and said, 'Can I give out your contact details?'…We were like, 'Yes!' This guy from Doncaster came down to see us in Caerleon, and sort of sub-signed us to Sony.[101]

Explaining their controversial switch to a major label, Andrea suggested to *NME* in January 1989 that the Buds wouldn't get into mainstream shops that were saturated with Jason Donovan and Kylie Minogue:

> When it came out that we'd signed to CBS, someone said to Native on the phone, 'Oh no, The Darling Buds on CBS! And they were such a good little indie band…' I thought, 'That's nice, good little indie band, but we're a shit major band!' [102]

Their classic debut, *Pop Said…*, arrived a month later. It was preceded by the effervescent singles 'Shame on You' and 'Burst'. 'Hit the Ground' was expected to both propel the band into the charts in December 1988 and provide the perfect preview for the album.

A sub-two-minute sugar rush of Stone Roses guitars, it turned out to be the ideal opener for the record and arguably its best track. Despite its lyric about feeling vulnerable and exposed, it reached No. 27, leading to their only appearance on *Top of the Pops* with Andrea decked in a leather jacket and 'Pop Said' shades. The single would've fared even better had it not been banned by BBC Radio 1. Shortly after its release, the Lockerbie plane crash happened, followed a few weeks later by the Kegworth air disaster, so concerned producers at the Beeb pulled the plug on 'Hit the Ground'.

Producer Pat Collier drew on his experience as bassist for The Vibrators to introduce just enough edgy punk into the Buds' brand of pop punk, while preserving the energy of their gigs. *Melody Maker* couldn't summon enough superlatives:

> 'Things You Do for Love', a slice of ravished relish, is a double-deckered blinding blend of Harley's spunky-punky buzzsaw guitars and Andrea's vivacious vocal aspirations…
>
> [Her] demi-lascivious deadpan ululations are as cute and deadly as cocaine-spiked Coke…Atomic and angelic, The Darling Buds palpitate, excitate and tantalize with 'Shame on You', a thrilling spillage of blazing instrumental radiance and Andrea's peach-perfect singing.[103]

Pop Said… paid homage to the band's Newport roots, while hinting at greater ambition. As *Wales Arts Review* said:

> Guitarist Harley Farr had evidently read all the right books, watched all the right films, and had styled himself in the prevailing '50s rebel chic of the mid to late '80s. While bassist Chris McDonagh was that most Newport of things – a seemingly reluctant refugee from the town's thriving American hardcore scene…
>
> It's a sound that aspires to venues much bigger and far beyond that of TJ's – at the time, a serious act of cultural heresy for anyone with a guitar and a NP postcode.[104]

Following the album's release, in August 1989 the Buds played their biggest gig, supporting Simple Minds in front of 50,000 at Cardiff Arms Park. Sandwiched between Texas and The Silencers, Harley recalled the experience in *Melody Maker*: 'I stood onstage and on the very first note, a can hit my guitar. I thought, "Ah, this is going to be good!"'[105]

A follow-up to *Pop Said…* was released in 1990. Sharing its name with a nightclub where The Beatles and Stones famously met in 1963,

Crawdaddy possessed a more complex, hard-edged sound including the lead single, 'Tiny Machine'.

Yet, the instantly catchy, jangly guitars are what make *Pop Said…* the Buds' crowning glory. Often compared to bands like The Mighty Lemon Drops and Shop Assistants (who featured amongst other '80s indie artists on *NME*'s cassette compilation, *C86*), they never possessed their twee social awkwardness. Arriving at a time of 'Madchester' and grunge, the Buds were never really part of a scene, too early for Britpop and Cool Cymru. Plus, they were already established and simply not loud enough to be associated with Newport's rebranding as the 'new Seattle'.

The scene the Buds were most associated with was a short-lived one. Continuing the annoying tradition of music writers to invent new movements, from 'Romo' to 'the New Wave of New Wave', the Buds were gathered into the 'Blonde' scene. Its intention was to recreate a scuzzy slant on Marilyn Monroe glamour. Therefore, they were grouped with bands featuring blonde female singers like Wendy James of Transvision Vamp and Tracy Tracy of The Primitives.

Understandably, the Buds distanced themselves from it. Andrea said to *NME*:

> When 'Burst' came out I opened one paper and there was just a picture of me. I rang up CBS and said, 'Look, we're a band, it's not just Andrea's Darling Buds.'
>
> The fact that I'm blonde shouldn't make any difference… People aren't stupid enough to think, 'Oh, she looks all right, I'll buy her record.' If they are, I don't want that sort of audience.[106]

Reminded of the 'Blonde' scene by the *Welsh Music Podcast* in 2020, Andrea still had little time for it: 'It's terribly lazy. There was, and still is, more to all the bands than hair colour.'[107]

———

'YOU CAN'T BE TRUSTED FOR A MINUTE! THAT NOISE IS UNACCEPTABLE FOR THE NEIGHBOURS…JUST MODERATE IT A BIT!'[108]

Blasts of gloriously fuzzy feedback finally come to a crescendo before there's an abrupt interruption to this impromptu studio session.

These sounds aren't emanating from Rockfield or Monnow Valley, but from a garage in Pembrokeshire where the teenage band should really be finishing their homework. It's music designed to piss off parents. The fact that the long-suffering mother's rant at the end of 'Barbed Wire' is left intact demonstrates Gorky's Zygotic Mynci's commitment to embracing their oddness.

Even their name is intriguing. Formed in 1991, when sixteen-year-old frontman Euros Childs's voice had barely broken, the band blissfully ignored convention and stuck with the 'most ridiculous, crap name' they could think of. It was an early sign of their unwillingness to play the game, and if they had any aspirations of a serious career outside Wales, they would've chosen a better one. Even by the mid-'90s when they were on *Jools Holland* and *The Chart Show*, the band delighted in presenters struggling to pronounce their name.

'Gorky's' derived from 'gawky' ('gork' being the school slang for 'dimwit'), while 'Zygotic' was 'hijacked from GCSE biology'[109] (a zygote being a fertilised egg cell). Lastly, 'Mynci' is a misspelling of the Welsh word for 'monkey' rather than the direct translation ('*mwnci*'). When Euros jokingly claimed the band were named after writer and socialist political thinker Maxim Gorky, they were soon pictured in *Melody Maker* posing in Russian hats at Red Square.

Alongside Gorky's, Ysgol Gyfun Gymraeg Bro Myrddin in Carmarthen boasts an impressive alumni including Welsh rugby internationals Stephen Jones, Rhys Priestland and Ken Owens; snooker champion Matthew Stevens; comedy writer Sian Harries; Steffan Cravos of Tystion (who was in an embryonic version of Gorky's); three members of psychedelic alt-rockers Zabrinski; and Elis James. The comedian is a Gorky's superfan, who arranged bus trips to their gigs. In his 2018 book, *The Holy Vible*, James dedicated an entire chapter to them:

One thing I am as sure of now as I was then is that Gorky's Zygotic Mynci are the best band of all time…

Just as I was beginning to worry that going to a small school in a small town meant that doing something creative for a living was something that happened to other people, the Gorky's appeared on the front cover of *Melody Maker*…And they had achieved this success by singing in Welsh, and not fitting in, and playing their first gigs in Carmarthen. It suddenly felt like having my brain turned off and turned back on again.[110]

Initially consisting of vocalist Euros Childs, guitarist John Lawrence and bassist Richard James, the trio often swapped instruments as they committed their first stabs at psychedelic strangeness to tape. These primitive recordings would evolve into Gorky's unique formula – an alchemical smorgasbord that was at turns weird and whimsical, achingly sad, eerily dark and saccharine sweet.

Best friends at primary school, the 'two-man cult' of Childs and Lawrence first collaborated as children, creating comic strips and videos before recording their own pretend radio programmes. 'We were getting into experimental recording, dabbling in very basic production techniques,' Lawrence told *Shindig!*.[111]

Far from being a throwaway project, these early endeavours inspired their first limited-edition, self-released cassettes, *Allumette* ('Matchstick'; twenty-five copies produced in May 1991) and *Peiriant Pleser* ('Pleasure Machine'; 100 copies in June 1992). Plundering their parents' record collections, it's evident that they were listening to lots of The Beatles. Living a bit too far from Swansea and Cardiff, the local charity shops also became their haven as they dusted off vinyl copies of Caravan, The Incredible String Band, Faust and Soft Machine (of whom Wales's greatest living composer, Sir Karl Jenkins, was once a member).

Outliers they may have been, but these unfashionable, left-field influences soon infiltrated their sound and secured them a record deal while still at school. In no time, Japanese fans camped on their front lawns and asked them to sign English-to-Welsh dictionaries.

Several songs on *Allumette* and *Peiriant Pleser* were taken from sessions on Nia Melville's BBC Radio Cymru show *Heno Bydd yr Adar yn Canu* ('Tonight the Birds Will Sing'), along with home recordings and live cuts. 'Heywood Lane' hinted at their future greatness and was later revamped on *Barafundle* in 1997. 'Peanut Dispenser' denoted the band's schoolboy mischief at a time when the fuzzy Fenders and three-chord doom-mongering of grunge was the in thing.

Their debut album, *Patio* – a precocious, early 'best of' compilation of sorts – was bursting with ideas and creativity. Recorded at Cardigan's Fflach Studios, the twelve-tune scattershot collection was released via Ankst in June 1992 after a falling out with Recordiau Fflach (before being reissued in 1995 with twenty-one tracks). Reinforced by the recruitment of drummer Osian Evans and Euros's sister Megan on violin, *Patio* combined naïve, childlike charm with a sound that belied their years.

It received high praise too, with John Cale (from nearby Garnant) labelling it his favourite album ever. The band quickly went from listening to John Peel's show to having their own songs broadcast by the man himself, and having their first session in January 1993.

With Childs and Lawrence hailing from south Pembrokeshire in first-language Welsh families, it was only natural they wrote songs in their mother tongue. Neither nationalistic nor political, Gorky's soon got it in the neck for their 'sitting-on-the-fence' bilingualism. They faced abuse and blacklisting from venues, while reviews in Welsh publications refused to mention their English-language compositions.

The majority of songs on *Patio* were in Welsh, but they were accompanied by hilarious explanations in the sleeve notes, which could've easily been written in the margins of a notebook (e.g. 'Written after lots of Russian Revolution history lessons').

Described by *Wales Arts Review* as 'The Raincoats on amphetamines',[112] 'Dafad yn Siarad' is a fascinating insight into how Gorky's would develop – before ending with a bleating sheep. If that wasn't random enough, there's 'Reverend Oscar Marzaroli' on the extended edition – a tribute to the post-World War II, Scottish-born photographer because…why not?

'Siwt Nofio' ('Swimsuit') is an early example of the band's love for naming songs after everyday, mundane items, while 'Mr Groovy' is impossible to pigeonhole, starting with a Christmas greeting before taking in disco, country and grunge. Elsewhere, 'Miriam o Farbel' sounds like two songs going on at once with a backing vocal seemingly sung down the phone, while the seven-minute pulverising drone of 'Sally Webster' remains the only song in rock that shares its name with a *Corrie* character. It ends with another stern telling off: 'BASS SOUNDS TRAVEL…YOU DON'T NEED THAT VOLUME IN A ROOM THIS SIZE!'[113]

Wales Arts Review continued:

[Gorky's] were a psychedelic band with other influences including punk, grunge, folk, frequent nods to The Stooges, The Fall, Grateful Dead…'Barbed Wire' starts as if they're about to cover 'Get Back', but lurches playfully into something much darker in tone…

Very much like *The White Album*, this is a disparate collection of beautifully juxtaposed songs…There is real maturity here and, while it feels wonderfully chaotic, there are moments of subtlety and poignancy rare for such young musicians.

Elis James said Gorky's genius was crafting infectious melodies that are idiosyncratic without being alienating:

There's an alchemy to a band working their way into your soul, and it doesn't begin and end at the songs.

One of the first things you'd notice about the Gorky's' releases were the brilliant record covers, which were great to look at, beautiful enough for you to want to put on your wall, totally different to anything else in the record shop, and told you exactly what the music would sound like.

Even the font the band's name was written in was perfect visual shorthand for: 'We're a quirky, offbeat band and if you like us, you'll become obsessed with us.'[114]

˻MILLION SELLERS˼

EXPLORING THE WELSH INDIE SCENE

The Manics' manifesto may have been to sell over 16 million copies of *Generation Terrorists*, but The Pooh Sticks set themselves a more modest goal – to shift *just* 1 million.

'It wasn't so much a million seller, as a 25,000 seller, which doesn't have quite the same ring to it,' laughed frontman Huw Williams.[115]

Despite making the switch to Zoo Records (a subsidiary of BMG) for their ironically titled third album, *Million Seller*, world domination was never going to happen for this staunchly indie band. For one fleeting moment, however, it looked like The Pooh Sticks would break through.

'The World Is Turning On' was a two-minute thrill ride of infectious melodies. In November 1992, *NME* said it was as 'catchy a guitar-pop record as anything Teenage Fanclub have concocted'.[116] Elevated to the BBC Radio 1 daytime playlist with Gary Davies spinning it between Whitney Houston and Madonna, it seemed like they were destined for chart success. It didn't quite pan out like that. Huw said:

> In order to get into the *Guinness Book of Hit Singles*, you need to get into the Top 75 rather than just the Top 40. The greatest one-hit wonder of all time is some band that got to No. 75 for one week. What I love about 'The World Is Turning On' is that it got to No. 76 for one week, which I think sums up The Pooh Sticks![117]

The band deserved better, but they were perennially stuck between two stools. In 1991, their album *The Great White Wonder* was pitched between 'Madchester' and grunge. Despite having Pulp and Cast support them, they were also a year too early for Britpop (and were the polar opposite of that scene's commercial-success-at-all-costs ethos).

Formed in Swansea in 1987, The Pooh Sticks started out as lo-fi indie kids before branching into bubblegum power pop. Steve Gregory (also the manager of Fierce Recordings) was the group's driving force, writing, arranging and producing their records, designing the sleeves and choreographing gigs.

At those live performances, Huw Williams defiantly wore his red dragon hoodie in the days long before Welsh bands proudly proclaimed their national identity. 'Nobody wanted to know then, but I like to think I had a hand in all this Welsh tub-thumping,' he smiled. 'Although at the time, we had to go to America and Holland to work because Wales was dead musically, no one was interested.'[118]

Named after the game played in A. A. Milne's *Winnie-the-Pooh*, they weren't a band in the traditional sense. Trudi Tambourine, Paul the guitarist, Alison the bassist and Stephanie Bass-Drum all had one thing in common – none of them existed! Hence, the Hanna-Barbera characters (depicted on the front cover of *The Great White Wonder*) joined them onstage as cardboard cut-out bandmates. The link with the famous American animation studio came via Swansea cult icon Stephen Harris (aka Kid Chaos), who was living in New York. Also co-managing Fierce Recordings, Harris was a bassist with Zodiac Mindwarp and the Love Reaction, The Cult and Guns N' Roses.

The Pooh Sticks followed in the footsteps of a fine tradition of make-believe bands from The Monkees and The Archies to The Partridge Family and The Banana Splits. It wasn't until 1991 when Amelia Fletcher (Talulah Gosh and Heavenly) unofficially joined the band that they had another living member.

Further mystique included the spelling of Huw's name as 'Hue' to portray a shadow version of himself. It also continued the indie tradition of musicians 'lying about their names because they were all signing on the dole'. There was also the rumour invented that he was the son of fellow Swansea musician Terry Williams (Man, Rockpile and Dire Straits drummer). Furthermore, their 'live' album *Orgasm* wasn't actually live at all, and their 'studio' album *Formula One Generation* was recorded at home with a drum machine.

Much to the delight of those in the know, The Pooh Sticks were one of the greatest in-jokes in music history. Like musical magpies, the band cherrypicked rock 'n' roll relics and shined them into brand-new pop jewels. They unashamedly borrowed song and album titles, lyrics, melodies and guitar solos before recycling them into something of their own.

Voted *Spin* magazine's 'No. 1 Album of 1991 You Didn't Hear', *The Great White Wonder* nicked its title from a Bob Dylan bootleg. If song titles like 'Sweet Baby James', 'Pandora's Box', 'Desperado', 'The Wild One, Forever', 'I'm in You' and 'I Saw the Light' seemed familiar, it was because they were filched from James Taylor, Procul Harum, Eagles, Tom Petty, Peter Frampton and Todd Rundgren repectively. 'The Rhythm of Love' was a cover of The Strangeloves as you've never heard them before, complete with a snippet of Smokey Robinson's 'Tracks of My Tears' and Neil Young's guitar solo from 'Powderfinger'. Other unconventionalities included the quarter-hour epic 'I'm in You', which jettisoned its lyrics early doors before settling in for ten minutes of relentless riffing.

The Pooh Sticks were never afraid to rehash old ideas either. 'Susan Sleepwalking' was a highlight of *Formula One Generation* before it got a sparkling makeover on *Million Seller*. Elsewhere, they gave the cover treatment to 'Dying for It' by The Vaselines. The Scottish indie icons' 1988 EP of the same name also included 'Molly's Lips' and 'Jesus Wants Me for a Sunbeam' (later amended by Kurt Cobain on *MTV Unplugged*, and they're still raking in the royalties). 'It's a shame Nirvana didn't cover one of our songs,' joked Huw.[119]

The Pooh Sticks were just as quick to mention a fashionable influence like Jellyfish as unfashionable ones like Meat Loaf and Bay City Rollers:

> Other bands lift things from obvious reference points like The Byrds and The Velvet Underground. We don't sit down for hours thinking it would be cool to nick this or that. A lot of these professed 'hip' indie bands are so unoriginal and boring, they don't have any personality…We're totally opposite to that![120]

A much-needed dose of humour and an antidote to the po-faced *C86* era, The Pooh Sticks revelled in the indie scene as much as they sneered at it. Their song 'On Tape' simultaneously indulged and mocked their geeky, fanboy collector mentality. Plus, tunes like 'Indiepop Ain't Noise Pollution' and 'I Know Someone Who Knows Someone Who Knows Alan McGee Quite Well' were self-deprecating barbs aimed at themselves as much as their contemporaries.

Huw said:

> There was a guy in university and he kept saying, 'I know Alan
> McGee quite well.' The 'I know someone, who knows someone'
> lyric came from that.
>   I've met Alan a few times over the years, including on a flight
> to South by Southwest. He came up to me and started talking
> about the radio rather than The Pooh Sticks as he gets me
> confused with Huw Stephens![121]

Both 'Alan McGee' and 'Indiepop' were issued as part of a box set
of five one-sided singles in February 1988, which sold out their
limited run. After a Peel Session a couple of months later and a
double-page *NME* spread, major labels started sniffing around.
Instead, the band signed a distribution deal with Rough Trade,
with whom the singles were reissued as a mini-album, shifting
20,000 copies and securing a Top 20 ranking in the indie charts by
October 1988.

Huw looks back proudly at that feat: 'When people say The Pooh
Sticks are underachievers, I'm like, "Fuck off!" If you understand
where we came from and what we were, we're the most overachieving
band in the history of rock 'n' roll!'[122]

While The Pooh Sticks' trips to Utrecht proved fruitful for *The Great
White Wonder* and *Million Seller*, they couldn't capture lightning in
a bottle for a third time in the Netherlands. Issued via cult US label
Seed, *Optimistic Fool* in 1995 was their final release before splitting.
The band themselves don't even rate it. Huw said:

> The funny thing is our only album on Spotify is the shit last
> one because we own most of our stuff and we choose not to do
> anything with it.
>   Steve Lamacq played 'Young People' on the radio the other
> day, and said [adopts Essex accent]: 'If you try to find this band,
> they don't exist in the twenty-first century – there's nothing
> online!' And I'm there thinking, 'Yeah, that's us!'[123]

'I knew even at a young age that Swansea was a backwater – "the graveyard of ambition" as Dylan Thomas called it – that's why pop music became my great escape.

'In my head I was in ABBA, flying on jets, being adored, like every other kid,' said Helen Love to *Classic Rock* in 2021.[124]

Mention the name Helen Love to most music fans and you're likely to get a blank stare. That's not surprising really considering her eponymous band have never bothered the charts since forming at college in 1992. Yet in the indiest of indie circles, Helen Love means the world. With a cult following including John Peel, Mark Radcliffe, Steve Lamacq, Dave Gorman and Phill Jupitus, she is one of Wales's most enduring, but underappreciated, artists of the last three decades.

Helen may have harboured childhood dreams of emulating the jet-setting lifestyle of Agnetha, Benny, Björn and Anni-Frid, but, ever the introvert, she's barely played thirty gigs in as many years. Away from the live circuit, Helen Love's music is probably best experienced as nature intended – the embodiment of bedroom pop.

Defiantly DIY and committed to unfaltering indie values, Helen and her bandmates laid down catchy bubblegum pop on four-track recorders with cut-'n'-paste Casio keyboards, fizzing guitars and angelically sweet vocals, all kept in time by a drum machine beat. 'I love all that bubblegum shit,' she told *Nation.Cymru*. 'I can't bear any pompous serious music. It's not fucking art.'[125]

Their 1998 single, 'Long Live the UK Music Scene' (which saw John Peel brand the band 'sarcastic bastards'), took aim at the mainstream music propagated by DJs like Chris Evans. Its message was that the pop of Gina G would always prevail over Britpoppers like The Bluetones. Helen said:

Chris Evans blocked me on Twitter. I was told when he first heard 'UK Music Scene', he thought it was a compliment. Twat.[126]

I sabotaged our so-called career with that song, but if anything looks like it's about to go right for us, I usually say something or do something to fuck it up…We were never going to get a deal like the other '90s bands, but that was fine. I would hate to tour for weeks at a time or have plans drawn up months in advance.[127]

Revelling in limited-edition record-store glamour, Helen Love's music is perfect for collectors looking for buried treasure. BBC Wales agreed: 'If there was a prize for being "proper" indie, Helen Love wouldn't let anyone else get a look-in.'[128] As Helen herself said:

> How those bands played all that *NME*, *Melody Maker*, *Select* circus, I'll never know…They must have had some great coke. When we played a show in London, we would drive up in the morning and then drive straight back home to Swansea afterwards, never went to The Good Mixer for a pint with Damon [Albarn], it was all bullshit.[129]

Rehearsing at Helen's mum's house, the band didn't issue an actual album until 2000. Instead, they preferred to issue a slew of multicoloured vinyl singles with artwork capturing the nostalgia of teenage magazines like *Smash Hits*.

Their debut single, 'Formula One Racing Girls' – with lyrics referencing 'girl power' long before the Spice Girls – was released in 1993 after Helen's brother sent a demo tape to Damaged Goods. The small but über-cool indie label then collected together the first three singles and the *Summer Pop Punk Pop* EP for the 1994 compilation *Radio Hits*, which included a special run of yellow glitter vinyl.

Mixing disco with Debbie Harry and The Sweet with The Shangri-Las, *Radio Hits* revelled in the warmth of bygone sunny days. Closing track 'Golden Summer' did exactly what it said on the tin, while 'Greatest Fan' was prefaced by a radio jingle that made it sound like you had discovered it while turning through the dials. Another of its best tunes, 'Punk Boy', was covered by Ash.

Decked in denim, shades, leather jackets and Converse baseball shoes, the major influence of Helen Love's career has been The Ramones – and more specifically their frontman, Joey Ramone. Helen once claimed semi-seriously that she *only* listened to The Ramones.

With lyrics referencing 'Sheena is a Punk Rocker', Helen Love's second single was called 'Joey Ramoney'. A play on The Ramones' 'Sheena is a Punk Rocker', the song was brought to Joey's attention by The Ramones' UK fan club. He not only loved the tune, but also invited them to New York.

Helen recalled the transatlantic phone call to *Classic Rock*:

> One evening out of the blue, the phone rings and it's Joey fucking
> Ramone! He sounded shy and nervous, but then so was I…We
> ended up going over to play a show he was putting on. It was our
> first gig, we only made records for a laugh really. We didn't know
> how to play live, we still don't![130]

Fast-forward one month, Helen and her starstruck bandmates found
themselves in the New York City apartment of the six-and-half-foot
punk pioneer. It hadn't been all that long since Helen bought The
Ramones' double album *It's Alive* from Swansea HMV.

> I got home, stuck it on the music centre and I was transfixed. Song
> after song after song, 1-2-3-4, 100 mph, catchy as fuck, perfect.
> How could you not love Joey Ramone? A cartoon superhero on
> speed, and such a great voice. Better than Elvis.[131]

Yet, the band would have to wait another four days to meet their
host: 'Even though we were under the same roof, he was too shy to
approach us and kept asking the girl from the fan club, "What are
they like? Should I say hello?"'[132]

The day before the show, Joey booked the group a rehearsal room
in a dodgy part of town, but it was luxurious within. Making the most
of the built-in stage, wall-to-wall mirrors and huge PA, the band ran
ten minutes over their allotted time. Waiting outside was another
icon. Helen's love of words stemmed from a childhood love of Dylan
Thomas, and tapping his feet impatiently at the studio's door was the
man who renamed himself after him – Bob Dylan!

'I found it amazing that this genius [Dylan Thomas] was from
Swansea – one of us,'[133] Helen said. 'When we kept Bob Dylan waiting,
we told him we'd come from Swansea and live next door to Dylan
Thomas's house, but he wasn't interested.'[134]

They say never to meet your heroes, but Joey Ramone paid for
Helen Love's studio time and was charming company compared to
the curmudgeonly Bob Dylan. He also later introduced the band's
first Peel Session and duetted with them on a 2000 remake of 'Punk
Boy' ('from Swansea Bay to the USA!').

Later, Helen said to WalesOnline:

> The Ramones were the greatest group in the world, they were the Bay City Rollers, The Beach Boys and The Who all rolled up into one magic pop explosion. The fact Joey took such time and trouble over our little band just shows what a cool and generous guy he was.[135]

Joey Ramone died in 2001 after a long battle with lymphoma, and Helen Love paid tribute with 'Debbie Loves Joey', 'The First Welsh Girl in New York City' and 'You Can't Beat a Boy Who Loves The Ramones'.

After thirty years, Helen continues to release music with DIY individuality pumping at its heart. It's music that Joey Ramone would be proud of.

———

The voice stopped Mark Roberts in his tracks.

Despite third-rate buskers caterwauling amongst the hustle and bustle of Cardiff's city centre being nothing new, this voice was something else. Immediately captivating, it moved from raspy and raucous one moment to soft and sweet the next. The chords and melody were familiar – 'That's Entertainment' by The Jam – but he had never heard it sung like this before.

Glancing across Queen Street, he locked eyes for the first time with Cerys Matthews, but she wore a pained expression. One of her strings had broken and, without any spares, her performance had come to an abrupt halt. From between the shoppers, Mark realised he had exactly what she needed in his pocket – the elusive guitar string (and a perfect icebreaker)…

This fairy-tale-like story of love at first sight had all the hallmarks of a Mills & Boon novel. If only it were actually true.

'That was a load of bollocks to make us sound more interesting,' laughed Mark to the *Welsh Music Podcast*.[136] Likewise, their pseudonyms of Mark E. Zaun and Cerys Ananzapela (her imaginary childhood name) were abandoned quickly.

In reality, Cerys had been one of Y Cyrff's biggest fans and they had been in a relationship since 1991, which was kept quiet during the early years of Catatonia. In Cerys, Mark had found his creative foil, and the couple formed a songwriting partnership while living together on Gold Street in Adamsdown.

Mark and Cerys busked together but those early efforts were a world away from the instant earworms they would become renowned for. Playing obscure songs to the indifference of shoppers, the duo were often off-tempo, out of tune and as high as kites.

Regardless, Cerys almost ended up in The Pooh Sticks when they were looking for a female singer. Huw Williams said:

> My partner at the time, Natasha, saw Mark and Cerys busking outside Debenhams, and thought she was really cool.
>
> We went to see them downstairs in Clwb Ifor Bach on a Meltdown open mic night, and they were pretty fucking awful! Mark said to me, 'We knew you were coming and wanted to make it special, so we all took acid.' Cerys wrote me a letter afterwards saying, 'I *can* actually sing and play guitar!'[137]

In 1992, Mark and Cerys formed Sweet Catatonia (as they were initially known). Their name derived from Aldous Huxley's autobiography, *The Doors of Perception*. Under the influence, Cerys and Mark chanced upon the word 'catatonia' and mistakenly believed it be a blissful feeling akin to nirvana.

The band's line-up was completed after they posted a tongue-in-cheek ad that read: 'Three gullible tossers required to make up dodgy beat combo. Laundry skills a must. Do you like Mud?' Soon finding applicants with an aptitude for sluicing and a love for the 'Tiger Feet' glam rockers, they recruited former Y Cyrff bandmate Paul Jones on bass, drummer Daf Ieuan (of Ffa Coffi Pawb, Anhrefn and later Super Furry Animals) and Clancy Pegg on keyboards.

Honing their craft in a cheap rehearsal studio at the Grassroots youth centre, the group gigged as often as possible, including at their favourite watering hole, The Yellow Kangaroo in Splott. Much of Cerys's dole money also went straight behind the bar of The City Arms as they hatched their masterplan.

For the next two years, Rhys Mwyn mentored them and advised that it was pointless endlessly playing to mates in south Wales that were already converts. He instilled a similarly dedicated approach to gigging as Anhrefn, with shows arranged across London and as far away as Brittany. Record company interest in Welsh bands was still low with the Manics only just breaking through, so live circuit visibility was crucial, and Mwyn's Crai label (an offshoot of Sain) became their new home.

Catatonia hit the ground running with the *For Tinkerbell* EP in May 1993. Mwyn was apprehensive about releasing its lead track in English and felt a Welsh song would better connect with Y Cyrff's fanbase. However, the EP mixed both languages, which Cerys argued was vital: 'I was bilingual, but I never came across contemporary Welsh-language music until I was eighteen, so it initially sounded really odd. We had always said we would sing in English as well because I wanted to be as successful as Shirley Bassey. That was the condition by which we all got involved.'[138]

Mwyn needn't have worried. After initial indifference, the EP gathered momentum in the national music press. Iestyn George (an acquaintance of Cerys's from back home) was sent a copy at *NME*, but had no idea she was a musician. After his regular championing of the Catatonia cause to his colleagues, Steven Wells named *For Tinkerbell* as the magazine's Single of the Week in September 1993. Regarded as a notoriously reactionary writer, Wells instead lavished praise, calling it 'a rollicking rollercoaster that will leave you shagged and gasping and screaming for more'.[139]

Another recipient of the EP was Mark Radcliffe at BBC Radio 1. He gave it airplay due to his exasperation with the deluge of 'identikit grunge bands and Nirvana-u-likes' and his desire to help an indie band 'who weren't trying to be anything but themselves'.[140]

Its B-sides included an embryonic version of 'Sweet Catatonia' (later to gestate into full form on *Way Beyond Blue*), and the gorgeous Celtic lilt of 'Gyda Gwên' ('With a Smile').

Self-produced, the EP featured a sleeve photo by Y Cyrff collaborator Rolant Dafis of a cherub ornament picked up from Poundstretcher. There was nothing cheap or throwaway about this release though. It may not have been a chart smash, but with their growing live reputation led by a remarkable voice, Catatonia were putting the music world on notice.

The follow-up *Hooked* EP did exactly as its name suggested and ensnared more fans and media interest with its hook-laden melodies. While *For Tinkerbell* secured a lead piece in *Melody Maker* by John

Robb, its successor culminated in a UK tour with Salad. Released via Crai in May 1994 and produced by Ken Nelson, *NME*'s John Harris labelled *Hooked* as 'nigh-on marvellous' and compared them with The Stone Roses.[141]

Meanwhile, the band demonstrated its flair for languages with 'Difrycheulyd' ('Snail Ambition' – reflected in the mollusc on its sleeve) featuring bilingual lyrics in Welsh and French. Mark Roberts penned the Gallic lyrics with aplomb before admitting he had borrowed them from a French phrase book.

Reissued as *The Crai E.P.s 1993/1994* at the height of Catatonia's fame in October 1999, *NME* wrote:

> Cerys's copper-plated holler was more of a kittenish simper back then, but it's still unmistakable – a gurgle that dared to be Welsh, well before the valleys became the heartland of UK pop.
>
> What's more though, these eight tunes display none of the awfulness you'd expect from the maiden recordings of a bunch of skint drinkers with guitars. They sound…well, like Catatonia.[142]

Even by 1994 though, Cerys expressed frustrations with being on an indie label. She struggled to source some of the limited copies of the EPs for her friends and family, and set her sights much bigger:

> It's sad like, but I can't understand all this ideology about independent music cos it's a bit of an elitist thing…
>
> We're the best tunesmiths of the '90s. Proper tunes, original tunes that will spook you, tunes that will seduce you. You'll go to hell and back with Catatonia!'[143]

———

Gruff was sitting on the roof of a train speeding briskly through the luminous green forests of mid-Wales. Sitting up alongside him was a teacher he'd met at the party happening below, which they had both agreed was crap.

The plan had been simple: Gruff would assist a band of hedonists in transporting a crate of booze between Llanuwchllyn and Bala, after which he could either crash at the party, or split with his share of the crate.

Something had gone wrong, however. The hedonists had drunk the booze on the train, and subsequently gone out of their minds. Gruff and the teacher (who was equally embroiled and equally confused) had no option but to sneak politely out of the window. [144]

There may be a liberal sprinkling of poetic licence in Ric Rawlins's hilarious Furries biography, but unlike the first meeting between Mark Roberts and Cerys Matthews, this was no PR concoction. As Gruff Rhys explained to Simon Williams in an *NME* band intro piece:

> We were sitting in the same carriage and it was a really nice day, so we looked at each other and said, 'Fancy going up on the roof?'…They kicked us off, so we had to walk a mile and a half to the nearest town, and we got to know each other. [145]

Ffa Coffi Pawb played their final gig at the National Eisteddfod in Builth Wells in 1993 with Gorky's supporting, and Gruff was suddenly kicking his heels again. Huw Bunford was also at a loose end. The son of classical conductor Clifford Bunford, he was in Cardiff band Edrych am Jiwlia until 1989 alongside future politician and YesCymru chair Siôn Jobbins. While working as a teacher, Bunf also played with punky space rockers U Thant, who counted Guto Pryce and Owen Powell amongst their number (the former was briefly in Catatonia, while the latter became a full-time member in 1996).

Formed at Ysgol Gyfun Gymraeg Glantaf and named after the former secretary general of the United Nations, U Thant gave the Furries a run for their money in the madness stakes. Drummer and ex-Catatonia member Stephen 'Frog' Jenkins was renowned for donning a pink catsuit and silver hat, and he'd play so hard he would collapse.

Rumour has it that U Thant also started 'The Ayatollah'. Cardiff City FC fans first performed the head-patting gesture at Lincoln's City Sincil Bank stadium on 15 September 1990 – the day after U Thant played Cardiff's Chapter Arts Centre. U Thant singer Rhys Boore had seen footage of attendants at the funeral of Ayatollah Khomeini patting their heads to express their grief. When Boore started mimicking them at gigs, the gesture was soon adopted by Bluebirds supporters, and it became a symbol of unity and celebration.

One of the first wave of Welsh-language bands in Cardiff in the mid-'80s, U Thant left behind a couple of great albums in *Bugeilio* and *Duwuwd*. Plus, there was the wonderfully titled *Plop Plops* EP featuring a picture of a toilet on the sleeve.

Gruff Rhys, Guto Pryce and Daf Ieuan initially played as a techno trio, touring with Anhrefn in France throughout the early '90s, but their winning pop-rock formula would soon get the nod, as Gruff told *NME*: 'There's no point in doing a Jesus Jones. We're not interested in any crossover music, you're either rock 'n' roll or a techno band.'[146]

The music press loved the Furries from the start. Everett True described them as 'the Welsh ELO, only minus the beards…Formed on a moving train while on acid…A fucked up Supergrass for the Prozac generation.'[147]

Named after T-shirts Gruff's sister was making for the fashion and music collective Acid Casuals, Super Furry Animals were formed in 1993. They briefly had a future Hollywood star as their frontman, as Rhys Ifans was a childhood friend and housemate of Daf's at Colum Road. An avid attendee at Welsh-language gigs in the late '80s, Ifans was in the front row with Daf and Gruff at Anhrefn's legendary gig atop Mount Snowdon in 1990.

In March 2022, the first-ever Furries song, 'Of No Fixed Identity', was dusted off after three decades in confinement. Recorded with Gorwel Owen in summer 1993 at the same time as an early version of 'The Man Don't Give a Fuck', it provided a compelling insight into the direction the band could have taken.

The Furries' line-up was complete once Daf added his younger sibling and technical whizz-kid, Cian Ciarán (sons of the late Carl Clowes – former chair of Public Health Wales and founder of the National Welsh Language and Heritage Centre at Nant Gwrtheyrn). Ankst were already well aware of Ffa Coffi Pawb, and had no qualms about signing Gruff's new group, starting in June 1995 with their gloriously idiosyncratic debut EP called (deep breath)…

Llanfairpwllgwyngyllgogerychwyndrobwllanty-
siliogogogochynygofod
(In Space).

The bumper title earned the Furries a spot in the *Guinness Book of Records* for the longest title for an EP (the legendary Anglesey village also lent its name to a Russian rock band formed in St Petersburg in 1993!). A melting pot of prog, psychedelia and pop, there was little deviation from the Ffa Coffi Pawb template on two of its tracks – the double-entendre-titled 'Organ yn Dy Geg' ('An Organ in Your Mouth') and 'Crys Ti' ('T-shirt'). But the Furries hit their stride with the ascending melodies of 'Fix Idris', while the epic finale of 'Blerwytirhwng?' was the first of their many wild sonic experimentations.

NME was hooked: 'Their pop sorcery combines '70s razzle metal, whizzing samples and ace la-la harmonies…in Welsh. The effect is akin to a spaceship crashing onstage on *Top of the Pops* in the middle of a Wizzard song.'[148]

The magazine was also in attendance at the Furries' first London show, at the Splash Club where Gruff screamed, 'Wake up, motherfuckers,' at a lethargic crowd. Simon Williams wrote: 'On vinyl, they display drippy, wistful, psychedelic tendencies. On stage, however, they're a far more stompy proposition, zipping by in a haze of implausibly fine melodies and magnificently blatant guitar solos, spiced with the odd blast of sonic intensity.'[149]

A later *NME* review of a show at the London Astoria heaped praise on their 'rabid dog-howling, Syd Barrett-style, honky-tonk piano and mis-tuned radio squeals to produce flog-worthy art of the highest order.' The Furries sounded utterly unlike anything else out there.

The weird, shimmering brilliance of the *Moog Droog* EP – their second and final release for Ankst in October 1995 – proved that the debut was no fluke. Combining pop flair with cheeky mischievousness, its multifaceted title referenced the synthesiser manufacturer Robert Moog, and the 'Nadsat' term for 'friend' from *A Clockwork Orange*. It was also a pun on the Welsh *'mwg drwg'*: meaning 'wacky baccy' (slang for cannabis, or more literally 'bad smoke'). The artwork was equally hallucinogenic and dystopian, depicting a faceless humanoid brushing dirt under a chessboard carpet.

'Pam V' and 'Focus Pocus/Debiel' quickly became cult classics and formed focal parts of their 1998 odds-'n'-sods compilation, *Out Spaced*, while 'Sali Mali' showcased their gentler, nostalgic side.

Named after the titular character in the fictional locale of Pentre Bach ('small village'), many Welsh-speaking children learn to read via Mary Vaughan Jones's books. In 2000, an animated series of *Sali Mali* was broadcast on S4C, narrated by Rhys Ifans and with a theme tune sung by Cerys Matthews.

The standout track, though, was the Furries' first foray into English-language music, 'God! Show Me Magic', which was an instant remedy to the '60s-obsessed Britpop scene. *NME* said:

> What sets Super Furry Animals apart is their intoxicating blend of idealism, realism, and pure optimism. They are sharp witted and genuinely earnest…You only have to check a few of their heroes to know that radicalism rather than retrovision stokes their ambition.[150]

1995 had been a promising start, but, like Catatonia, the band were yearning to sell far more than the hundreds they were shifting via Ankst. Ric Rawlins said:

> Throughout the year, Daf's catchphrase had been 'We'll be signed by Christmas', but in reality, the band's expectations were more grounded.
>
> In the seven years that Ffa Coffi Pawb had been together, they'd played London just once, while Radio 1 and MTV might as well have existed on a different planet.[151]

Little did they know that the stars would soon align, and by 1996, Super Furry Animals would be signed to the coolest record label in the country…

———

Meanwhile, Gorky's returned on St David's Day 1994 with their second record and first album proper, *Tatay*.

Sharing its name with a Spanish classical guitar, the follow-up to *Patio* on Ankst was a beguiling mix of psychedelic folk, prog rock and whimsical pop. Co-produced with Alan Holmes (who also supplied the trippy artwork) and engineered by Gorwel Owen at Stiwdio Ofn, it retained that magical DIY, field-recordings vibe of its predecessor.

With sixteen tracks crammed into forty-one minutes, *Tatay* was bold, but never boring, using a broad palette of Moog synthesisers, trombones, violins and steel guitar.

While Oasis were snorting white lines and singing 'Cigarettes & Alcohol', Gorky's rarely addressed conventional, hedonistic tropes. *Tatay* began with the domesticated 'Thema o Cartref' ('Theme from Home'), and, unlike Liam and Noel, Gorky's were 'about as laddy as probiotic yoghurt'.[152] This extended to their between-song chatter, as Elis James further observed: 'My favourite example is a late-night argument at what sounds like a sleepover when Steffan, the then violin player, replies to pleas to be quiet with an indignant "Oh sorry, owner of the house"'.[153]

Elsewhere, Gorky's unearthed magic from the everyday mundane with song titles like 'Gegin Nos' ('Night Kitchen') and 'Silff Ffenest' ('Windowsill'), while their playful weirdness comes to the fore on 'Beth Sy'n Digwydd i'r Fuwch?' ('What's Happening to the Cow?') They couldn't have been further away from the formulaic, overproduced mid-'90s zeitgeist, and they mined different influences to their '60s-fixated contemporaries. The Beatles are a major reference point for Gorky's, but on *Tatay*, they pile that Lennon-and-McCartney piano-based approach with bizarre twists and exotic instrumentation. All the while, they celebrate simple, pastoral pleasures, usually in Welsh.

Melody Maker said:

> Who cares what they're singing about? Gorky's songs make you feel warm all over and when things start to get a little weird, shit happens. Suddenly, you're in the middle of a musical temper tantrum…How do they do it? Fuck knows, but you know they have to be good to get away with it.[154]

In the *Sunday Times*, comedian and fan Stewart Lee added:

> Where Britpop bands creep out from between Paul Weller's legs to create a cultural orthodoxy of second-hand Beatles albums and Small Faces CD reissues, Gorky's have chosen to plunder a different back catalogue of late British psychedelia. Their audience is a weird mixture of supportive peers and a few delighted former hippies comforted by traces of Soft Machine and Kevin Ayers.[155]

Indeed, *Tatay* is Gorky's homage to the Canterbury scene of the '60s and '70s, which practised improvisational styles of prog rock, jazz and psychedelia. Kevin Ayers's 1970 album, *Shooting at the Moon,* is cited as 'the best LP of all time',[156] and they pay tribute with a track named after him.

There's also a cover of 'O, Caroline' by Robert Wyatt's post-Soft Machine band, Matching Mole. His influence looms large throughout – 'Beth Sy'n Digwydd i'r Fuwch' and 'Naw. E. Pimp' feature backwards cymbal and keyboards, but still manage to be melodic earworms. 'Amsermaemaiyndod/Cinema' sounds like a different song in each ear through headphones (before finishing with an impromptu argument about teabags). The avant-garde randomness of 'When You Hear the Captain Sing' recalls another maverick musician – Captain Beefheart.

The sleeve notes continue to be a joy too. 'Y Ffordd Oren' ('The Orange Way') is inspired by reading a stranger's diary. Likewise, the idea for 'Gegin Nos' was nicked from the children's book *In the Night Kitchen* by Maurice Sendak. 'Silff Ffenest' revolves around a girl called Anna, who falls out of the window – only to discover she can fly. Long before Noel Gallagher's High Flying Birds had a lady playing the scissors, Gorky's invented their own forms of improvised percussion including a chair, a kettle, knives and forks, Sellotape and cardboard boxes.

Raw, innocent and eccentric, *Tatay* remains Gorky's weirdest album and is often cited as their best, but probably not advisable as a starting point!

THE NEW SEATTLE

REVISITING NEWPORT'S
EXPLOSIVE UNDERGROUND SCENE

'I'M GONNA CHOP YOU UP, YA CUNTS!!!'[157]

In one fell swoop of a samurai sword, three dorky-looking Californians were stunned into silence.

One second they had been innocently fooling around; the next, an irate, tattooed, muscle-bound Welshman was wielding a deadly weapon in their faces.

Fresh from the release of their second album, *Kerplunk*, in December 1991, Green Day were virtual unknowns in the UK, but they were looking to attract a following in south Wales.

'Newport is the last town you hit when you leave Wales and head for the Severn Bridge. It's the first town you hit when you come from England, so it has a sort of no-man's-land quality,' said 60 Ft. Dolls singer Richard Parfitt. 'We felt like the other – not particularly Welsh, definitely not English.'[158]

Living between suppression and expression, Newport was in a halfway state of otherness during the '90s. Yet, it would also become home to one of the country's most exciting underground scenes. At its heart was an unlikely club: TJ's.

Green Day were bottom of the bill for the eighth annual Cheap Sweaty Fun Christmas party – a night Billie Joe Armstrong, Mike Dirnt and Tré Cool would never forget…

'I WARNED YOU ONCE, YA AMERICAN BASTARDS!'[159]

Dressed only in his underpants, with eyes bulging and neck veins throbbing like bass guitar strings, Dean Beddis glared at his lodgers as they hid by the Christmas tree. Promoter Simon Phillips had requested the band stay with Cowboys Killers' formidable frontman, who was clearly expecting better behaviour.

'I had to go to work the next day, so when I went to bed I told them to be quiet,' Beddis told WalesOnline in 2017. 'They were jumping up and down in their sleeping bags. They looked like caterpillars. I had a samurai sword on the wall and said, "I FUCKING TOLD YOU TO BE QUIET!"[160]

Fearing for their lives as he swung the weapon around his head, the cowering Californians were only too happy to accede to his demands.

Beddis can afford to laugh about it now:

> They've got no sense of humour, these Americans…I thought I'd shit them up enough, but the following morning they asked if they could stay for Christmas! I said no.
>
> A few years later, we were playing in London with The Offspring and NoFX. Green Day's drummer, Tré, came over and said they had stayed at my house. I said, 'You've become a millionaire since then,' and he was like, 'Yeah, we're doing OK!'[161]

───

Located on Clarence Place and named after its owners, partners Trilby Tucker and John Sicolo, TJ's was the opposite of glamour.

A dingy, cave-like dive with masses of dog-eared gig posters and an endlessly sticky floor that could suck your soles off, TJ's revelled in its grittiness. Green Day's brush with a samurai sword was just one of the legendary tales etched into its folklore. Andrea Lewis Jarvis said:

> If you started pogoing in there, you'd probably end up with a concussion. I remember people jumping up and hitting themselves on protruding bits of ceiling…
>
> When The Darling Buds first played TJ's, it was still in its very early days, but every time I went away and came back, it had just grown that little bit crazier…It became this mysterious place as well as an exciting kind of place to get absolutely off your face in.[162]

Spattered in graffiti, the bogs were a piss-ridden mess where flies flittered around urinals, which were sometimes booted off the wall. Loo seats were often missing and toilet paper a rare luxury. Completely out of place near the front entrance was a fake palm tree (a nod to TJ's past as a themed restaurant), while the snooker table was stained by all sorts of fluids.

A constant fug hung heavy in the air as Sicolo could often be heard telling people to put out whatever they were smoking. Yet you only had to glance at the photos behind the bar to realise how many icons had played there.

There was the time when Iron Maiden ventured into the club looking to borrow a local band's instruments for their Newport Centre gig, but Trilby sent them packing.

Also, there was the night when it was rumoured The Stone Roses were coming back from an extended hiatus to play a secret gig at TJ's. The posters for Oasis's 'Supersonic' tour date in May 1994 said 'Plus Very Special Guests'. With the Roses spending an eternity recording *Second Coming* just up the road at Rockfield, fans flocked to the gig (when they released their comeback single, 'Love Spreads', later that year, John Squire's artwork featured one of the stone cherubs on Newport Bridge).

As it turned out, it was 60 Ft. Dolls, who received the £50 offer for the support slot from Oasis's Ebbw Vale-born manager, Marcus Russell. It was that early in their career, Richard Parfitt hadn't even heard of them. The Gallagher brothers had already fallen out by the soundcheck and Liam was threatening not to sing. When Noel was informed that the Manics would be in attendance, he challenged them to a fight!

Oasis took half the venue back to the Kings Hotel on High Street. Welsh photographer Rob Watkins snapped pics of Liam posing beneath the sign of its aptly titled Oasis Bar. Following a mammoth drinking session, Bonehead emptied the contents of his room out of the window.

Most memorable of all was Tuesday, 10 December 1991. A line-up featuring Hole, Therapy? and Daisy Chainsaw was impressive enough, but Courtney Love brought with her someone who would soon become arguably the most famous musician on the planet. Incredibly, Nirvana frontman Kurt Cobain stood unassuming and unbothered at the back despite having released *Nevermind* – the most important record for a generation – only three months prior.

Shortly before the gig, Kurt and Courtney had been in a car crash on the Old Green Roundabout, which wrote off booking agent Russell Warby's Škoda. Shuffling into the venue with his head down, promoter Simon Phillips asked for the £4.50 entry fee before Cobain swept his fringe out of his face and the penny dropped. After the shaky start to their night, legend has it that Kurt proposed to Courtney.

Phillips also somehow managed to turn down two Nirvana shows in Newport. Firstly, he couldn't meet the £400 fee for them in their very early career, and then he couldn't find them a date when they came calling again six months later.

While running Rockaway Records at Newport Market, Phillips devised Cheap Sweaty Fun after left-wing students visited the shop during the miners' strike. Not only did he guide them to the coolest releases, but he also encouraged them to support the food fund for miners' families and attend benefit gigs in local venues, including one featuring The Pogues.

Initially, Cheap Sweaty Fun nights were held at Stow Hill Labour Club until the gigs came to TJ's in 1987. That same year, they promoted a Butthole Surfers gig at Newport Centre where frontman Gibby Haynes almost burned the place down after igniting bottles of surgical spirit.

Hosting American punk and hardcore bands like Sonic Youth, The Offspring, The Misfits and Melvins at TJ's was a master stroke. Combined with the explosive crop of local bands like 60 Ft. Dolls, Dub War, Novocaine and Flyscreen, Newport was the place to be for alternative music fans. *New York Times* writer and rock biographer Neil Strauss labelled it the 'new Seattle'[163] and thus continued the '90s journalistic trend for compartmentalising scenes away from London.

As is often the case with media-created tags though, there's pushback, especially when they're not entirely accurate. Richard Parfitt recalled:

> Neil Strauss had been sent over to cover Welsh-language music at the Eisteddfod, but somehow, he got waylaid and stayed at the Kings Hotel. He wandered over the bridge and went to TJ's, and found himself seduced by this venue...
>
> When he went back to America, he wrote an article for *Spin* magazine and he did *not* say, 'Newport is the new Seattle'. What he actually said was, 'Wales is the new Seattle', which doesn't make any sense! But there was so much attention on Newport, that it became that.[164]

The Rock of Newport filmmaker Nathan Jennings added: 'The "new Seattle" was one moment, and lot of Newport bands don't agree with it. There's a mentality in Newport of "it's a shithole, but it's *our* shithole…" We don't need that outside validation.'[165]

Even more condemning was Funeral for a Friend frontman Matthew Davies-Kreye in his 2015 piece for *Vice* titled 'South Wales was the New Seattle – Total Bollocks!':

> What was happening in Wales was probably happening other places in the UK too, but for some reason the quirkiness of 'Oh, it's got an accent and it's got bilingual road signs' seemed to appeal to the marketers.
>
> It started happening in the '90s with the Manics, 60 Ft. Dolls and Novocaine. You'd pick up *Kerrang* and it would say 'Newport is the new Seattle.' Then the millennium happened and it was like, 'OH CHRIST, ALL OF SOUTH WALES IS THE NEW SEATTLE.' It was total bollocks. They were nothing alike other than the fact that we're by the coast, it's depressing, and it rains for 290 of the days of the year.[166]

Sam Dabb now runs the Le Pub venue in the city centre. As a teenager, she was fully immersed in Newport's bubbling scene and was in the band Disco (immortalised with 'Ragdoll' on the 1997 compilation *Dial M for Merthyr*). Attitudes towards Welsh music were transforming thanks to the Manics in nearby Blackwood, combined with Catatonia and the Furries in Cardiff and Gorky's in Pembrokeshire. Newport more than held its own and punched above its weight. Sam feels it was the strength of the bands and promoters that were the real driving force rather than any outside influence:

> The mid-'90s scene was something really special and attracted attention from all over the world. Being in a band back then was absolutely crazy. As soon as you mentioned Newport, people wanted to book you for a gig or interview…
>
> Every pub had a gig on. There wasn't a day of the week you couldn't find original live music somewhere – Le Pub, The Riverside, Grooves and, of course, TJ's being the main four venues.
>
> Touring artists were coming to Newport weekly thanks to

the amazing work of Simon at Cheap Sweaty Fun and Conal Dodds…We don't really give credit to the promoters that brought the bands to Newport…They were the real orchestrators.[167]

Another influential figure was journalist Andy Barding, who recognised Newport's in-between state. Not close enough to London to lure the attention of the mainstream music media, Newport also wasn't 'Welsh' enough to get coverage from the Welsh national press either. Therefore, he took it upon himself:

> My fanzine was called *Frug*, which is a '50s expression for a free-form dance.
>
> The reason I set it up was because the *Western Mail* wasn't going to let me write about the music coming through Newport, which I felt was some of the most important music being made in the world at that time…
>
> These bands would come over and play Newport and London and then they would bugger off to Europe. We weren't part of a circuit – we were the circuit.[168]

'At one point, they switched our electricity off…I'd dangled the TV out of the window, still switched on and hanging from the power cable.'[169]

It was a rock 'n' roll tale that would make even Mötley Crüe blush. These things weren't supposed to happen in a plush hotel, let alone in sleepy Oswestry. But a young band called 60 Ft. Dolls were in town to record a BBC Radio Wales session, and carnage was about to commence.

Drummer Carl Bevan recalled to band biographer Roy Wilkinson:

> When we got back to the hotel, I asked the receptionist who was paying for the extras bill. 'The BBC,' she said. Our next words were, 'Six pints, three double brandies please,' followed closely by, 'Same again…'
>
> They chucked us out at 11.30, so me and Mike broke into the restaurant, loaded a service trolley with champagne and whisky and barricaded ourselves in our room…
>
> I was still a student and Mike and Rich were on the dole. We'd

just signed with Rough Trade and were waiting for the cash to come through. We literally had a fiver between us…

The next day our manager turned up and said, 'The money's in boys. You're all having a lump sum of £5,000 to get started, plus a wage. Apart from Carl and Mike, whose hotel bill is £10,000…' A lot of that was for devastating one of the oldest bowling greens in Britain.

We went through tour managers very quickly. Dick, one of our roadies, had a clause in his job description saying he wasn't allowed to go to sleep before me and Mike. Dick fixed smashed-up guitars in record time…And kept me out of hospital and jail for years![170]

Although the band baulked at the media's 'yob rock' tag, 60 Ft. Dolls' music was undoubtedly an aggressive experience. Yet it spoke more of hedonistic highs than brawling in the back streets. '[The Dolls] were well known for hell-raising,' said Parfitt. 'I was a bit older, but I was never a big drinker really. I was the Gary Barlow of the band. I was the straight guy compared to Mike and Carl.'[171]

In the early '90s, Parfitt was living in a small two-bedroom flat with his wife and baby. He was also broke, and making ends meet by delivering pizzas for Nicolino's in Newport. Donna Matthews was a waitress there, and lived above TJ's. Parfitt said:

I remember her as a teenager busking with her sister dressed like The Bangles. At the end of each shift, her inebriated boyfriend would come to meet her. I remember thinking, 'That boy's got an excellent haircut – let's put these haircuts together!' The first version of the band was actually me, Mike and Donna, but she was smart enough to leave and go to London![172]

Aged twenty, Donna answered an ad in *Melody Maker* and became the lead guitarist for post-punk, Britpop front runners Elastica. An alcoholic at fifteen, Mike Cole had already been long committed to the rock 'n' roll lifestyle. He was briefly in The Darling Buds before being asked to leave after just three gigs. With the Dolls, Cole later sung the single 'Hair', which he wrote about Donna.

Carl Bevan's introduction came via a more unconventional route –

an evangelical church band. His father, Ray Bevan, was the founding minister at King's Church in Newport, sometimes leading thousand-strong congregations.

'I got to about seventeen, eighteen and the seeds of atheism had taken hold,' said Carl. 'I started to do a kind of Tom Sawyer routine where I'd shimmy down the drainpipe, go off to town and get hammered, and then someone saw me: "Pastor's Son Drunk and Disorderly". I got thrown off drums; I was gutted!'[173]

Carl heard there were a couple of local guys looking for a drummer, and approached them next to the jukebox at the Riverside Tavern. 'When we played together for the first time, it was instant sparks and we all knew it,' he said.[174]

The triangle was complete – a cherubic pixie smashing away on drums, bolstered by a whippet-thin bassist with a Brian Jones moptop, and fronted by a scowling Robert De Niro lookalike with razor-sharp vocals. Three-piece bands always have to work harder as there's less room to cover each other's mistakes, but the Dolls instantly locked in tight together.

The magic was in the band's brutal beauty – stripping back their sound to keep the essential ingredients, and jettisoning anything extraneous. 'We were from the Hemingway school of rock 'n' roll,' said Parfitt. 'Simplicity is more effective than complexity, and harder to achieve.'[175]

Four years Cole's senior and ten years older than Bevan, Parfitt was the wise head. Raised on a diet of Beatles, Bowie and Beach Boys ('the Shakespeares of rock 'n' roll'[176]), he was already a music veteran compared to his bandmates, having played with The Messengers, The Colours, The Truth and Blood Brothers. Alongside schoolmate Jeff Rose (later of Dub War and Skindred), The Messengers even supported The Jam after Parfitt found Paul Weller's number in the phonebook and left a demo tape with his mother.

Described by John Harris as 'mod-grunge proto-pub metal blues',[177] 60 Ft. Dolls lashed together the songwriting styles of Lennon and McCartney, Weller and The Who with the guitars of the Rolling Stones and The Yardbirds. The eviscerating punk rock of Iggy Pop and the lo-fi and American hardcore heard at TJ's also influenced their sound.

The Dolls gained early momentum thanks to an ecstatically received support slot with Throneberry at TJ's. Parfitt said: 'In those days, the *NME* meant a lot, and after that review I started to get labels ringing me up asking me for demos.'[178]

In 1993, Pooh Sticks singer Huw Williams became the Dolls' manager and within a year they released their debut single, 'Happy Shopper', via his Townhill label. Awarded *Melody Maker* Single of the Week, Everett True hailed it as a 'three-chord, two-finger salute to a world, which long ago gave up caring about them'.[179] Plus, *NME* called it a 'riff-chomping pop metal belter that recalls The Wildhearts' breed of rock 'n' roll scuzz.'[180] The same paper's Simon Williams said: 'Say hello to 60 Ft. Dolls and "Happy Shopper" – their viciously crunchy 45, which dares to shag The Jam and the Manics at the same time and not apologise for the mess afterwards.'[181]

After support slots with Elastica and Dinosaur Jr., the Dolls joined the first *NME* BratBus tour in 1995 with Veruca Salt, Marion and Skunk Anansie. A one-off single via Rough Trade followed with the wonderfully raucous 'White Knuckle Ride'. By the time of their next release, 'Pig Valentine' ('a cauldron of hatred' according to the Stud Brothers[182]), the Dolls had already signed with Indolent – an imprint of RCA – partly thanks to heavy rotation by Steve Lamacq on BBC Radio 1. Likewise, influential American DJ Rodney Bingenheimer of KROQ-FM gave them regular plays, leading to a deal stateside with Geffen Records.

Accompanied by a video filmed on the Newport Transporter Bridge, 'Talk to Me' landed in the Top 40. By now one of the hottest prospects in the country, impressive names were bandied about, like Pete Townshend and Bernard Butler, to produce the debut album. Renowned for his work with the Pixies, it was Al Clay who got the nod. Parfitt told WalesOnline in 2015:

> Al was great, he was the right guy for us. The wrong guy would've been somebody who turned up with a bottle of Jack Daniels, who wanted to join the band…
>
> Al was like a sergeant major figure, he told us we weren't leaving the studio and he'd lock the door. It was like bootcamp.
>
> He had an air rifle that he would fire at us when we were playing. It was his way of keeping us on our toes![183]

Carl Bevan added: 'Al Clay made me clean and polish my drums and cymbals and then stand to attention by the side of kit.'[184]

Recorded at Rockfield and featuring a photo (by acclaimed rock photographer Pennie Smith) of the band looking mean and moody at the Crindau industrial estate, *The Big 3* was lauded with equally big praise. Its title was borrowed from one of John Lennon's favourite groups, The Big Three – a Liverpudlian band of the early '60s.

Released a week after the Manics' *Everything Must Go* and the Furries' *Fuzzy Logic* in May 1996, *The Big 3* introduced an underrated talent in Richard Parfitt. His kitchen-sink lyrics and intricate guitar skills were often overlooked, but not in these reviews.

NME said:

> The Dolls celebrate their hard-drinking, hard-rocking, road-hogging reputation with 'No.1 Pure Alcohol', a song that could be an anthem for their hometown of Newport, where boozing is second only to breathing, but it's a deceptively sharp love/hate paean to life chained to the bottle…
>
> Never let it be said that the Dolls can't articulate the underbelly of this torrid existence as well as any gutter poets.[185]

Melody Maker agreed:

> You'll hear words about duplicity, escape, consumerism, desperation, hatred, aspiration, [but] far from being witless hedonists, 60 Ft. Dolls have created a surprisingly serious album.[186]

Wales Arts Review added:

> *The Big 3* is a compelling argument that the Dolls remain undervalued, and that they are probably the greatest rock band ever to come out of Wales, forged in the snakebite-and-black-flecked night streets of post-industrial Newport in the early '90s.[187]

Nothing could stop them. Not even *Select* hailing *The Big 3* the best album since *Definitely Maybe* – a kiss of death for many a young group. Even the biggest band in the country couldn't break their bond. When Noel Gallagher approached Mike Cole to come onboard as Oasis's bassist following the temporary departure of

Guigsy in 1995, he was given an instant response – just not the one he was expecting. Parfitt said:

> I was worried. If he'd gone, I wouldn't have blamed him because he would've made himself rich and famous…Mike told me he'd been asked and I was like, 'Oh, OK, are you gonna go?' He just said, 'No fucking way!' And that was the end of that. I really think it would be impossible for us to exist with any other drummer or bassist.[188]

The Dolls came face-to-face with Noel Gallagher once again when they watched the Sex Pistols from side-stage on their reunited Filthy Lucre tour at Finsbury Park in June 1996. Rubbing shoulders with celebs like Johnny Depp and Kate Moss, the Dolls didn't look out of place in a support line-up including Iggy Pop, The Wildhearts, Buzzcocks and Stiff Little Fingers. After a few missiles, the Dolls fronted up to 30,000 ageing punks with Cole taunting them: 'We're not scared of you…We're Welsh!'

Within two years, the Dolls ceased to exist though. The band always veered too close to the precipice, and were lucky to get to the end of each week, let alone each year. The perils of a rock 'n' roll lifestyle matched with a relentless schedule and big label pressures took their toll. Cole had a breakdown in Japan and was hospitalised for nearly a year. Parfitt said:

> We had great chemistry, and there was no way we were going to get anyone in to replace Mike. Being in a band was the absolute worst place for him, but it was our group, the three of us. I didn't think we could be the same with anybody else.
>
> I'm a big believer in alchemy…A great band is usually great because of the chemistry between its members. John and Paul from The Beatles are an obvious example in that it couldn't have been so great without one of them. They were so much more together than they were apart.[189]

The follow-up to *The Big 3* should've been eagerly anticipated, but by its release in 1998, the band had already split and have since viewed it with ambivalence. Meaning 'Magic Jewel' (which Carl Bevan nicked from the back of a video game), *Joya Magica* was an understandably patchy and unfocused effort given what the band were going through.

Overproduced and lacking the raw, 'live' feel of its predecessor, Lou Giordano was the wrong choice as producer. *Joya Magica* had some good tunes, but it didn't have the collective sound of *The Big 3* and too often it failed to replicate the brilliance of its lead single, 'Alison's Room'.

Parfitt prefers to remember the band at their best:

> I remember doing T in the Park and I started to play 'Stay', which just starts off with me singing on a guitar, and drums kick in, and then the band takes off. There were about 10,000 people there. The song had just been released on the radio, and everyone started singing it at the same time as me.
>
> I looked over at Mike and he looked over at me, and for that moment at least, it was like, 'This is it – all these people are singing our song!'[190]

———

The good, the bad and the ugly of the Newport scene were collated on *I Was a Teenage Gwent Boy* – a 1994 compilation released on Andy Barding's Frug! label.

Its titular pun may not have aged well, but the album offered a fascinating snapshot of the mid-'90s Newport scene across its eleven tracks. Obviously present and taking aim at the capital were 60 Ft. Dolls on 'London Breeds'. Cowboy Killers replicated their ferocious Dead Kennedys-esque live sound on 'Growth Change', while Newport cult favourites Deep Valley Orgasm contributed 'Lacey'.

Two names synonymous with the scene were Flyscreen and Novocaine, and both were featured on *Gwent Boy* with 'Acid Incest' and 'Culture Me'. The former recorded several mini-albums including *Dap Bag* and *Council Pop* on the Cowboy Killers' imprint, Words of Warning. A punk-pop cocktail of thrashing guitars with pithy lyrics about football and school, Flyscreen released their debut album in 1998 featuring the playground-inspired title of *Girls Can't Make Gun Noises*.

Inspired by Nirvana, and with a name apparently thought up while sitting in the dentist's chair, Novocaine should've reached greater heights with their raw, post-grunge sound riding the mid-'90s zeitgeist. Fronted by the throat-shredding vocals of Steve Evans alongside local legend Richard Jackson on guitar, the group were prolific in their output before inexplicably splitting. Most notable were their 1997 releases – the mini-album *Frustration No. 10* and their full-length debut, *Nervous Disposition*.

Rollerco were featured as part of a promising trio of Newport bands who ultimately remained also-rans. Five Darrens were perhaps hamstrung by their terrible name, while Flemgods never quite made it despite John Peel airplay and support slots with The Lemonheads, Sebadoh and Shampoo.

Elsewhere, *I Was a Teenage Gwent Boy* immortalised the long-forgotten. Tearooms of Babylon, anybody?

There was one notable Newport band strangely missing though…

———

'I remember going to see the Manics on their *Holy Bible* tour at the Astoria in Cardiff in 1994, and I'd got in there early to see the support acts, who were Sleeper and this band called Dub War,' said Dan Griffiths, a curator at the National Library of Wales. 'Benji Webbe came onstage with this extraordinary vocal in a Newport accent, and he just floored me.'[191]

Melding metal, rock and punk with rap, reggae and hip-hop, Dub War concocted a sound that was entirely their own despite comparisons with Rage Against the Machine, Faith No More and Bad Brains – the latter two of whom they weren't even familiar with.

Formed in 1993, Dub War forged their reputation from their frantic live shows, starting with a support slot with Therapy? at TJ's. Front and centre was the magnetic, extrovert personality of Benji Webbe, who could often be seen cranking away on an air raid siren or orchestrating the 'Newport Helicopter' (an overhead mass swinging of clothing). Joining him were three Newport stalwarts in guitarist Jeff Rose, bassist Richie Glover and drummer Martin 'Ginge' Ford.

Webbe said to *Metal Hammer*:

> It all started because I wanted to do some real rock music. I always liked rock music, but I'd been travelling around the country doing these reggae sound systems and I just got pissed off with it.
>
> Then I heard about this local rock band that were looking for

a singer, so I went down to the rehearsal room and that's where I met the rest of Dub War.

It all felt right straight away, but I really didn't want to do the reggae vocals anymore. I wanted to try being a rock singer, so I deliberately didn't do any of the reggae stuff. But one day Jeff asked me to try some reggae vocals over a new song we were writing, and that was it.[192]

Dub War started life with a couple of vinyl singles including a 12" split with Cowboy Killers before issuing their 1994 debut, *Dub Warning*. With artwork featuring the aforementioned air raid siren, the mini-album caught the attention of the aptly named extreme music label Earache.

Recorded with producer Bryan New and featuring the singles 'Respected', 'Mental', 'Gorrit' and 'Strike It', their 1995 debut album, *Pain*, was an adrenaline-soaked rush that captured the incredible raw energy of their gigs.

Not only were Dub War unafraid of tackling social and political issues in their lyrics, but one of their most distinctive characteristics stemmed from Webbe's world-view and willingness to portray a positive message:

We were just trying to deliver a social message of people coming together, of unity and pushing the bullshit out the window.

We didn't think about using the band to escape from where we were brought up. We just wanted to be uplifting. You might not be able to do anything about the madness on your streets, but you could become a better person and that was our philosophy.[193]

In a 2022 retrospective of *Pain*, *Wales Arts Review* wrote:

[Webbe's] voice moves from soaring rock god to gatling gun ferocity. The musicianship behind him is deceptively excellent…

Jeff Rose's guitar work is packed with ideas, and although *Pain* is clearly the album with which Dub War was looking to break America (it is full of flashes of Guns N' Roses and Soundgarden), the distinctive musical personalities of Webbe up front and Rose to his side mean this is an album that stands solid to this day.

There are very few rock albums from the mid-'90s anywhere near as good as this one.[194]

Never ones to rest on their laurels, Dub War became more experimental on their 1996 follow-up, *Wrong Side of Beautiful*. Inspired by Bob Marley and The Clash, the new material was generally softer. Although the likes of 'Enemy Maker' and 'Cry Dignity' weren't vastly different to their previous singles, fans had come to expect a particular sound. Still pure dynamite live, working with a different producer had shorn off their ragged edge on record.

Webbe said:

> Brian [Bryan] New did a great job and I think that's why *Pain* still sounds really fuckin' great all these years later. We ended up working with Paul Schroeder on the next album, and he was a great friend of ours, but I don't think we ended up with a great album.
>
> Brian was like a chemist, and Paul was a free spirit, and it sounded like he'd thrown the tapes in a washing machine and spun them around! If I could do the second album again, I'd do it with Brian.[195]

Subsequently, Dub War even made a brief foray into dance music with the *Soundclash* EP before releasing a remix album, *Step Ta Dis*, in 1998. After an initial honeymoon period with Earache, relations soured and Dub War split in 1999.

Webbe, Rose and Ford regrouped and achieved far greater success worldwide as Skindred. There would be one final hurrah for Dub War though, and a repairing of their relationship with Earache.

After twenty-six years away, their long-awaited third album, *Westgate Under Fire*, was released in August 2022. Its title referenced the 1839 uprising when 4,000 Chartists led by John Frost marched into Newport to protest against the government and demand the right to vote in a secret ballot. The event ended in a bloody battle resulting in the deaths of twenty-two Chartists and many more injured when gunshots were fired outside the Westgate Hotel. Bullet holes remain visible on its walls today.

Still living where he was raised in Pillgwenlly, Webbe holds his hometown close to his heart. In the 2023 BBC Radio 4 documentary *Sound Towns: Newport*, he paid tribute to one of the city's favourite sons, John Sicolo:

> We supported an American band at TJ's called El Niño [later known as Ill Niño], and John came over and grabbed me by the neck and said: 'You gotta get out of here; you're better than this. I've been talking to people in London about you; they expect great things from you. Believe in yourself because other people do believe in you.'
>
> Newport needed John, and I think he brought something very special to us all.[196]

LAND OF
MY MOTHERS

ALTERNATIVE TAKES ON
WELSH-LANGUAGE MUSIC
IN THE MID-'90s

Anhrefn made their bold first venture into English-language music in 1994, but their choice of song was even more surprising.

Teaming up with TV presenter and actress Margi Clarke, they recorded Cole Porter's theme tune from the musical *Anything Goes*. The band's change of direction must've left their hardcore fans spitting out their tea rather than at each other. It was an about-turn akin to Paul Weller when he switched from the punky tunes of The Jam to the jazz, New Wave and blue-eyed soul of The Style Council.

Yet, Rhys Mwyn had been itching for something different, and another 1994 collaboration with Margi Clarke sealed the deal. The *Clutter from the Gutter* EP included a techno remix of the title track by Neil McLennan and Dave Pemberton, which got Mwyn's mind buzzing with ideas.

Hen Wlad Fy Mamau ('Land of My Mothers') would be the new project. Mwyn met Bill Drummond of The KLF through iconic punk artwork designer Jamie Reid. The initial concept was to record the Sex Pistols' 'Pretty Vacant' in Welsh.

Another brainstorming notion was to release an EP of the Celtic nations and reinterpret their anthems. Mwyn asked Côr Eifionydd to sing the Welsh national anthem, but with new words and from a feminist perspective. His music wasn't just punk anymore – it could be performed by a choir. However, Drummond refused to participate, and the idea temporarily lay dormant.

Mwyn had also been invited to contribute music to a new Welsh-language TV movie called *Rhag Pob Brad* ('Against All Treason'). Directed by Rhys Powys and written by Russell Gascoigne, the film starred a young Rhys Ifans and allowed Mwyn to move into urban music. Assisted by Y Cyrff and Anhrefn drummer Dylan Hughes, he sourced hip-hop samples with influences including Public Enemy and NWA. The producer at Stiwdio Sain, Ronnie Stone, gave them one guiding principle: 'Keep the Groove.'

Rhys Powys wasn't that keen on the hip-hop songs though, so the band decamped to Cardiff's Famous Studios to work on more punk-oriented tunes with producer Tony Etoria.

Rhag Pob Brad signalled the start of Rhys Mwyn's short-lived acting career. After (his brother and Anhrefn bandmate) Sion Sebon and Daf Ieuan refused to participate, it was left to Mwyn to play an extra breaking up a fight. But he couldn't utter a word as he wasn't a member of Equity. Mwyn and the cast had a great laugh sneaking lager into their cans instead of water. The only problem was that they were trying not to be too pissed, while simultaneously acting out a drunken brawl!

When Crai released the *Hen Wlad Fy Mamau* album in 1995, it was a diverse world-beat collection of remixed Welsh folk music, samples and electronica. Amongst the roll call of contributors were Punjabi rapper Harvinder Sangha, African dub collective Zion Train, Alarm keyboardist Steve Allan Jones, backing singer Kandina Jane and the ubiquitous Gorwel Owen.

Featuring photography by Mwyn's partner, Nêst Thomas, and artwork by Jamie Reid, the album's front cover featured Welsh suffragettes at Snowdon, while the back included Gwilym Cowlyd's poem 'Y Llynnau Gwyrddion Llonydd' ('The Calm Green Lakes'). The sleeve also depicted a brief history of the Welsh Not, which shared a title with one of the tracks. A 'Welsh Not' was a wooden board strung around a schoolchild's neck in a bid to shame them from speaking Welsh. These oppressive objects were used in some Welsh schools during the nineteenth century as a way to punish any child caught speaking their mother tongue.

Elsewhere, 'Nid Cymru Fydd Cymru' ('Wales Won't be Wales') contained a sample of Saunders Lewis's *Tynged yr Iaith* speech, while 'Brad' ('Translation') was revisited from the *Rhag Pob Brad* sessions. As well as snippets from the film, the track also included the former Welsh secretary George Thomas's quote: 'The nationalists of Wales have created a monster they cannot control.'

Jamie Reid's artwork was projected as a backdrop at gigs, and an old video of Tryweryn accompanied 'In This Dis-United Kingdom'.

Reid also used a bootleg of *Braveheart*, and, ever the provocateurs, the band launched their subsequent single 'Dis-UK' at the House of Lords with a helping hand from former Plaid Cymru leader Dafydd Elis-Thomas. Another idea was for the London Welsh Male Voice Choir to sing outside their shows in the English capital.

Following *Hen Wlad Fy Mamau*, the band were invited to become the first Welsh-language artist to play WOMAD, where they headlined the second stage. Such prestige lured V2 Records, who signed the band as their second Welsh act behind Stereophonics. At the London launch gig, they supported the Cwmaman boys, but the night was memorable for another incident.

Mwyn said:

> The KLF were there with their tank with a sodding Union Jack on it. That was them being pricks like Noel Gallagher and everyone else. We had two rastas in the band with us that night, and both of them were getting really wound up about the flag.
>
> We stayed backstage, but it was rammed with press and pop stars like Boy George…I said, 'I've got it – we're gonna go out there and take the flag down in front of everybody.'
>
> Jimmy Cauty [of The KLF] was really annoyed with us. I was like, 'Bloody hell, you've just burned a million quid! What's your problem?!' We had brilliant publicity though; it got into all the magazines. You had this totally unknown, obscure band taking down the Union Jack – great![197]

Mwyn wanted to be radical *and* in the charts on his new label. One of his first visions was to record a drum-and-bass version of 'Myfanwy' with Tom Jones. It never materialised though, and the band's union with V2 was an unhappy one, lasting just seven months.

> I honestly think they didn't know what we were on about from the Tom Jones drum-and-bass 'Myfanwy' thing onwards. They said it was a novelty record, and yet they brought out *Reload* a few years later, and we had this conversation *before* that.[198]

Problems with V2 started early on when they brought in producers who the band felt didn't grasp the project. There were musical differences within the group too. They drafted in talented vocalist Nicole Patterson from Robbie Williams's band, with Mwyn wanting to record demos in the vein of Massive Attack and Soul II Soul: 'I was always a bit of a Sade fan, so I thought if we can't do *Top of the Pops* with Tom Jones, let's do more soul. Daf thought I'd lost my marbles as he wanted to do techno!'[199]

The new songs were promising, but unfortunately, they never saw the light of day: 'V2 sent reps up from London on the train to meet us in Llanberis. They told us we were dropped. It wasn't completely unexpected, but we were still looking at them in shock – one of the most bizarre experiences of my life.'[200]

———

On the evening of 17 May 1980, a middle-aged Welsh stone-cutter named Rheinallt H. Rowlands sat in his kitchen miserably looking into a bowl of broth.

Unemployed following the closure of the quarry he had toiled at for the last thirteen years and with no future prospects, Rowlands was feeling very bleak.

Turning on his radio for comfort, yet more bad news filtered through. The familiar, sombre beats of Joy Division emanated across the airwaves, but this time tinged with more melancholy. In between the tunes of the Manchester band were tributes from John Peel for Ian Curtis, the group's enigmatic frontman who had died by suicide at his Macclesfield home aged twenty-three.

Perched at his dinner table, a stunned Rowlands dropped his spoon and had an epiphany – becoming a singer would be his pathway to fame and fortune.

The only problem was Rowlands never existed. Instead, he was the onstage persona of north Wales singer-songwriter Owain 'Oz' Wright. Nevertheless, the story circulated the Welsh alternative music scene and Wright's native Anglesey in 1991 as if it were all true.

Joined by Dewi Evans – a devotee of John Barry and Philip Glass – their music under the Rheinallt H. Rowlands moniker mixed the whimsical pop of Brian Wilson with the lushly orchestrated sweep of Spector, Steinman and Serge Gainsbourg. The concoction was all wrapped in a rich Johnny Cash-like drawl, but delivered as if 'The Man in Black' hailed from near Menai Bridge and not Nashville, Tennessee.

Wright added further layers of mystique by initially performing live alone, accompanied by a tape machine of Evans's pre-recorded backing tracks, while adorning a dark cloak, hat and clogs. Evans's presence was added at gigs following the release of the 1993 debut cassette, *Hendaid Brân a Straeon Eraill* ('Grandfather Crow and Other Stories'), and a request to support Gorky's. Having grown up near each other in the famed Anglesey village of LlanfairPG, Wright (vocalist, guitar and harmonium player) united onstage with Evans (composer, keyboardist and arranger) to play synth rhythms that sprouted into unexpectedly grand orchestral flourishes. Think Scott Walker fronting Burt Bacharach's band in a smoky rugby club.

As Ben Thompson said in *Seven Years of Plenty: A Handbook of Irrefutable Pop Greatness, 1991–1998*:

> There's always been a place in pop for the driven outsider – the writer or performer spurred on by their own personal bob-a-job scout pack of demons to create sounds and songs the like of which have never been heard before…To this illustrious list, another name must now be added. That name is Rheinallt H. Rowlands.[201]

Wright said:

> We don't want people to think we're a novelty band. We're trying to do something that has a sense of humour, but isn't a joke. There's nothing more ridiculous than people, especially musicians, who take themselves absolutely seriously.[202]

Another legend affixed to the Rheinallt H. Rowlands story was that it was formed at the request of Alan Holmes (Fflaps and Ectogram) for a spoof Geraint Jarman tribute album. Paying homage to Ian Curtis, the band's first performance was a cover of Joy Division's 'New Dawn Fades' (retitled 'Gwawr Newydd Yn Cilio') on Nia Melville's BBC Radio Cymru show.

This live take was later included on the 1996 Ankst compilation, *Triskedekaphilia*. A thirteen-song collection of session tracks curated by Melville, it featured the usual suspects of the Furries, Gorky's, Catatonia and Datblygu alongside Ectogram, Fflaps, Ann Matthews and Celfi Cam. Also covered by Moby and John Frusciante, there's no interpretation quite like the folky cadence of Rowlands's rendition of 'New Dawn Fades', which evolves from minimalist restraint to a crescendo of spectral synths.

Building upon the reputation of an impressive debut, Rowlands had no such trouble with the 'difficult second album'. Produced and engineered by Alan Holmes and Gorwel Owen and released via Ankst in 1996, *Bukowski* was a concise collection of ten songs saturated with lavish strings and Morricone squiggles capped off with a Bryn Terfel-esque baritone.

Named after the legendary Californian novelist and poet Charles Bukowski, the title track is an extraordinary, eleven-minute epic befitting the whisky-soaked writer's life. Formed from two songs sewn together, the ambient intro with the 'It's Not Unusual' trumpet fanfare was included on their debut before Bukowski died in 1994, while a subsequent section was written posthumously. The end result provided a stunning centrepiece to the second album.

'Charles Bukowski' was also featured on the 1995 compilation *S4C Makes Me Want to Smoke Crack*, which was released via north Wales label Atol on a limited run of 500. Appearing alongside Catatonia, Ectogram and Paladr (a Penygroes band later known as Topper), the EP's title was a direct lift from Beck's wry take on MTV. *NME* said of Rowlands's 'quite insane paean':

> As a wise old owl noted just the other pint, 'tis a thin line between John Barry and Barry John…'Charles Bukowski' is cheesier than a mouse's larder and hence exactly what Bryan Ferry should sound like in 1995. 'Gwyrthiol' (miraculous) in any language![203]

Feeling that S4C had become 'a Disney channel pumping out a Welsh culture that seemed a bit mediocre and crap' (as Emyr Glyn Williams described it[204]), Ankst released a follow-up compilation in 1996 also featuring Rowlands on 'Merch o Gaerdydd' ('Cardiff Girls'). Included on *Bukowski*, it was a playful ditty where Herb Alpert horns juxtaposed with Oz's Ian Curtis-like vocal. Elsewhere, 'Dydd Gŵyl Giro Sant' ('St Giro's Day') may have been a string-soaked piss-take of the patron saint of social security payments, but even music this gorgeous was unlikely to result in endless riches as Ben Thompson indicated: 'Wright has developed an imposing selection of intimidating stares and baroque microphone manoeuvres which – in tandem with his potent baritone – add up to one of the '90s' most compelling, if least widely celebrated, pop spectacles.'[205]

Interestingly, the English songs on the album weren't penned by Wright, but by poet Zoë Skoulding. Explaining their flittering between languages on *Bukowski* (which also features French), Wright said: 'Although I speak English and Welsh pretty indiscriminately, the Rheinallt persona tips the balance. Because of the nature of the music, it just seems more suitable especially for the dramatic stuff. For those who don't speak the language, it adds an element of mystery.'[206]

After a third and final album, *Rheinallt III*, in 2000, the duo took a break due to Wright's vocal problems. Their hopes of releasing sparser, stripped-back music never materialised. Sadness was an intrinsic part of the Rheinallt H. Rowlands story starting with the death of Ian Curtis, and likewise it ended in tragedy.

In the early hours of 23 December 2005, Owain Wright was killed at the age of thirty-five by a car on a Bethesda mountain road while walking home from Euros Childs's gig at Hendre Hall.

———

It's truly psychedelic because rather than it being about jangly guitars and sunshine, you can hear people on the edge of a bad psychedelic experience…And that's what makes a really psychedelic record. There's darkness to the trippiness.[207]

Richard King's quote to the *Welsh Music Podcast* encapsulated the unpredictable nature of *Bwyd Time* – Gorky's third album in July 1995, which exemplified their psychedelic peak.

Barely out of their teens (it was released on John Lawrence's twentieth birthday), *Bwyd Time* signalled a turning point in the band's development. The thirteen-song collection combined their youthful enthusiasm and anything-goes attitude with a growing maturity for making cohesive recordings.

Like an errant radio station spiralling out of control and splurging out strange interludes, the album sounds so unfocused at first though. After the initial jingle of the title track, 'Miss Trudy' is a sweet childhood tale about an unpredictable violin teacher – one minute she's fine, and the next she's flown into a rage throwing around instruments.

Awarded *NME* Single of the Week, 'Miss Trudy' is the album in microcosm in that it flies between moods without warning. Likewise – taking its title from a friendly Welsh phrase meaning 'Good Health' – 'Iechyd Da' (co-written with Rheinallt H. Rowlands) begins as a bright and breezy drinking song complete with clinking glasses and chatter. Over the next four minutes it corkscrews into an inebriated breakdown featuring the most discordant rendition of 'Calon Lân' you'll ever hear.

The light and shade throughout are like before and after a bad trip on magic mushrooms. Although the Furries don't descend into quite the same darkness, there are definite parallels between the bands, as Richard King explained:

> Both *Mwng* and *Bwyd Time* make me feel like if you're in rural Wales and there's a village hall, you're seconds away from it turning into this sort of psychedelic space – rainy, leafy green environments that can host a weird introspective happening… and probably the things you need to make that happen are growing all around you![208]

Not all is as it seems on *Bwyd Time* (not least the enigmatic, bilingual melding of its title, meaning 'Food Time'). There's the hallucinogenic fairy tale of 'The Telescope and the Bonfire', creeping horror on 'The Game of Eyes' and queasy imagery on 'Eating Salt Is Easy'. The great single, 'Gewn ni Gorffen', fluctuates between lilting melodies and sinister synths that are outright unsettling. Plus, the Japanese bonus track, 'Impressionistic Soundscapes', is an utterly bonkers arrangement of strange samples stitched together.

All of this chaotic improvisation suggests that *Bwyd Time* shouldn't work – and yet this beautifully bizarre mess of contradictions hangs together perfectly. Swapping instruments and languages on a whim, Gorky's threw everything into the mix and came out the other side with a smouldering selection of quirky curios.

The band tossed everything from strings to stylophone into the mix and out the other end came surrealistic gems. The kitchen-sink approach to instrumentation extended to Childs frequently swapping English for Welsh, sometimes in the course of the same song. It's this blend of bilingualism and surrealism that make it Richard King's favourite Gorky's album:

> I loved the idea of this very young group of people growing up in Pembrokeshire and finding inspiration in old, cheap, hippie records. *Bwyd Time* is perfect because you've got a lot going on – its English and *Cymraeg*, and they really go out there with experimentation and psychedelia.
>
> But even when they do on songs like 'Blood Chant', it's still very controlled and self-contained…After a lot of the songs break down, they often return to a melodic centre.
>
> This was a record prior to the success of Catatonia and the Super Furries, as well as Gorky's later success. It feels like a record that's apart from that success, and isn't in that context.
>
> I think it's all the stronger in that it appeared in its own moment before that dreaded phrase [Cool Cymru] had been coined…This was released in '95, which was the year of Blur vs Oasis, and you couldn't get further away from that lot with this record. [209]

With Megan Childs increasingly adding violin melancholia, *Bwyd Time* also demonstrated her brother excelling as a vocalist.

Richard King again:

> Euros Childs has one of the great voices. I think it's an incredible instrument, and it can reduce me to tears – not just the words, but the way he sings.
>
> It's quite a soft, quiet voice at times, but it's strong and has such integrity because he's so good at hitting the high notes and not disguising the fact that he's young doing it. [210]

As Ben Thompson said in *Seven Years of Plenty*: 'Childs's vocal style veers from choirboy to banshee and back again in the blink of an ear.' [211] Gorky's added The Incredible String Band, Captain Beefheart and the Bonzo Dog Doo-Dah Band into their bubbling cauldron of influences to create a cult classic. Like a darker version of The Beatles' *Magical Mystery Tour* mixed with Brian Eno's *Here Come the Warm Jets*, *Bwyd Time* saw the group making music entirely on their own terms with no concession to commercialism. True to form, it stalled at No. 150, but it's never impenetrable.

Produced at Stiwdio Ofn by Gorwel Owen and released on Ankst, *Bwyd Time* featured the band's best imagery too. Like with the Manics on *The Holy Bible*, the album's artwork (by Alan Holmes) entirely embodies the music within – from the psychedelic swirls of calligraphy to the maniacally grinning druids holding flaming torches. Retreating to the woods to dress in medieval garbs (or the 'Saturn branch of Toys R Us' as *Melody Maker* put it[212]), the band look simultaneously cool, ridiculous and menacing in the sleeve photos as they stare down the camera lens with complete confidence.

Drummer Euros Rowlands's father was actually an arch-druid at the Eisteddfod, but Megan Childs felt that the media jumped to the wrong conclusions with their Tolkien chic:

> We always have these really silly ideas. We do it for a laugh to make things a bit more interesting, but you tend to be taken very seriously.
>
> We did this photoshoot, and suddenly we're all wizards, and deadly serious about our Celtic history. People didn't get the irony, and that's a danger. It can come across as a bit pompous.
>
> When we first started, the press was, 'Well, if we're from Wales and our music is a bit strange, we must all be living in the middle of nowhere.' People would ask us how we would hear music. They decided our parents were all hippies and we'd grown up on communes taking magic mushrooms.[213]

As Britpop swallowed up everything in its path, the music press even positioned this most eccentric of bands on the fringes of the movement. Typically though, Gorky's would secure national acclaim for singing about something as unconventional and mundane as a patio

BRITPOP VS COOL CYMRU

TWO MOVEMENTS GO HEAD-TO-HEAD

'YANKS GO HOME!'[214]

As Brett Anderson swooned in front of a Union Jack, Stuart Maconie's *Select* cover story in April 1993 kickstarted a home-grown musical movement. Its subheading read: 'Suede, St Etienne, Denim, Pulp, The Auteurs and the Battle for Britain'…and so started Britpop.

The term had previously been bandied around to describe the British pop groups of the '60s, as well as '70s punk and glam, plus the '80s indie scene. For five years after that *Select* piece, Britpop became inescapable.

Its origins can be found in two key reactions to what was happening in America. As Britain was submerged in an anti-melodic shoegaze scene in the early '90s led by My Bloody Valentine, Ride and Slowdive, grunge ignited stateside as Nirvana, Pearl Jam and Soundgarden became unlikely poster boys for MTV.

With a timespan of 1993–8 (with its peak years being 1994–5), Britpop was the antidote to the doom and gloom of grunge with an emphasis on melody, bright guitars and catchy choruses.

It's easy to criticise the relative simplicity and derivative nature of Noel Gallagher's songwriting, but it spearheaded a positive, feel-good scene about fulfilling dreams. Tunes like 'Some Might Say' and 'Acquiesce' are full of euphoria, hope and unity, while 'Live Forever' was written as a reaction to one of Kurt Cobain's songs. Noel said: 'I remember Nirvana had a tune called "I Hate Myself and Want to Die", and I was like, "Well, I'm not fucking having that."'[215]

The potential for American culture to infiltrate British life and become predominant was an even bigger fear for Damon Albarn. When asked in 1993 if Blur were an anti-grunge band, he responded: 'If punk was about getting rid of hippies, then I'm getting rid of grunge.'[216]

That same year, Blur released their second album, *Modern Life Is Rubbish*, with lyrics that David Cavanagh in *Mojo* said captured a 'Ray Davies-like characterisation to investigate the dreams, traditions and prejudices of suburban England.'[217]

Jon Savage pointed out that Britpop was actually more like 'Engrock'.[218] Where The Kinks sang of preserving village greens, Blur's imagery evoked aspects of Englishness (not Britishness) that were outdated by the early '90s – a steam train for the artwork of *Modern Life Is Rubbish* and greyhound racing for *Parklife*.

In its most reductive sense, Britpop was a movement obsessed with recreating the past and, more specifically, the 1960s. Prime Minister-in-waiting Tony Blair was emulating Harold Wilson, and Oasis were aping The Beatles. Soundtracked by a new No. 1 single singing of 'three lions on a shirt', England were looking to avenge 'thirty years of hurt' since winning the 1966 World Cup by hosting a major tournament (Euro '96) again under the Twin Towers at Wembley.

Indeed, critics decried that anyone in possession of a Fab Four songbook and a knowledge of three chords could make it big in the mid-'90s. Yet, Britpop's front runners – Oasis, Blur, Pulp, Suede and Supergrass – were all great bands.

Other than feeling the need to produce more uplifting music, the only thing connecting those groups was their national identity. A multitude of wholly disparate bands were quickly corralled under the same umbrella because they held British passports. Even Placebo and Garbage – who only included one band member each born on these isles – were claimed as Britpop.

Meanwhile, Wales's very own Britpop equivalent was gaining momentum. Likewise, there was nothing linking their sound or influences. Regardless, the Manics, the Furries, Catatonia, Gorky's and 60 Ft. Dolls were gathered together based on their nationality as 'Cool Cymru'.

Variously reported as originating from the *Western Mail* or the English music press, Cool Cymru was nevertheless a media invention, leading to inevitable pushback from the bands. As amazing as the memories of the era are, the mere utterance of the words can still make musicians and fans wince.

Nia Mai Daniel of the Welsh Music Archive at the National Library of Wales said:

You could compare 'Cool Cymru' to the 'Land of Song,' which was a label placed on Wales by the Victorians. It was a label given by people from outside of Wales looking in, and there was a backlash to that as well because it wasn't how we described ourselves. These labels could sometimes be used in a patronising way.[219]

Yet as Rhys Mwyn is keen to point out: 'It's better than being Uncool Cymru!'[220] And while Britpop began fizzling out by summer '97 after Oasis's album *Be Here Now*, Cool Cymru grew stronger for the rest of the decade.

———

'I'm feeling supersonic, give me gin and tonic…'[221]

For a band who always enjoyed a line or two, this was a relatively simplistic one. Yet with their debut single in April 1994, Oasis captured the growing, euphoric zeitgeist that brighter days were ahead in Britain.

John Smith's Labour leadership had seen the party surge to poll leads of over twenty percentage points. Finally, it looked as though there would be a Labour prime minister after nearly two decades.

Scowling down the camera lens, the Burnage brothers Liam and Noel Gallagher introduced themselves to the world with their first release after a couple of years of gigging the country's less glamorous venues. Starting as they meant to go on, the video accompanying 'Supersonic' was a nod to The Beatles' farewell concert atop the Apple headquarters. Filmed on a hotel roof opposite London's King's Cross station, it captured a very British vibe with smoking chimneys, satellite dishes, swirls of litter and rainy puddles.

Its opening lyric further encapsulated British individuality, which had been drummed into the nation after eighteen years of cold Tory rule where there was 'no such thing as society'. Introduced with Tony McCarroll's drumbeat as Noel ground out a George Harrison-esque riff, his younger sibling drawls the opening line: 'I need to be myself, I can't be no one else.'

Four months later, 'Supersonic' became a focal part of *Definitely Maybe*, which steamrollered to No. 1. Partly recorded at Monmouth's Monnow Valley Studio with Caernarfon-born producer Owen Morris, it was Britain's fastest-selling debut album at the time. If *Definitely Maybe* celebrated the hedonistic, carefree abandon of youth, then an album released the same day was its complete antithesis.

Described by the *NME* as a 'vile record',[222] the Manics' magnum opus, *The Holy Bible*, was a searingly intense examination of man's potential to inflict cruelty. As Richey Edwards said: 'I'd like to be able to write, "I'm feeling supersonic, give me gin and tonic"…but I haven't felt supersonic since I was about ten years old.'[223]

Eschewing the glam-punk metal of their debut, *Generation Terrorists*, and the stadium-rock sheen of its follow-up, *Gold Against the Soul*, *The Holy Bible* was ironically very much inspired by Britain, but definitely not Britpop. While their contemporaries set about rediscovering the Swinging '60s, the Manics harked back to the post-punk bands of the late '70s like Magazine, Public Image Limited and Skids. Their newfound military chic was borrowed from Echo and the Bunnymen, while aspects of *The Holy Bible*'s sleeve were directly lifted from *Empires and Dance* by Simple Minds.

Bereft of any kind of humanity and with a working title of *The Poetry of Death*, the album is best summed up by one of its samples. During the instrumental break of 'Mausoleum' – a song recalling the horrors of the Holocaust – J. G. Ballard utters: 'I wanted to rub the human face in its own vomit and force it to look in the mirror.'

The author was referring to his controversial 1973 sexual fetishism novel, *Crash*, but his sentiments could easily apply to the Manics' motivations two decades later. 'I really enjoyed how *The Holy Bible* confronts the audience, but that album confronts us too,' James Dean Bradfield said to *Select*. 'You play it onstage and you can feel Damien round the corner. It feels like handling a cursed chalice. You can feel the lesions breaking out all over your body.'[224]

Feeling they had indulged too much in rock 'n' roll excesses while recording *Gold Against the Soul* in Hook End Manor, the Manics retreated to the tiny, awkwardly shaped Sound Space Studios on the fringes of Cardiff's docklands, the city's (then) red-light district. Forming a tight unit with engineer Alex Silva, their nightly entertainment was to peek through the letterbox to observe besuited businessmen looking for cheap favours.

The peculiarity of the anachronistic music they were creating at Sound Space wasn't lost on them. While recording 'Revol', Nicky Wire heard Blur's 'Girls & Boys' on the radio. The former was a scattergun song outlining the apparent sexual perversions of Russian dictators, while the latter was a sleazy slice of Europop portraying working-class lads and lasses having it large in Club 18–30 holiday resorts. Nicky Wire recalled to *NME*: 'I thought, "Fuck, we've just written a song about group sex in the Politburo, and really the biggest thing out there from an indie band is going off on holiday in Ibiza." We couldn't be fucking further from the musical explosion!'[225]

An overriding statement for its parent album, 'Girls & Boys' was the lead single and opening track of *Parklife*, which reached No. 1 in April 1994. Meanwhile, *Definitely Maybe* burst into life with 'Rock 'n' Roll Star', which at least contained a more positive message of chasing dreams.

Conversely, *The Holy Bible* opened with 'Yes'. Starting with a soundbite declaring 'everything's for sale' from a Channel 4 documentary about prostitution, it was inspired by seeing the exploitation of sex workers on their ill-fated trip to Bangkok. Several of the album's songs can be interpreted as a metaphor for the band and Richey Edwards in particular, and here the Manics referenced becoming 'willing prostitutes' by signing with Sony. With an ingenious piece of marketing that aped the slogan of TSB, the band further pissed off their detractors by stating: 'MSP – The Band That Likes to Say Yes.'

Originally intended as the album's fourth single, its obscene content would've ensured that 'Yes' didn't receive radio play. While the music throughout the record is far from impenetrable, there's no concession to commercialism. If any further proof was needed that *The Holy Bible* was a confrontational album and an artistic statement unlike any other, 'cunts' was uttered in just its fourth word. The Manics' management at Hall or Nothing were inundated with calls from journalists double-checking lyrics.

A day after *The Holy Bible*'s release, the Manics recorded with Jo Whiley and their old nemesis Steve Lamacq for a BBC Radio 1 Evening Session (which later won an *NME* Brat Award). Censorship was already creeping in with Bradfield changing 'fuck' to 'suck'. Thankfully, a clean version of 'Yes' was never released as it would've completely nullified its impact.

With their shackles off onstage, summer '94 marked the band's uncompromising peak as a live proposition. Yet this coincided with the escalating mental health problems of Richey Edwards, who wrote 75 per cent of the album's lyrics. With his rudimentary slashes of rhythm guitar uncharacteristically high in the mix against a backdrop of *Apocalypse Now* paranoia, the Manics delved into their heart of darkness with a gloriously pissed-off set at Glastonbury. There was a genuine risk of electrocution amid the downpour. The occasion was most (in)famous for Wire's withering verdict of Worthy Farm: 'I say build some more fucking bypasses over this shithole.'[226]

Before hearing a note of the album, its artwork is mesmerising. Britpop, *TFI Friday*, Page 3 and *Loaded* magazine may have openly encouraged the male gaze to ogle the female form, but *The Holy Bible* presented a version of womanhood the 'new lad' preferred to avert his eyes from.

Richey had fallen in love with Jenny Saville's *Strategy (South Face/Front Face/North Face)*. After being quoted £30,000, the artist agreed for its free use following a phone call where Richey outlined each album track in depth. The painting depicts a triptych of an obese woman stripped to her underwear. Originally a nine-foot painting, its angled orientation sees the woman looking down at us, and it seems she's judging us as much as we are examining her. In doing so, she breaks the fourth wall and stares straight into the souls of record buyers.

The imagery most evokes the song '4st 7lb' – a harrowing, first-person portrayal of a self-loathing anorexic, who's starving herself to death to avoid looking like the 'fat scum' that surround her. If what she's seeing in the mirror is the subject of Saville's triptych, it's a terrifying thought that sets the tone for an endlessly uncomfortable album.

At the time in 1994, Damon was telling *Loaded* that he had given up reading to concentrate on 'football, dog racing and Essex girls'.[227] Meanwhile, Noel later said: 'Booksellers, book readers, book writers, book owners – fuck all of them.'[228] Conversely, the Manics were reproducing *The Holy Bible* line by line in a double-page *NME* ad spread and encouraging fans to 'analyse, despise, scrutinise'.[229]

While Oasis were reeling off twelve-bar blues and ripping off The New Seekers' 'I'd Like to Teach the World to Sing' on 'Shakermaker', the Manics were talking about the hypocrisy of US gun laws on 'Ifwhiteamerica…' Elsewhere, Liam sang, 'You and I are gonna live forever,' while Bradfield screamed, 'I want to die in the summertime.' On 'She Is Suffering', the Manics explored the reluctant attraction of 'lust, vice and sin', but Noel released a song called 'She's Electric' with lyrics inspired by children's TV show *You and Me*. There was never going to be a bonus track on *The Holy Bible* à la 'Bonehead's Bank Holiday' either.

Richey's words are beyond poetry and seem impossible to use as lyrics. Subject matter is occasionally cloudy even to his bandmates. Lines collide without punctuation and words not often used in conjunction tumble alongside each other.

Bradfield's herculean effort in wrapping his tongue around every syllable and hauling melody out of each line cannot be underestimated. With its breathless delivery, Bradfield has often likened singing it to a sporting challenge: 'The bridges in "Mausoleum" have no concept of punctuation, health and the bodily organ called the lungs.'[230]

Performing tracks from *The Holy Bible* also means descending into a bleak mentality, not least on 'Of Walking Abortion' where Richey surmised that it's blissful indifference that allows evil to prosper. In *33 Revolutions Per Minute: A History of Protest Songs*, Dorian Lynskey said:

['Of Walking Abortion' is] a song about the evils of fanaticism. The names of Mussolini and Hitler are rata-tatted out, but it sounds fanatical. It's like the final report of someone who has been commissioned to investigate the cause of an atrocity and who, instead of producing a series of wise, humanitarian recommendations, concludes that the moral contagion is everywhere and the blame is bottomless.

The singer delivers the final verdict: 'Who's responsible? You fucking are!'...At which point, the traditional contract with its listener – 'you and me, we're on the right side' – is irrevocably shattered. So, what then?[231]

Halfway through *Parklife*, there's a nice break by way of the jaunty instrumental 'The Debt Collector' whereas *The Holy Bible* is unrelenting. It brings to mind Richard Burton as O'Brien in *1984*: 'If you want a vision of the future...imagine a boot stamping on a human face *forever*.'

The album's lead single, 'Faster', coincidentally starts with a sample of John Hurt as Winston Smith in Michael Radford's film adaptation of George Orwell's dystopia. At exactly the same point on *Definitely Maybe* comes 'Digsy's Dinner'. The message of 'your friends will all go green for my lasagne' isn't quite as hard-hitting as 'I hate purity, hate goodness. I don't want virtue to exist anywhere. I want everyone corrupt.'

Days after its release, the Manics played their new single with a frenetic performance of alienation and rage on *Top of the Pops*. Flanked by flames, Bradfield cuts an intimidating figure decked in khaki, Doc Martens and a balaclava, which many viewers mistakenly construed as sympathy for the IRA.

In 1998, Nicky Wire reminisced to Jools Holland:

> It had the most complaints on the BBC ever, it had 17,500 phone calls, so it must've been good…Bands can look back at their careers and feel embarrassed and they can blame it on drugs, but we were all completely sober – that's the scary thing![232]

One thing often overlooked with the Manics is their dark sense of humour. Bradfield's formidable presence was undermined by the fact that 'JAMES' was written across his balaclava as if his mam had labelled it and sent him off to London. The sight of guest hosts Vic and Bob pogoing in the background as he rasped, 'I am an architect / They call me a butcher' makes the moment even more surreal.

The burgeoning national mood of optimism had been halted the previous month. On 11 May 1994, Labour leader John Smith made a speech highlighting the party's 'opportunity to serve our country – that is all we ask.' The following morning, he died of a heart attack.

Defeating John Prescott and Margaret Beckett in the July 1994 Labour leadership election was Tony Blair – a baby-kissing, charismatic leader and great speaker. Hindsight may leave a bitter taste in the mouth, but when the Labour Party swept to a landslide victory in May 1997 soundtracked by D:Ream's 'Things Can Only Get Better', it was an inspired choice of campaign song.

The song's promise of a brighter day may have hooked the national mood, but there was also a creeping sense of history repeating. A right-wing resurgence swept across Europe with the British National Party and Jean-Marie Le Pen's *Front National* Party in France.

Consequently, the Manics' world-view in 1994 was anything but optimistic. As David Evans said in *33⅓: The Holy Bible*:

'I hope you're not going to mug me.' Rhys Mwyn met John Peel in the mid-'80s and kickstarted the Welsh-language music revolution. (*Peter Telfer*)

Opposite: Datblygu frontman David R. Edwards flicks the V's to his detractors. (*Medwyn Jones*)

Above: Flamboyant four-piece Tigertailz added a touch of glamour to the south Wales scene. (*George Chin/IconicPix*)

Below: A mess of eyeliner and spray paint, the Manics burst out of Blackwood with their 1992 debut *Generation Terrorists*. (*Paul Rider*)

Opposite: The Alarm ventured into bilingualism with their albums, *Change / Newid* and *Raw/ Tân*. (*Alamy*)
Above: Newport band The Darling Buds were signed to Sony and propagated an infectious brand of jangly pop perfection. (*Paul Rider*)
Below: Huw Williams of The Pooh Sticks proudly wore his Welsh dragon hoodie in the days before Cymru was cool. (*Andrew Cadmore*)

Above: Indie-pop star Helen Love was invited to New York City by Joey Ramone in 1993 to play a gig with the punk-rock icon. (*Veronika Kofman*)
Opposite: Led by charismatic frontman Benji Webbe, Dub War spearheaded the mid-'90s Newport scene by melding metal with rap and reggae. (*Rob Watkins/Alamy*)

Opposite top: The Big 3! 60 Ft.Dolls delight the happy shoppers at Cardiff's Virgin Megastore. (*Alamy*)

Opposite bottom: SFA OK! After two typically madcap EPs for Ankst, Super Furry Animals justified their early hype with *Fuzzy Logic* on Creation Records. (*Alamy*)

Above: Former Y Cyrff members Mark Roberts (right) and Paul Jones (left) joined forces with Cerys Matthews to create Catatonia, who twice topped the UK album charts. (*Alamy*)

Opposite: Cardiff singer, Donna Lewis became a global sensation with her ubiquitous 1996 hit 'I Love You Always Forever.' (*Alamy*)
Above: Gorky's Zygotic Mynci were one of the most inventive and idiosyncratic bands of the '90s with a prodigious talent that belied their young age. (*Rob Watkin/Alamy*)
Below: Stereophonics throw their support behind the 'Yes' campaign for Welsh devolution with Labour MP Peter Mandelson in a 1997 referendum event at Cardiff's HMV store. (*Jeff Morgan/Alamy*)

Opposite: Featuring the married couple of Paul and Andrea Adams, Melys weaved tales of torment, bitter break-ups and betrayal on their 1998 debut album, *Rumours and Curses.* (*Rob Watkins/Alamy*)

Above: Alongside the late Jon Lee (left), Grant Nicholas (centre) and Taka Hirose (right) formed Feeder, whose debut *Polythene* was awarded *Metal Hammer*'s Album of the Year in 1997. (*Mirrorpix*)

Below: You Can Leave Your Hat On! Tom Jones performed with Robbie Williams at the 1998 BRIT Awards before returning to the top of the charts with Reload. (*Fiona Hanson/Alamy*)

Catatonia kicked off the Rugby World Cup in October 1999 with a rousing performance of 'International Velvet' at the Millennium Stadium. (*David Jones/Alamy*)

You Love Us! In 1989, the Manics played to just two people at Radcliff's Square
Club in Cardiff. Ten years later, they closed out the '90s in front
of 57,000 fans at Manic Millennium. (*Rob Watkins/Alamy*)

In May 2000, Super Furry Animals released *Mwng*, which became the biggest selling Welsh-language album ever. (*Edd Westmacott/Alamy*)

[Richey's lyrics] peer outwards, addressing issues that lie beyond the scope of traditional rock: capital punishment, suicide, gun violence, political correctness, religious fundamentalism, genocide, the sexual proclivities of dictators, Cold War paranoia.

Like Sylvia Plath, Richey runs together personal traumas and world historic tragedies, often in the same lyric. Part of his intention was to puncture the sense of complacency he saw in Britain in the mid-1990s. First teaching of *The Holy Bible*: Things Can Actually Get Worse.[233]

Indeed, this would sadly prove to be the case for the Manics themselves. It was hoped that Richey was indulging in character writing and journalistic collage, but it's difficult to now separate *The Holy Bible*'s content from his state of mind.

After spells at the Priory and Whitchurch Hospital, Richey disappeared from the Embassy Hotel in Bayswater on 1 February 1995 ahead of a US promotional tour. His car was found two weeks later at Aust services near the Severn Bridge, and he hasn't been seen since.

——

'This is history, this is history! Right here, right now, this is history…'[234]

Those were the words of Noel Gallagher as he entered the stage for Oasis's second night at Knebworth. Never a man short of a confidence, he had assumed a Christ-like pose while soaking up the adoration at his beloved Maine Road only a few months earlier.

Yet beneath the bravado this time, there was a hint of incredulity. After all, it hadn't been that long since Noel took control of his younger brother Liam's rudderless Rain outfit and transformed them into all-conquering chart juggernauts Oasis.

By August 1996, every word of his songs was being sung back verbatim as 250,000 fans swarmed like ants to the Hertfordshire stately home. Oasis may have lost the previous summer's Beatles-versus-Stones-like battle for No. 1 to Blur, but they would've loved the irony of winning the war at a country house.

If performing a pair of warm-up gigs in front of 90,000 at Loch Lomond a week before hadn't been impressive enough, the stats surrounding Knebworth were jaw-dropping. A staggering 2.5 million applied for tickets – one in twenty people and 4 per cent of the population. Over 3,000 crew helped stage the event, and there was a rumoured guest list of 7,000. Demand was so huge that Oasis could've sold out a further eighteen nights.

There was a bumper support bill across the weekend, but the only band warming up the hordes on both nights was the Manics.

Nicky, James and Sean had agonised about whether they could continue following Richey's disappearance, and modestly entered the live circuit again with a one-off show with The Stone Roses in December 1995. Emerging under the lights at Wembley Arena in a Cardiff Devils ice hockey shirt, a nervous Nicky Wire said, 'It's only us.'[235] His greeting straddled the indifference of the Roses' fans and acknowledged the Manics devotees, who had made the pilgrimage to London just to see their support slot. Within months, the trio were showcasing their newfound melodic direction and commercial allure across UK arenas on tour with Oasis.

Following in the footsteps of New Order after the death of Ian Curtis, the Manics adopted a similar non-image. They may now have been dressed like any other Britpop band, but the way they returned from suffering such trauma with quiet dignity and an incredible album was admirable to say the least.

Central to its success was lead single 'A Design for Life'. A heart-on-sleeve tribute to working-class resilience, it encapsulated everything they had been trying to say since forming in the mid-'80s.

In the summer of 1995, Wire sprawled two potential ideas across twenty pages of A4. One was 'The Pure Motive' and the other was 'A Design for Life' – the latter's title inspired by Joy Division's *An Ideal for Living* EP. Once it was whittled down into one coherent piece, James Dean Bradfield devised the song's trademark spiralling riff.

Since the Manics had been away, Oasis had become huge, and it was going to take something very special to shift them. Bradfield recalled:

> I was watching 'Some Might Say' on *Top of the Pops* and Noel lifting up his Union Jack guitar, and I just got up and walked out and went around London for four or five hours totally bewildered – 'How the fuck did this happen to us? We've lost our best mate and we don't know what we are or what we're going to do.'
>
> Nick had sent me some lyrics and said to me: 'Let's see if we've got anything,' and the song came out in about five minutes. I was

scared, as I'd done the verse and I was so pleased…It was do or die, forcing myself to keep the rest simple, and then I took a deep breath and dug down inside myself and there it was on tape.

I called up Nick and knew we had it, that we could carry on. It was like finding the final piece…Then I was pacing around the house for half a day thinking, 'God, I don't think I've ever been this close to potentially writing a No. 1 single with a perfect lyric.'[236]

In late 1994, Bradfield admitted: 'At the end of the day, we haven't written the song that the milkman can whistle.'[237] Now, seemingly they had.

The Manics had previously approached producer Mike Hedges for *The Holy Bible* thanks to his work with Siouxsie and the Banshees. This time, they had another of his masterworks in mind – the widescreen 'Wall of Sound' production that had sprung 'Yes' by McAlmont & Butler into the Top 10 the previous year. Their very own George Martin, Hedges immediately labelled 'A Design for Life' a 'jukebox' record[238] that people would want to listen to again and again.

Call it serendipity or divine fate, but the Manics were about to mount one of the most miraculous comebacks in rock 'n' roll. With the rough mix in the bag by September 1995 and production finalised with a gorgeous string section at Abbey Road around Christmas, the single was finally ready to test its mettle in April 1996. By the time a slogan-heavy video and Sean Moore's drum solo finale had been added to the amalgamation of Ennio Morricone and Phil Spector, the end result was pure gold.

After the commercially problematic *Holy Bible*, the Manics faced the very real possibility of being dropped by Sony. Therefore, 'A Design for Life' couldn't have been timed better. Briefly No. 1 in the midweek charts, it agonisingly missed out on the top spot to Mark Morrison's 'Return of the Mack'. Nevertheless, it was by far their biggest hit to date – quite the transition from their previous single, 'She Is Suffering', peaking at No. 36.

Part of Wire's incentive in writing the lyric was his reaction to Blur's portrayal of '*Parklife* Britain'. In Kieran Evans's docufilm *Escape from History*, he said: 'The working-class symbols of a miners' institute and stuff like that were being bypassed and turned into some sort of *On the Buses* caricature of working-class Britain, and it was being done by people who weren't even working class.'[239]

> *Everything Must Go* was dedicated to Tower Colliery in the Cynon valley where 239 miners led by Tyrone O'Sullivan each pledged £8,000 from their redundancy payouts to buy back the mine for more than £1 million amid strong UK government resistance. Within its first year it ran a £3 million profit.

In 1996, Bradfield said to *Melody Maker*:

> There are songs of his where [Damon] treats characters as completely disposable. As if life's a peep show for him from the perspective of a well-off pop star. He pays his pound, looks at all the funny little lives, writes a few lines about them and that's that.
>
> I don't think we've ever done that. If we use characters in our songs – 'Kevin Carter', '4st 7lb' – they're never, ever treated like that.[240]

In *Escape from History*, he added: 'We weren't walking around saying Britpop was shite or anything; there was some good records coming out...But that representation of cheeky, saucy, seaside working-class-postcard desires just seemed a bit condescending.'[241]

Wire's depiction of the working class was very different. In 2016, he said to *The Quietus*:

> It was a reaction to the arch raised eyebrow of bands like Pulp. That was my only problem with Pulp – it always seemed to be done with such a sense of irony, and everything was presented as some sort of *Carry On* film, which was anathema to me.
>
> The humour in the valleys is absolutely vicious piss-taking, but it's never that arch, ironic raising of the eyebrow. It's just fucking verging on violence, so everything was turned into a greyhound race, and I just didn't get it.[242]

The hugely powerful opening line of 'A Design for Life' was inspired by the inscription 'Knowledge Is Power' above the door at Pillgwenlly Library (while its less discussed second line, 'Then work came and made us free', originated from the '*Arbeit Macht Frei*' sign at

Auschwitz – you don't get that with Shed Seven). It was the antithesis to Liam, *Loaded* and laddism. Simon Price found it hard to stomach that the Manics were suddenly supporting Oasis:

> Nicky Wire's wife and brother both worked in libraries. One suspected that Liam Gallagher would feel out of his depth if a woman told him she was a Libran, never mind a librarian... Nicky dedicated 'A Design for Life' to Dennis Potter, Dennis Skinner, Arthur Scargill and Antonio Gaudi, and now here he was backslapping with this proudly illiterate apeman, who had probably never made it to the end of an Enid Blyton.
>
> Everything the Manics hated about Madchester was true of Oasis: anti-education, anti-intelligence, anti-femininity, anti-glamour, pro-getting wasted. Oasis was a worst-case scenario, lowest common denominator cliché of what the working classes can be, encouraged by a southern bourgeois media clearly aroused by a northern bit of rough.[243]

John Robb continued:

> 'A Design for Life' has got everything that's great about the Manics...You don't have to do nothing all your life. I think there's something really powerful in that...
>
> If you like a rock 'n' roll record, why can't you read a book by Camus? Intelligent things aren't that hard to get into. They can make you feel as good as drinking ten pints of lager on a Saturday night.[244]

Wire has often said it couldn't have been written anywhere other Wales – or more specifically, the south Wales valleys. Manics superfan Michael Sheen said:

> I remember once driving back to London from Wales and as I crossed the Severn Bridge, 'A Design for Life' was playing, and I was just weeping.
>
> It's ridiculously nationalistic, but there was something so incredibly moving about that song, and the meaning it had for me and particularly crossing the Severn Bridge to leave Wales...[245]

There's a peculiar kind of Welsh bigness and the Manics are absolutely in that tradition: dramatic and passionate. We have the word *'hwyl'* in Wales – that sense of it coming from somewhere deeper than your bootstraps, in your gut.

Music can be popular and anthemic and have a political edge and a real integrity to what it's talking about at the same time as being soaring and transcendent…It is possible to have both.[246]

Speaking to Mark Goodier, Bradfield added:

We won an Ivor Novello for Best Contemporary Song for 'A Design for Life', which is one of my favourite moments in the band…

I don't think there are many examples in British rock/pop history where every line of the song means something…It talks about boom-and-bust economy, it talks about the gap between the haves and the have-nots where the haves don't give a damn about tax, but you know the have-nots constantly get preached to about not spending above their means…And being told, 'Stay in your place,' but also, 'You can't enjoy yourself either.'[247]

In June 2009, the Manics opened the new Cardiff Central Library.

At the ceremony, Cardiff Arms Park Male Choir performed a rousing rendition of 'A Design for Life', and in doing so, united the past and present traditions of Welsh music.

With a working title of *Sounds in the Grass* (inspired by a series of paintings by Jackson Pollock), *Everything Must Go* featured four Top 10 singles. Intrinsic to its success was that it had Richey Edwards's influence etched across it.

Continuing the non-image aesthetic was the album's artwork, which featured another triptych like *The Holy Bible*, but not as striking this time, as Simon Price explained:

You only needed to glance at the cover of *Everything Must Go* to know that something had changed: this band had been redesigned...

Mark Farrow's sleeve was a masterpiece of neat, uncluttered modernism. For the first time, the band's faces – clean, scrubbed, blank – appeared on the front. Its only conscious statement seemed to be that there was no statement. Below the title stood a pair of wide-spaced parentheses containing no text, just a yawning void (which spoke louder than words ever could).[248]

One concept for the album that didn't come to fruition was Richey's idea of 'Pantera meets Nine Inch Nails meets *Screamadelica*'. However, the feeling amongst the group was to become more uplifting and melodic as several demos recorded at House in the Woods studios in 1995 testified. Simply making *The Holy Bible* Mk II would've seen them slip into self-parody. Wire told *Buzz*:

The Pantera thing wasn't explored at all. Music just wasn't me and Richey's department, so you can come up with all these ideas in the world, but we had already written 'No Surface', 'Further Away' and 'Small Black Flowers' when he was still around. We all felt we didn't want to do something as intense as *The Holy Bible*.[249]

Richey had written full lyrics for three songs: the achingly beautiful 'Small Black Flowers that Grow in the Sky', the Nirvana *Unplugged* acoustic strum of 'Removables' and an unlikely hit in 'Kevin Carter'. The fact that a bleak lyric about a Pulitzer Prize-winning photographer (who died by suicide) could reach No. 9 demonstrated that the Manics were still brilliantly subverting the British mainstream.

The Manics later revisited the folder of lyrics that Richey Edwards left behind in 1995 to create their ninth album, *Journal for Plague Lovers*.

Recorded at Rockfield with Steve Albini and released in May 2009, the band sculpted songs exclusively around the words of Edwards, who had been declared legally dead the previous year.

Wire and Edwards co-wrote the Sylvia Plath-inspired 'The Girl Who Wanted to Be God', and 'Elvis Impersonator: Blackpool Pier', where the Manics actually found themselves in agreement with Blur about a creeping stateside influence in British life. It conveyed that Brits would lap up anything American even if it was dead culture, and a cheap imitation at that.

Richey's uncomplicated guitar playing from the 'No Surface All Feeling' demo even found its way onto the final record underneath Bradfield's Smashing Pumpkins-esque riffing. Plus, a band who vowed they would never write a love song had now written two; both were included. 'Enola/Alone' and 'Further Away' were written by Wire for his wife, Rachel.

The most poignant (and heartbreaking) lines of the whole album came via its title track: 'I just hope that you can forgive us, but everything must go' and 'I look to the future, it makes me cry'. Across four minutes, Wire agonises about their decision to continue without Richey. Not only had they lost their driving force, but also their manager Philip Hall, who died from cancer in 1993.

Following Richey's disappearance, Bradfield came back to live with Terri Hall in Shepherd's Bush where the new songs brought her to tears: 'He was often found in the kitchen banging away on the guitar, whether that be one in the morning or one in the afternoon…[The album] sort of drew a line under the painful period and nodded towards a future – a future without people that we loved, but a future nonetheless.'[250]

Likewise, the fourth and final single, 'Australia', referenced Wire's yearning to get away as far as possible from all the press intrusion and rumours surrounding Richey's disappearance. Belied by its euphoric guitars and catchy chorus, it became the Manics' very own 'Life of Riley' as it soundtracked the goals on the Nationwide Football League coverage and provided the theme for *Renford Rejects*. It was also used for promotional campaigns by the Australian tourist board and various sporting montages. Wire told *NME*: 'One of the best moments was when Australia beat England 76–0 at rugby. I was happy enough anyway, but when they played "Australia" afterwards…'[251]

At the 1997 BRIT Awards, the Manics scooped British Group and Album of the Year, while at the *NME* Awards they won Best LP, Live

Act and Single. Reaching No. 2, *Everything Must Go* was only kept off the top spot by George Michael's *Older*. Nobody could've anticipated all this overwhelming success, not least the band themselves.

Wire has often spoke of the album as the moment when Britain's biggest cult band came overground, and it's easy to see why. From the Queen Vic to the Rovers Return, the Manics were *everywhere*. As Marc Burrows said in *Manic Street Preachers: Album by Album*:

> *Everything Must Go* had been one of those albums that transcended a usual indie-band audience. At one point, it was playing in the background on BBC1 school drama *Grange Hill* as a student pulled an all-nighter.
>
> We checked back on him every once in a while, and the fact that a different song from *Everything Must Go* was playing each time was used to mark the passage of time. It was assumed that enough of the audience would own the album to get the point. That's one hell of a penetration.[252]

As time passed, the band's non-image began to fade. Wire's trademark tiaras and frocks came back – as did his acid tongue. Thankfully, he emerged from purdah at their first headline show at Cardiff International Arena in December 1996 where he roasted his Britpop contemporaries: 'If any of you out there own any Ocean Colour Scene or Kula Shaker records, burn the fuckers!'[253]

When Nicky Wire collected the Manics' BRIT Award for British Album of the Year in February 1997, he premiered a bold new look.

Cocooned in 'Y *Ddraig Goch*' ('The Red Dragon'), he arrived onstage at Earls Court as if 'gift-wrapped from Wales'.[254] With both commercial and critical acclaim secured, the Manics were now in a position to readdress and embrace their Welsh roots without media derision – something that was unthinkable in their early days. The Welsh flag has been proudly draped across Wire's amp ever since.

Simultaneously, Britpop and the wider Cool Britannia scene were saturated with Union Jacks from Noel Gallagher's guitar and Geri Halliwell's minidress to the works of the Young British Artists and the flood of flags that greeted Tony Blair's arrival at No. 10 Downing Street. Only a few years removed from the furore Morrissey caused cavorting with the Union Jack and skinhead imagery while supporting Madness at Finsbury Park, the British public had seemingly grown comfortable again with its flag's associations.

Welsh historian Martin Johnes said:

I think in England it's much more difficult to be patriotic because patriotism is associated with the right whereas it's not in Wales. In England, if you wave a St George's flag anywhere apart from an England football match, it's just a bit weird.

If you've got Welsh flag flying in your garden here, nobody thinks anything. But if you put up a Union Jack...[255]

However, the Manics's embracing of the Red Dragon drew a divided reaction from fellow Welsh bands, which Wire acknowledged:

By that point, even if people didn't like us, there was a begrudging sense of 'They've taken a lot of shit and flak, this lot, just for being from Wales.'

I think some of the Welsh-language bands were slightly narky that I had a Welsh flag on my amp, I think maybe it was Gorky's.[256]

In their promo video for 'Iechyd Da', Gorky's playful flag-waving certainly looked like piss-taking.

Some artists weren't comfortable with patriotism being mixed up with nationalism. Richard Parfitt of 60 Ft. Dolls said, 'We *never* ever put a Welsh flag on anything...

We definitely felt that we were a Welsh band, but we never really gave a shit about it.'[257]

Meanwhile, Rhys Mwyn was unequivocal: 'Passports, flags, anthems – they can all go to hell.'[258]

Gruff Rhys was more nuanced about the Manics' subversive removal of the masculinity associated with national symbols: 'I like the way Nicky Wire uses the Welsh flag because it's often side by side with a feather boa, which takes the machismo out of it.'[259]

It's safe to say that Gruff wasn't a fan of flags generally though. In a 1998 interview, *The Guardian* described Super Furry Animals as 'the perfect antidote to Britpop's offensive nationalism' and a band who are 'non-regional, non-patriotic and non-fussed about conquering everything in their path'.[260] Gruff responded: 'There's something violent about the terms "cracking America" and "British invasion". It's militaristic, colonial gobbledygook.'

Speaking to *Magnet* in 2016, he added: 'We had a relationship to Britpop in that we were interested in melodic songwriting, but we were politically opposed to it as Welsh speakers, as members of a minority group. We saw it as a conservative, jingoistic movement.'[261]

Bandmate Guto Pryce agreed: 'Britpop was quite a risible scene. We didn't like the idea of flag-waving, and we never waved a Welsh flag...There was a backlash against that scene, and rightfully so.'[262]

As the Manics' relationship with their Welshness became more comfortable, so did their reputation as a band that could fill huge venues. The peak of the *Everything Must Go* era came via their biggest gig to date in front of 20,000 at Manchester's NYNEX Arena in May 1997.

It was a night that epitomised how the Manics had somehow been co-opted into Britpop. Battles raged amongst their old-guard support wrapped in feather boas and leopard print against the casual wear of new fandom.

Yet, both camps would end up featuring obsessives that few other bands could match.

Simon Price argued that it was more a problem of the diehard versus the fair-weather fan (though some of the later converts were equally as encyclopaedic as the long-term devotees). However, some of the Ben Sherman brigade who came the band's way via Britpop took the ironic, beer-swilling chorus line of 'A Design for Life' a bit too literally.

Bradfield said to *NME* that there was room for everyone:

At the NYNEX, when crowds of lads were singing 'We only want to get drunk', I think there was a big mistake made there. This idea of [adopts condescending tone]: 'Oh God, what are Nicky and James thinking about in this moment? They must be cringing at that lot there.'

Part of that lyric has no irony at all. For a start, I've been in many a situation where I know not what to say, but I know what to do, where I'm not articulate enough to make myself understood and yeah, sometimes I do just want to fucking get drunk...

Sometimes the most base reaction is the only one I've got, and those were the working-class considerations in the song.[263]

Regardless of how you construed the lyrics, there was one common theme between both sets of fans – Welsh flags.

Biographer Mick Middles said:

There's a swell of warmth spreading around the arena. There are Welsh flags billowing everywhere. Not rebel flags, but flags that create a curious feeling of homecoming.

It was impossible to tell if these people were Welsh, or were pretending to be Welsh, [but] it was an acknowledgement of Welsh talent that had at last really arrived in the pop world.[264]

We the Super Furry Animals have acquired a Super Furry tank. The tank is our very own non-violent, travelling sound system.

Given the opportunity, we will de-commission all existing armed vehicles. They will be adapted to shoot food over long distances to famine-struck areas, providing thousands of ex-soldiers with employment.

In the meantime, our iron-plated mobile disco will be visiting a location near u in the near future.

THINK TANK! SFA.

In the above fax dated 3 June 1996, Super Furry Animals announced their new mode of transport. Not just any old vehicle, but a techno tank bought from Nottingham for £10,000.

Just a fortnight after the release of their debut album, *Fuzzy Logic*, the band and Creation Records were seemingly blowing vital marketing budget. But buying a tank proved to be a master stroke as it provided more publicity than any ad or positive review ever could.

Bilingual, internationalist and pacifist in their ethos, an army vehicle had never been used in such a way before, especially being driven directly into the National Eisteddfod.

Blasting out The Beach Boys and painted bright blue with the band's name emblazoned in yellow block caps, the tank trundled towards the fields of Llandeilo where far more civilised events like poetry recitations and clog dancing were happening. Ironically, in keeping with the traditions of the Eisteddfod, a question was spelled out above its headlights: '*A oes heddwch?*' ('Is there peace?')

As harps were serenely plucked and bards were being anointed, the group rolled into town. Dating back to the druidic rites of the twelfth century, the Eisteddfod had never experienced anything like the Furries. Even worse, they performed some of their '*Saesneg*' songs at this strictly Welsh-language only festival (and to further take the piss, they *whistled* the banned lyrics).

An organiser had earlier assured the media that the Furries would be on their best Welsh-speaking behaviour, but he was in for a bit of a shock, as Ric Rawlins recalled:

The festival spokesman wandered down to the stage where Super

Furry Animals were playing…The crowd were singing along to an instrumental performance. Stranger still, although some were singing in Welsh, others were singing in English…and was that even Japanese he heard? He walked into the audience and spotted a girl handing out lyric sheets.

'Would you mind if I took a look at this?' He smiled, grabbing a pamphlet…The lyrics were printed in a variety of translations with a simple instruction: 'SING ALONG IN WHICHEVER LANGUAGE YOU LIKE.'

The spokesperson put his quivering hand over his mouth… The contradiction of voices as they blended into one another made for an almighty sound – indecipherable, certainly – but also a strange kind of international language.[265]

In a S4C documentary, one interviewee accused the band of being the 'sons of Thatcher' for their move into the more lucrative English-language market. He argued that as they grew up with a prime minister that preached greed-empowering individualism, they clearly had no social responsibility. In another scene, a bunch of teenagers drive across the Severn Bridge only to find their Welsh radio morphs, horror film-like, into the English language.

Thankfully, by May 1998, Gruff's fear of being disowned by his own country had died down, as he told *The Guardian*.

It was greatly exaggerated. We were the subject of a radio phone-in. Then the Welsh-speaking news wheeled in a few farmers to slag us off. It wasn't national outrage, just paranoia.

They thought we were undermining thirty years of political groundwork for the Welsh language. I do feel a certain responsibility, but we just love singing and have no phobias about the English language.[266]

The tank continued to transport the band around the UK festival circuit with the twin purpose of pumping out techno that could challenge the Criminal Justice Act. Gruff said to *Vice*:

The government had banned repetitive beats on a loud sound

BRITPOP VS COOL CYMRU

system, so anyone caught playing repetitive beats in public could have their sound system confiscated. We wanted to DJ at music festivals, so we thought if we converted a tank and put some decks inside and speakers on top, nobody could shut us down.

I remember going to the Reading Festival and our sound system was louder than the second stage![267]

Alan McGee added: 'Our record plugger found a by-law where you could drive armed vehicles around London between four and six in the morning, so he drove the tank to Radio 1 and parked it outside and plugged the record.'[268]

After the summer, the tank was put into retirement – or more specifically, sold to Don Henley of Eagles.

'He got it shipped over to his ranch in Texas,' said Gruff. 'But he had no interest in the band and I think he got it painted back to its original colours. It was just a weird kind of epilogue.'[269]

———

'I thought I was signing an out-and-out Britpop, Blur kind of band. Little did I know that I was signing The Beach Boys meets Gong meets Isaac Hayes on a fucking acid trip.'[270]

Creation Records once had a semi-serious, unwritten rule that they would never sign a Welsh band. By 1995, though, they were breaking one of their Ten Commandments as Alan McGee was smitten with the Furries.

With Britpop fast becoming a homogenous scene, you couldn't blame him for not being initially enthused at another group of fellas bearing guitars, decked in combats. Simon Price thought the same:

At first, I didn't get it. The image of Super Furry Animals as presented via the English media was a turn-off. Yet another cagoule-wearing band signed to Creation by Alan McGee with the Oasis millions. The way in which the press played up SFA's drugginess misrepresented them as a laddish herd of gonzo hedonists…

But SFA's reputation as wacky funsters almost did them a disservice, taking attention away from the transcendent gorgeousness of their music.[271]

Splott-born Creation Records A & R man Mark Bowen had alerted the

127

Scottish Svengali to their charms after seeing only their second-ever gig in Aberystwyth in March 1995. The band had only just debuted at Lampeter University Students' Union (where they were billed as 'Super Fury Animals'), and now here was a rep from a prominent label inviting them to London.

With Iestyn George at *NME* lavishing praise on their debut EP and Simon Williams giving their gig at the Splash Club a glowing review, Alan McGee decided to check out this exciting cult act. 'My passion at the time was either women or football,' he said. 'But I thought, for once, I should do my job, so I went to their next show.'[272]

McGee was renowned as the man who spotted Oasis at King Tut's in Glasgow in 1993 and propelled them to stratospheric heights. It may have been only the Furries' second gig outside Wales, but labels were already vying for Britain's coolest new band, so he needed to act fast. Approaching them after their short set, McGee asked if they would like to rub shoulders with Primal Scream, Teenage Fanclub, My Bloody Valentine, The Boo Radleys and, of course, Oasis on Creation Records. Swiftly adding the band to his ranks, he famously implored them to sing in English – only to be told they already were!

Released on the same day as *Everything Must Go*, *Fuzzy Logic* was produced by Gorwel Owen at Rockfield. With two classic Welsh albums arriving on the same day, it's only in hindsight that we can acknowledge what a landmark day in Welsh music that was. In August 2020, James Dean Bradfield recalled to *The Line of Best Fit* his first memories of hearing *Fuzzy Logic* at Big Noise Recorders (formerly Sound Space Studios):

> From the title and the cover, I had no idea what this band was going to be like…And then looking at some of the titles, I saw 'Hometown Unicorn' and I was like, 'Fuck me, that's a great title.'
>
> Nick put it on in the office, and we sat down and listened to it, and it was just a lovely, exciting moment of having almost a sense memory of what a band is going to be like before you even hear it.[273]

Everything Must Go may have topped *Melody Maker*'s end of year album poll, but *Fuzzy Logic* finished close behind it at No. 3, and Nicky Wire declared it as his favourite record of 1996: 'It reminds me of *Bummed* by Happy Mondays, the way the chaos and disorder comes together at certain moments into perfection.'[274]

Initially, the most striking thing about *Fuzzy Logic* was its brilliant sleeve by Britpop artist-of-choice Brian Cannon. His classic covers already adorned Oasis's *Definitely Maybe*, Suede's *Dog Man Star* and The Verve's *A Northern Soul*, but *Fuzzy Logic* is perhaps his most iconic.

Gruff Rhys had sourced a collection of passport photos of the Bridgend-born drug smuggler Howard Marks, who had over forty aliases during his time at large. When Cannon arranged the shots in a collage across the table, he envisaged a record that would jump off the shelves. Add into the mix a track called 'Hangin' with Howard Marks' and Creation's decision to coincide *Fuzzy Logic* with the release of Marks's autobiography, and the campaign was off to a flyer.

Marks was sent an advance copy of the album while in prison in Indiana. Upon release, legend has it that he attended the Furries' Pontypridd Town Hall gig in June 1996 with a plus-ten request for the guest list. Coincidentally, he met Rhys Ifans that night, who would go on to portray Marks in the 2010 biopic *Mr Nice*.

Rejecting inward-looking schools of thought, the Furries saw Marks as a progressive, revolutionary icon sharing their own internationalist vision. Ric Rawlins said:

They were consciously trying to create what they termed 'outlaw culture' – a reaction against certain notions of Welsh nationalism. This had been cemented in their minds one night when they had visited Clwb Ifor Bach, which that evening was operating a Welsh-speakers-only door policy.

When the gig came to a close and Heather Jones came on to sing 'Land of My Fathers', they were disheartened to see everyone standing up to sing the national anthem. 'We made a point to sit down,' said Gruff. 'We're not interested in any anthem, it's such an antiquated notion and so exclusive. We're all about inclusion.'[275]

Founded by Cymdeithas Clwb Cymraeg Caerdydd in 1983, Clwb Ifor Bach has provided a vital space for Welsh and grassroots acts for over forty years.

Located on Cardiff's Womanby Street on the site of a

former British Legion club, it's named after Ifor Bach –
a rebel leader against English rule in the twelfth century –
and the venue's title translates as 'Little Ifor's Club'.

Known simply as 'Clwb' by locals and 'The Welsh Club'
by students, it operated a strict Welsh-language-only policy
throughout its early years, which David Owens labelled
'separatist snobbery' in *Cerys, Catatonia and the Rise
of Welsh Pop*:

> Whenever I wanted to see a band play at Clwb, I was
> excluded – even though I was an enthusiastic supporter
> of Welsh-language bands...
>
> The only way I could see Y Cyrff was to play my trump
> card and say I was a journalist reviewing the gig for a
> fanzine...
>
> It worked but even then, I was begrudgingly allowed
> in only if I was signed in by a Welsh speaker. I remember
> going up to the bar and debating whether I should
> attempt to order a pint of lager in my pidgin Welsh ('Un
> paint o'r lager' – I think!), or just ask for it in English.
>
> Feeling sure I'd make a fool of myself either way, I
> stumped for the English option and was shot such a look
> of abhorrent horror by the barman that I had spoken
> English, that I made that pint last all night. Talk about
> feeling like a stranger in your own land![276]

Realising that music should be a universal language, Clwb
gradually softened its Welsh-only stance, and it's now a
totally integrated, non-exclusionary experience. Welsh and
English are spoken equally, and staff are generally required
to be bilingual. No anti-Welsh sentiment is tolerated in
either language.

As well as hosting some huge names on their early
upward trajectories, like Coldplay, The Strokes and The
Killers, Clwb has staged countless Welsh artists, from the

Furries and Stereophonics to Duffy and Gwenno.

In March 2022, the Manics played Clwb for the first time as part of the BBC Radio 6 Music Festival. In October 1990, they had been due to play an anti-poll tax gig organised by Plaid Cymru at the venue. Advertised below headliners Tynal Tywyll on a bill also featuring Beganifs and Hanner Pei, the Manics cancelled last-minute as they were off to London to sign a record contract!

The Furries' first performance on *Top of the Pops* with 'Something 4 the Weekend' was prefaced with an on-screen graphic saying *'O Gymru'* ('From Wales'). It may seem a tokenistic, simple stab at the Welsh language, but it demonstrated how quickly the perception of Welshness had changed. The single gave the band their highest ranking at the time of No. 18.

Hearing such a strong Welsh accent belting out a Top 20 hit on national TV was a thrill, but Gruff attempted to make his words more decipherable:

> I was twenty-five and singing in English for the first time, so it took me a while to settle on my singing accents because I was kind of winging it.
>
> On *Fuzzy Logic*, I'm trying on a few different accents. I think I'm trying on a Birmingham accent on 'Something 4 the Weekend' because I was listening to a lot of ELO and The Move, so it's pretty weird.[277]

Lead single 'Hometown Unicorn' offered an early instance of the strange subjects found in the Furries' songs. It referenced the reported UFO abduction in 1979 of Franck Fontaine, who reappeared a week later lying in a cabbage patch with little memory of what happened. While guest reviewing for *NME*, Pulp loved it and awarded it Single of the Week.

A rerecorded version of 'God! Show Me Magic' secured the same accolade a couple of months later. Its inlay featured the quote *'Gorau Chwarae, Cyd Chwarae'* (the motto of the Football Association of Wales, meaning 'It's Better to Play Together' – a precursor to the simplified 'Together Stronger').

With the SFA techno tank adorning its artwork, the fourth and final single, 'If You Don't Want Me to Destroy You', also reached No. 18. Amongst its B-sides was a delightful rebuttal to their detractors in the language debate, '(Nid) Hon Yw'r Gân Sy'n Mynd i Achub yr Iaith' – meaning 'This Is (Not) the Song That Will Save the [Welsh] Language'.

There was also the guitar-pop perfection of 'Frisbee', while the outro to 'Long Gone' sampled Rhys Ifans in the midst of an acid frenzy captured via answerphone. 'Gathering Moss' was a welcome dose of dreamy, balalaika-infused prog-psychedelia, while 'Fuzzy Birds' was dedicated to a late friend – a swan, who exploded into a flurry of sparks outside Rockfield when it flew into the power line. As darkness descended, the band believed the studio was cursed, especially as they were blighted with continual instances of the number twenty-three.

The twenty-three enigma is a belief popularised by books, conspiracy theories and even a movie starring Jim Carrey, which suggests that the number appearing in regular frequency could be a symbol of some larger, hidden significance. The control panel at Rockfield was far larger than Gorwel's production desk at Stiwdio Ofn, and he found gremlins in its twenty-third channel. Gruff then counted twenty-three beams above Gorwel's head. When the bird got fried outside the studio, it was also the twenty-third day of the month. No prizes for guessing where *Fuzzy Logic* charted!

Melody Maker's review offered both plaudits and casual racism:

> Never mind that the band are a bunch of scamps with names like Grumph and Bumble, that their first language is gobbledygook and their second is Welsh, that they worship 'cute' dope smuggler Howard Marks to the extent of putting him all over the cover and writing a song about him. All that's just a blind distraction from the little baroque box of baubles to hand.[278]

With lyrics reading like the end credits to a film, 'For Now and Ever' was perfectly placed as the album's arms-in-the-air denouement. *NME* said:

> *Fuzzy Logic* closes with the smashingly cheesy 'For Now and

Ever' wherein Gruff howls, 'We'll be together 'til the end', and the punters hold their SFA scarves aloft and weep a particularly tearful finale. It then ends with what appears to be the BBC sound effects workshop being blown up. The prog's bollocks![279]

———

The Furries closed out an amazing year by entering the record books, and true to form it would be for something unconventional.

Released in December 1996, their new single was never likely to challenge for Christmas No. 1 especially as it contained 'fuck' more than any other song. A sticker may have been strategically placed on the sleeve to cover the profanity, but it still gleefully boomed: 'WARNING: THIS TRACK CONTAINS THE WORD **** 50 TIMES!'

Ever the nonconformists, their anarchic anthem 'The Man Don't Give a Fuck' was an incendiary missile aimed at oppressive governments and corrupt politicians. After a slowbuild to the chorus, the song explodes into life before cascading into a two-minute outro with the oft-repeated line 'You know, they don't give a fuck about anybody else…'

Gruff Rhys said to *Vox*: 'Radio 1 did a really crap version of the song with bleeps…If we'd known they were going to do that, we wouldn't have agreed to it because it takes away the whole point. I think Radio Wales played it once complete with "fucks".'[280]

The Furries were keen to emphasise that it was the establishment who didn't give a fuck, and not themselves. When a company approached them with the idea of selling T-shirts featuring the slogan 'SFA: We Don't Give a Fuck', the band were quick to inform them they had the wrong end of the stick.

Previously an exercise in dub, it was cobbled together from a day-long improvisation at Daf's parents' house inspired by the drummer's love of Steely Dan's 1973 tune 'Show Biz Kids'. He sampled its key line into a loop, which the band played over with a dance-influenced sense of hypnotic repetition. With its various elements coalescing, the band loved their new composition. Yet, not everyone was happy.

Steely Dan frontman Donald Fagen refused permission for 'The Man Don't Give a Fuck' to be used on *Fuzzy Logic*. Subsequent promo copies of 'If You Don't Want Me to Destroy You' featured the song as a B-side, but again Fagen wouldn't grant clearance, so 'Guacamole' ended up replacing it. It was looking like 'The Man

Don't Give a Fuck' wouldn't see the light of day, but then Alan McGee came to the rescue, proclaiming to the Furries: 'You're on the label that doesn't give a fuck too. We're putting it out.'

Speaking to *Nation.Cymru* on the single's twenty-fifth anniversary in 2021, McGee said:

> 'The Man Don't Give a Fuck' was the best thing I'd ever heard them do, so I said, 'Why are we giving away this song as a B-side?' I was told, 'Steely Dan want £7,000, so we're just going to put it out as a B-side and pay them a royalty.' I said, 'Well just pay them the £7,000,' so we did and it was fucking great![281]

Reaching No. 22, it premiered live a couple of days after its release at the Hippo Club. A crammed sweatbox of a venue behind Cardiff Central train station with a saucer-eyed clientele who loved rave culture, it was the perfect location for such a song.

NME may have been prohibited from writing its title in full ('Mildy Peeved Against the Machine'[282]), but they still awarded 'The Man Don't Give a Fuck' with Single of the Week. Its artwork featured a personality who shared the same maverick spirit as Howard Marks (who provided a remix of the song). It depicted, in a colourised shot, enigmatic Cardiff City striker Robin Friday – known as a nonconformist always fighting against 'the man' – running past stranded Luton Town goalkeeper Milija Aleksic while flicking the Vs in his direction. Ric Rawlins said: 'Who exactly was not giving a fuck in this context was admirably ambiguous – fuzzy logic indeed.'[283]

A quarter century later, the legacy of 'The Man Don't Give a Fuck' lives on as the Furries' frenzied set-closer. Accompanied by a video featuring Lenin, Stalin and Trotsky, it's now renowned for its wild improvisation including an extended techno wig-out that allows the band time to don their trademark yeti suits.

Detroit hip-hop duo Insane Clown Posse broke its record by using the F-word 105 times in their 1999 single 'Fuck the World'. The Furries have since reclaimed that honour thanks to an epic twenty-three-minute live version at London's Hammersmith Apollo in 2004.

———

'When our debut album comes out, it'll have *every* sort of sound on it…I'm talking about a record that'll be better than *The Stone Roses*.'[284]

As manifestos go, it's not quite promising to outsell *Appetite for Destruction*, but it's still hyperbole that Richey Edwards and Nicky Wire would've been proud of.

Catatonia were nevertheless in unstoppable form in an early interview with *NME*'s John Harris. Mark Roberts continued: 'I'm not talking about orchestras, that's the usual thing – "Our album's got strings on it." Wow. The Bunnymen did that sixty-five years ago.'[285]

Beside him, Cerys Matthews was increasingly warming to her theme: 'Echobelly, These Animal Men…They've got the gift of the gab, they know what to say, they live in the right places, but you put their records on and you're fucking disappointed…You're not going back to listen to them in ten months, let alone ten years.'

Harris recalled this first meeting with Mark and Cerys:

> I thought they were mad…[But] this pair clearly knew the drill. I set my tape recorder down on a pub table, and in a rather incoherent but undoubtedly passionate style, out it all came…
>
> The usual deal was that the band dispensed such quotes in between knowing smirks, the journalist faithfully wrote them up, the article appeared, and both parties eventually agreed that it was probably one of those things they'd have to forget. These two, by contrast, clearly meant every word.[286]

Aided by Mark's uncanny knack for a pop hook, Cerys was a force of nature even before Catatonia's 1996 debut album, *Way Beyond Blue*. The band had signed to Blanco y Negro Records the previous year and the label had money allocated for a glamorous shoot set up for their new charges with renowned rock photographer Gered Mankowitz. However, he couldn't get the band's singer (and most marketable commodity) to look right.

Lumbered with pictures they didn't really like, they were already at loggerheads with their new label – until an ingenious bit of quick thinking from their PR, Jayne Houghton.

A review of their Splash Club gig by *Heaven Up Here* fanzine had included the line: 'Cerys' voice is an angelic choir girl one moment and fast-rising, beer-soaked, rip-roaring pop tart the next!'[287] The phrase lampooned Pepsi's 'lip-smacking, thirst-quenching' ad campaign, and Houghton had the brainwave to splash it across a T-shirt and snap some moody, black-and-white pics of the singer alone. The end result was simple, but devastating in its impact.

Cerys also walked it like she talked it. After disappearing on a three-day bender in France, Cerys astonished everyone by arriving back just in time for a *Melody Maker* interview.

Just three months on from the *Hooked* EP, Catatonia returned with 'Whale' in September 1994 – a three-minute wedge of sparkling pop with a sublime vocal that once again earned them *NME* Single of the Week. With its Noel Gallagher-like guitars, it didn't suggest anything beyond the zeitgeist, but Mark was undeterred: 'You know how Oasis make good songs for just before you go out to the pub? Well, our songs are going to cater to every human emotion.'[288]

'Whale' was an essential stepping stone. Released via the Rough Trade Singles Club, its founder, Geoff Travis, also ran Blanco y Negro (a subsidiary of Warner Brothers), who the band subsequently signed with. In the interim, another catchy, stand-alone single, 'Bleed', was issued before the album campaign started in earnest.

Strangely, it was a rerecorded song from the *For Tinkerbell* EP that kicked things off in January 1996, but 'Sweet Catatonia' certainly warranted a wider audience and it jumped over forty chart positions compared to its predecessor.

Their next single, 'Lost Cat', fared even better, but agonisingly missed out on the Top 40 by one place. At the filming of its promo video, the London Fire Brigade were called out by a passer-by to assist a lady stuck up a lamp post looking for the titular lost cat…The lady in question? Cerys Matthews!

In late August, Catatonia unveiled their latest secret weapon with the perfect pop of 'You've Got a Lot to Answer For'. Described by David Owens as a 'shrewd snapshot of love '90s-style,'[289] the song popped into Mark's head while queueing in Spar. It concerned the perils of pregnancy tests: 'If it turns to blue, what are we gonna do?' Thanks to its 'Made of Stone' guitars, the media were quick to summon the name of a certain Mancunian band. *NME* said: '"You've Got a Lot to Answer For" sounds like on-form Stone Roses, a ten-storey love song with a killer twist, sonorous church-bell guitars and a towering alpine tune.'[290] It charted at No. 35, their first

Top 40 hit.

A month later, *Way Beyond Blue* was released. On the one hand, it was a missed opportunity in that it offered very little new material and instead largely collected tracks from their EPs and singles. Yet it also served as an early 'best of', and you couldn't deny the sheer songwriting talent.

'Some Half-Baked Idea Called Wonderful' and the incessant earworm of 'This Boy Can't Swim' could've been singles, while 'Infantile' and the title track showcased Cerys's vocal range. The hypnotic and sleepy 'Dream On' is one of Catatonia's finest-ever compositions, which *NME* described as 'a post-coital, opiated haze – like a '90s "Je t'aime".'[291]

Featuring artwork by their friend Elfyn Lewis, *Way Beyond Blue* is still regarded by many fans as Catatonia's best work. With its diverse styles, though, it feels more of a compilation than a cohesive album. The revolving door of musicians didn't help. Keyboardist Clancy Pegg was ousted from the line-up following the *Hooked* EP, while Daf Ieuan drummed on half the tracks before joining the Furries. His replacement, Aled Richards, was recruited from The Hepburns (a criminally unheralded Llanelli indie band formed in 1985 mixing Prefab Sprout with Burt Bacharach). Owen Powell of Crumblowers and Colour 45 was also drafted in as a second guitarist to allow Cerys more freedom to sing.

Added to that were the fragmented recording sessions while on tour in studios across Wales and England with producers Paul Sampson and Stephen Street, and mixers TommyD, John Smith and Julian Mendelsohn. There were also issues with distribution and sales were relatively low (perhaps from song duplications). The band felt *Way Beyond Blue* would've done better with an earlier release around Christmas '95.

Plus, Mark and Cerys's relationship was breaking up – a wound publicly scratched on the classic B-side 'Do You Believe in Me?' You can feel Cerys's pain in its chorus line: 'Do you believe in me, or are you leaving me?' It was their most personal lyric to date, and bassist Paul Jones joined Mark and Cerys as a co-writer, resulting in some promotional stickers erroneously stating that the song was a collaboration with Tom Jones!

The inclusion of 'Do You Believe in Me' could've made *Way*

Beyond Blue even better, as would 'Gyda Gwên' (which was featured as a hidden track) – a nice rebuttal to accusations that they had sold out by not including any Welsh-language songs.

For a music press insistent on pigeonholing everything, critics just couldn't accurately define Catatonia. Lazy comparisons were drawn with female-fronted acts like Sleeper, Echobelly, Björk and Blondie. While *NME* corralled Catatonia into the usual talk of Welsh bands (as if that were a genre in itself), they also placed them on a pedestal:

> What you hear on *Way Beyond Blue* is not some provincial cousin to the Gorky's Super Manic Dolls school, but archetypal rock themes handled with passion, imagination and a heroic disregard for fashion.[292]

Catatonia recoiled at being labelled indie too. Owen Powell said to the *Washington Post*: 'We've always just tried to make pop music. Even if it's pop music with a hard edge and quite a twisted little view of life.'[293]

Regardless of their clunky comparisons, *NME* nailed Catatonia's collision of catchy pop and irresistible guitars:

> Even Radiohead-sized anthems such as 'Painful' and 'Way Beyond Blue' boast the sleek melodic sensibilities of Bananarama in their prime…
>
> Underneath their polished pop sheen, these uniformly majestic tunes are big-hearted, lived-in, lusty, boozy, heartbroken, and ready for a fight – or a shag – at all times. That's why *Way Beyond Blue* is this year's best guitar album.[294]

John Harris saw signs of their genius from the start: 'I have long since adjusted my initial impressions of Catatonia. Cerys Matthews and Mark Roberts weren't mad; they were just brilliant. As any ex-wunderkind will tell you, people tend to get the two mixed up.'[295]

———

Edging onto the rooftop, the band exchanged nervous glances in the knowledge that the plug could be pulled on their impromptu set any moment.

With time of the essence, the group burst into song. As the sound of their guitars cascaded across the city centre, sullen businessmen cast irritated glances up, while policemen bustled about wondering where the sound was coming from.

Parodied by the likes of The Rutles, U2 and *The Simpsons*, *that* 1969 Beatles performance atop the Apple headquarters – their last live performance together before their split – is the most legendary spontaneous gig ever.

With the addition of keyboardist Billy Preston, the Fab Four were actually the Fab Five that day, and they inspired another quintet to climb up to the rooftop and create history eleven years later. There may not have been big beards, Yoko Ono and certainly not Ringo's red PVC mac, but Screen Gemz's spur-of-the-moment gig in May 1980 eventually led to one of the era-defining tunes of the '90s: 'Born Slippy' by Underworld (or 'Born Slippy: NUXX' to give it its original title).

Unlike the grey, windswept conditions for The Beatles' gig, the weather gods looked down fondly on five scraggly-haired youngsters atop Cardiff University Students' Union. Dressed in a gaudy shirt and red trousers, Bewdley-born frontman Karl Hyde was even strapped into a white guitar akin to John Lennon's trusty Epiphone Casino semi-acoustic.

Strewn around him were broken TVs and a giant yellow fridge covered in red spots that opened to disgorge party balloons. The quirky stage set reflected Hyde's bohemian lifestyle at a Riverside 'punk house', and the creativity stemming from his degree at Cardiff College of Art.

In the late '70s, Screen Gemz were briefly *the* band in the Welsh capital, proffering their own synth-based slant on New Wave power pop by mixing it with Kraftwerk and reggae.

In his 2016 book, *I Am Dogboy: The Underworld Diaries*, Hyde said: 'Like the original [Beatles] rooftop gig the police closed this one down, but not before a young student on an electronic engineering course had become temporarily smitten with the band. The young man's name was Rick Smith.'[296]

Smith, a childhood friend of Screen Gemz guitarist Stuart Kelling in Ammanford, moved to Cardiff for university after a wild weekend together there. After being recruited into the group as keyboardist, he quit uni. 'It seemed so glamorous,' Smith told *The Independent*. 'Then after a month I thought, "Shit, what have I done?"'[297]

Smith soon departed the band, but kept in touch with Hyde via

Cardiff's Queen Street haunt, The Lexington, where they worked washing dishes and cooking respectively. Impressed by Smith's burgeoning grasp of electronics, Hyde disbanded Screen Gemz.

'We started recording on borrowed drum machines, processing voices through guitar pedals, fusing Germanic electronics with Jamaican dub,' said Hyde. 'We sent tapes to Peel in cornflake boxes… and he started playing them!'[298]

Long before The Artist Formerly Known as Prince, their new band, Freur, was initially known by a symbol. With garish haircuts, glam garbs and jewellery, they even delved into Welsh-language music by learning borrowed phrases for live performances.

Freur were snapped up by CBS with whom they recorded two albums. The latter – *Get Us Out of Here* – was prophetically titled as they were dropped by the label soon after. Before splitting, there was still time for one last 'butterfly effect' moment.

The band had been working on a score to the 1985 horror film, *Underworld*, which revolved around a subhuman species addicted to a mind-expanding drug. Clive Barker's dystopia ended up being an unlikely inspiration for Hyde and Smith's new electro-dance venture, Underworld.

They released two albums of funky synth-pop to relative indifference before hitting their stride following the addition of pioneering DJ Darren Emerson. In July 1996, Underworld unleashed 'Born Slippy'. An epic tune named after a Romford racing greyhound, it went on to soundtrack a generation.

Somehow it began life as a B-side, but after the success of *Trainspotting*, 'Born Slippy' became an emblem of Cool Britannia, described by director Danny Boyle as the 'heartbeat of the film'.[299]

Despite its association with house music and repeated references to a 'mega mega white thing', 'Born Slippy' largely revolved around another drug – alcohol. 'A drunk sees the world in fragments and I wanted to recreate that,' Hyde told *The Guardian*. 'I was inspired by Lou Reed's *New York* album and Sam Shepard's *Motel Chronicles*. I was into flash photography as well, so I was walking around Soho with a notebook and camera, just observing things.'[300]

At first, Underworld refused permission for it to be used in *Trainspotting* as they disliked how their music was aligned with negative portrayals of clubbing. Nevertheless, 'Born Slippy' evoked the hedonistic '90s zeitgeist of lads and ladettes, Liam and *Loaded* – and, of course, lager. Like 'A Design for Life', its lyrics were often misunderstood.

Hyde continued:

> Rick came up with a rhythm and I started singing over it. The vocals were done in one take. When I lost my place, I'd repeat the same line – that's why it goes, 'lager, lager, lager, lager'.
>
> The first time we played it live, people raised their lager cans and I was horrified because I was still deep into alcoholism. It was never meant to be a drinking anthem, it was a cry for help.[301]

Selling over 1 million copies and storming to No. 2, Underworld somehow managed to Trojan Horse a ten-minute epic to the top of the charts in an era when the guitar was king. *Wales Arts Review* described 'Born Slippy' as 'the first dance track to enter the popular consciousness'.[302] Could Karl Hyde and Rick Smith have dreamed of that in their Cardiff days?

David Owens said:

> History is littered with chance meetings, of fate dealing its hand and synchronicity in action, but if there was no Screen Gemz, if there was no rooftop gig, if Rick Smith hadn't bothered to show up that one sunny lunchtime, destiny takes a wrong turn and an altogether different story is written…
>
> Underworld – from Cardiff to dance music canonisation. A fifteen-year overnight success story. Made in Wales.[303]

———

If 'Born Slippy' captured '90s hedonism, then an equally ubiquitous song in 1996 seized an altogether different emotion.

Initially delivered with an angelic, breathy vocal before cascading into irresistible synths, Donna Lewis's 'I Love You Always Forever' was *everywhere* in 1996. The English author H. E. Bates previously cropped up with one of his books lending its name to The Darling Buds. Likewise, his 1952 novel, *Love for Lydia*, inspired the lyrics here.

'I Love You Always Forever' transformed the little-known Cardiff singer and Royal Welsh College of Music and Drama graduate into a global star. The song had even more impact stateside, where it was released first in May 1996. 'I Love You' not only topped the pop charts, but also stayed at No. 2 on the US Billboard Hot 100 for nine weeks, making it the highest charting single by a Welsh artist since Bonnie Tyler's No. 1 hit, 'Total Eclipse of the Heart', in 1983.

Only Spanish duo Los del Río's 'Macarena' kept Donna off the top spot. Regardless, Donna's song was a VH1 mainstay and remained the most-played record on US radio for thirteen weeks, amassing over 1 million spins.

Donna said to BBC Wales:

> The craziest moment of 1996 was probably being asked to perform at a stadium show in Chicago and when arriving there, realising that I was the only non-R & B artist! I remember thinking, 'What am I doing here?'
>
> The radio guys said, 'Most of the people have come to see you,' and as soon as we played the song the stadium went nuts.[304]

The beginnings of the song were conceived as Donna daydreamed while wandering the streets of Birmingham. Once she returned to her home studio, she whipped out her keyboard and laid down the complete song onto an eight-track recorder. Once Atlantic Records chairman Doug Morris heard it, he flew Donna to New York and signed her in 1994. Several changes followed as producers floated around ideas, but Donna trusted the instinctive magic of her demo:

> It just seemed to work on American mainstream radio. I had tried to get a record in the UK and wasn't successful, but I tried America and fortunately my dream came true. It's all down to the right place, right time and a little bit of luck.
>
> The promo work was madness. Flying into a different country most days, arriving at TV studios at 4 a.m. to sing live, then off to radio interviews, then flying off again.[305]

A subsequent release on these shores in August 1996 ensured that the song was certified gold on both sides of the Atlantic. 'I Love You' reached the Top 10 in fifteen countries, including No. 5 in the UK (where it remained in the charts for fourteen weeks) and No. 1 in

Canada.

On its parent album, Lewis paid homage to her Welsh homeland with its wonderful title *Now in a Minute*, which she remembers having to explain 'all the time' stateside. Co-produced with Kevin Killen, the album also included the singles 'Without Love', 'Mother', 'Fool's Paradise' and 'Love & Affection'.

Yet, it was Killen's work with Kate Bush that came most to the fore, with his perfect pop production on 'I Love You' leading to a 1997 BRIT Award nomination for British Female Solo Artist. The following year Donna reached No. 1 on the US dance charts with 'Love Him'.

In 2023, she collaborated with Nick Gale (aka Digital Farm Animals) on a remixed new version of 'I Love You Always Forever'. Being universally remembered for a single song could frustrate some musicians, but not Donna Lewis:

> I do look back at that time with affection. It was my dream and an amazingly exciting time, and even though it was incredibly hard work I loved every minute.
>
> Even though I now live across the pond, I'm still very proud to be Welsh and my Welsh flag always flies here in New York![306]

A VERY GOOD MORNING IN WALES

WELSH DEVOLUTION IN 1997

'Good morning…And it is a very good morning in Wales.'

As quotes go, it's up there with the most iconic in Welsh history. Stood at the podium at Cardiff's Royal Welsh College of Music and Drama in the early hours of Friday, 19 September 1997, Secretary of State for Wales Ron Davies cut an exhausted figure.

The pause in the middle of the sentence wasn't just for dramatic effect. Davies was brimming with emotion and, like the very best quotes, it came about spontaneously.

Speaking on ITV Wales in 2022, he said:

> There was a lump in my throat, and I looked at the piece of paper…'Good morning…' I was either going to say something else or I was going to burst into tears, and that's the way it came out – 'And it is a very good morning in Wales…' That pause gave me chance to take a deep breath and get back on track.[307]

Not only did he realise that the 'Yes' vote had been achieved after a strenuous campaign, but that victory had been snatched from the jaws of defeat. Early results indicated that it was going to be another overwhelming 'No' like in 1979.

In 1997, Dafydd Wigley was the leader of Plaid Cymru and Westminster MP for Caernarfon:

The votes came in from some of the city areas like Newport early on, and it was going one-nil, two-nil, three-nil, four-nil against. We were wondering where things had gone wrong. It appeared that we were going to be slaughtered, and I did a television interview saying, 'Well, Scotland has voted yes...We may have lost this time, but the third time will come.' But I knew in my heart, if we'd lost on that night, it was dead for a generation and perhaps forever.[308]

Even Ron Davies considered his position at one point: 'I said to [advisor] Huw Roberts, "Have you got a speech written for me if we lose?" His face dropped.'[309]

The polls were agonisingly poised at 49 per cent for 'Yes' (510,304) to 51 per cent for 'No' (526,579) until Carmarthenshire came to the rescue by returning a positive vote of 49,115 to 26,119 at 3.50 a.m. Voter turnout was low at 51.3 per cent, but those who did turn up at the ballot box returned a final result of 50.3 per cent to 49.7 per cent (559,429 to 552,698) in favour of 'Yes'. If the Brexit referendum was close, the difference here was miniscule (less than 1 per cent of the overall turnout). However, Wales finally had devolution.

> The overall majority was just 6,721, and so overjoyed was Carmarthenshire's own Dafydd Elis-Thomas that he made it his pin number (he's since changed it!).
>
> Two years later, the former head of Plaid Cymru held the gavel as the assembly's first presiding officer.

Welsh musicians were generally delighted at the victory even if some thought that devolution offered a diluted version of parliament. Labour MP for Neath Peter Hain said:

I tried to get the Manic Street Preachers to endorse us. I spoke to Nicky Wire – and I'm a big fan of Nicky and the band – but he said, 'No, we don't think it's sufficiently radical enough.'

Afterwards he apologised to me and said, 'We should have endorsed you,' and I said, 'Yeah, you should have, particularly since it was so close!'[310]

In the run-up the election, Stereophonics joined high-profile sports stars like Neil Jenkins in nailing their colours to the 'Yes' flag by staging an event at HMV in Cardiff. Stuart Cable said: 'It's basically to give Wales a voice really – everything from education to the health service to bringing in more work – to give Wales a bit more power.'[311] Gruff Rhys also appeared as part of the BBC's coverage from City Hall in the Welsh capital. Despite such serious debate, Gruff was ironically in town to record 'Smokin'' – a light-hearted tune revelling in the Furries' love of spliffs.

On the night itself, their eyes were glued to the telly. In *Brittle with Relics*, Gruff said:

> We stayed up all night at my house for the referendum result after leaving some live TV media party with free booze when the result seemed in the balance. The euphoria at the end of the night was like winning the pools. It was very emotional. I was phoning around all my family at 6 a.m. I was elated the next day – though Daf was in a foul mood because the result was so close and Cardiff had voted 'No'.
>
> I've still got the papers from the day – the *Daily Mirror*, who briefly had a Welsh edition, had a full-page dragon on the front cover with a 'Vote YES for Wales' headline…The state did pull out all the stops. It felt like a rare window of opportunity.[312]

Catatonia had steadied their election-night nerves with an ample supply of alcohol at Giovanni's restaurant. Located next to Spillers Records, S4C had the bright idea of quizzing them on their political views, but they were completely pissed and the debate wasn't scheduled to start until 1 a.m.!

Fresh from a *Melody Maker* interview at the Grosvenor Casino, Mark Roberts and Cerys staggered across town already under the influence. The band had made no secret of their wish for devolution and Cerys in particular had regularly sported a 'Yes for Wales' T-shirt. She had one important question up her sleeve…

'Who's Siân Lloyd shagging tonight?' she asked loudly in Welsh as her bandmates tried to stifle their laughter.

Cerys had won the £10 bet to get the unlikely question televised, but understandably she was excluded from any further discussion.

Previously immortalised on the Furries' *Fuzzy Logic* track 'For Now and Ever' ('It's been a funny kind of day / Siân Lloyd says the sun will come and play'), the weathergirl and pro-Welsh-assembly campaigner was furious. A legal writ was issued for defamation of character, but was subsequently revoked when it was pointed out that Catatonia's backing of the 'Yes' campaign was essential for the youth vote.

'Afterwards, I got a nice letter from the head of S4C, which read, "Dear Cerys, you are no longer welcome on Welsh television, particularly live shows"…And I'm the biggest talent in Wales!' Cerys explained.

'There was a flurry of legal letters, and then she [Siân Lloyd] issued a statement saying she liked our last album and listened to it all the time in the car.'[313]

'They're not allowed within ten miles of each other,' laughed Mark.

Cerys bristled at the backslapping and nepotism of the event: 'There were all these media darlings air-kissing and telling each other how much they loved each other…and I just questioned their nightly habits.'[314]

Her next foray into political debate was just as infamous. While accepting a Q Award for Best Single with 'Road Rage' in November 1998, Cerys said: 'This one's for Ron Davies. What the hell was he doing?'

Cerys was referring to the incident that had led to Davies's unfortunate resignation. In September 1998, he defeated Rhodri Morgan to become Labour's candidate for first secretary of the assembly. Sadly, the 'architect of devolution' wouldn't get the chance to lead Wales's first parliament. Just over a month later, Davies was gone. If the 'Good morning' quote was iconic, then two other phrases became equally synonymous with his name.

'An error of judgement' and 'a moment of madness' was how Davies described the incident that cost him his job. The latter statement was devised by Tony Blair's press secretary, Alastair Campbell, after Davies had been mugged at knifepoint while walking on Clapham Common. Married in a heterosexual relationship and with a daughter, Davies became the focus of extensive (and quite homophobic) tabloid coverage that revealed his car was stolen in a well-known homosexual meeting place. In an interview with the BBC, Davies even had the word 'sorry' written on his hand.

Another memorable phrase coined by PR guru Alastair Campbell was 'the people's princess' following the death of Diana, Princess of Wales in late August 1997.

This was one of the first major situations Tony Blair's new government had to address, and the sombre-looking prime minister concluded his statement with the sobriquet in the immediate aftermath of the fatal car crash in Paris: 'She was the people's princess and that is how she will stay, how she will remain in our hearts and our memories forever.'

After so many years of cold and inflexible Tory rule, there was a feeling the country would become more liberal and compassionate again. Mass gatherings had been prevalent throughout the '90s (raves, Knebworth and Euro '96), and once again masses of people flocked together. Evoking a strong sense of Britishness, the prolonged mourning perhaps suggested a collectivist reaction to a previous decade when Thatcher had preached individualism, and that there was no such thing as society.

As Elton John's 'Candle in the Wind 1997' topped the charts (on its way to becoming the biggest-selling UK single of all time), a wide range of music was banned across the media. BBC Radio 1 exclusively played songs that weren't too upbeat or bleak, and crucially lacked any lyrics that could be construed as offensive.

The tragedy even halted Kylie Minogue's rebranding as an indie chick. Featuring collaborations with the Manics, the release of her sixth album was delayed by two months due to its title, *Impossible Princess*.

––––––

Devolution was another early issue for the new Labour government in 1997.

Despite it being a major part of their campaign in the run-up to the general election, historian Martin Johnes claims that Blair wasn't actually that interested: 'It was John

Smith's baby; he was deeply committed to it. After Smith died in 1994, Blair inherited the policy and had to go along with it.'[315]

Eight months after the referendum, the National Assembly for Wales held its first election where a couple of surprising results were returned.

Perhaps paying the price for its drift towards the interests of 'Middle England', Labour lost its heartland seats in Islwyn and Rhondda.

In his book *Wales Since 1939*, Johnes recalled an infamous incident where Blair's mask slipped: 'A senior Labour figure asked, "What sort of an election is it where we hold Cardiff North, but lose Rhondda?"

'On seeing the result Tony Blair reportedly retorted, "Fucking Welsh..."'[316]

Much ridicule followed and Cerys wasn't the only Welsh musician taking aim. In Stereophonics' video compilation *Call Us What You Want but Don't Call Us in the Morning*, Stuart Cable offered his own crude impression (which definitely can't be repeated here).

The biggest shame was that Davies was a charismatic and wholly competent politician at the peak of his powers, who made a huge difference in such a short space of time. After the May 1997 general election, he had delivered the referendum by September and passed the legislation for the Government of Wales Act 1998.

After John Major's Tory government had been mired in scandal, Tony Blair was desperate to avoid repeating such uproar. Accepting Davies's resignation perhaps solved the headache of sacking him.

Replying to Davies's resignation letter, Tony Blair said: 'I do so with a real sense of sadness. You have done an excellent job for the people of Wales...Many people will share the profound sympathy I feel, that your Cabinet career has come to an end in this way.'

Regardless of his 'moment of madness', Ron Davies was a breath of fresh air compared to previous secretaries of state like John Redwood, who refused to sign documents written in Welsh.

While in the job from 1993–5, he also said that Welsh speakers are likely to switch to their mother tongue the second an Englishman enters a shop. Most memorable was his excruciating attempt at singing 'Hen Wlad Fy Nhadau' at a Conservative conference where he awkwardly swayed his head and mouthed the words like a goldfish – a mortifying clip that he'll never live down.

If a song titled 'Welsh Bands Suck' had come out in 1990, it would've been accepted at face value.

Writers would've lapped up its lyrics and lauded it as Single of the Week, and yet just seven years later nobody was missing the irony.

A bold opening track to the 1997 compilation *Dial M for Merthyr*, the song was written by Swansea's John William Davies (aka Teen Anthems) and wryly stuck a middle finger up at the detractors. It simultaneously celebrated DIY indie and joked about Wales being the hip new thing: 'Oh no, it can't be true / Everybody's saying Welsh bands are cool / Oh no, that can't be right / Apart from Helen Love, they're a load of shite.'

Aptly, Helen Love appeared next with 'Beat Him Up' – a two-and-a-half-minute rush of brilliant bubblegum pop masking a darker subject matter of domestic violence and revenge. With the compilation being the brainchild of Pooh Sticks frontman Huw Williams, it's no surprise that it started with an indie double-header

A joint venture between his Townhill Records and *NME* writer Simon Williams's Fierce Panda label, the album's title was a piss-take of Alfred Hitchcock's classic crime thriller, *Dial M for Murder*. The artwork depicted Merthyr Tydfil's legendary bantamweight boxer, Johnny Owen (aka 'The Matchstick Man'), who tragically died in November 1980 aged twenty-four following a fight with Lupe Pintor.

Inspired by the previous year's Splash tour where Community Music Wales organised gigs across the south Wales valleys showcasing new Welsh talent, the album was launched at TJ's. All three bands who played that night were present here too: Newport's own Novocaine contributed 'Cellophane Wrapped New Head'; Armstrong offered the ridiculously catchy 'You Deserve to Succeed'; and Swansea punks Parc Troli provided the abrasive 'Desensitised'.

Also representing Newport were Dub War, Flyscreen and The Jonah Hex, the last of whom offered the instant earworm of 'Birds and Trees and Flowers'. Plus, there was 60 Ft. Dolls, whose squall of guitars and raucous vocals on 'Ballerina' could've made *The Big 3* even better.

The compilation also gave welcome prominence to songs like Catatonia's 'To and Fro', which had somehow been tucked away on their 'Lost Cat' single. The origins of Welsh music were recalled throughout with a haunting church organ.

Other early treasures included Stereophonics on their limited edition first single 'Looks Like Chaplin', and the Manics with a B-side from their second ever release, the *New Art Riot* EP. Fellow Blackwood band Ether also featured with 'When She Woke', taken from their infectious (but sadly, only) album, *Strange*.

Elsewhere, there was a feast of hidden treasures. Melys's cult classic, 'Puppet' (from their 1996 debut EP, *Fragile*), juxtaposed sinister synths and angelic vocals, while ex-Catatonia keyboardist Clancy Pegg played on the dark and moody 'Rollercoaster' with her new group, Crac.

Originally known as Beganifs, until a Dutch promoter misheard their name, Big Leaves delivered a superb debut in *Pwy Sy'n Galw?* ('Who's Calling?') before venturing into the English-language market for their underrated second album, *Alien & Familiar* in 2003. Likewise, it's an English tune, 'Mill Lane,' that featured on *Dial M…*

Described by *NME* as a 'post-hardcore Monkees',[317] Derrero were a vibrant kaleidoscope of inventiveness and idiosyncrasies (one of their songs, 'Stoned Rider', included a band review shouted by the drummer). They supported Catatonia, the Furries and Gorky's, while James Dean Bradfield selected *Radar Intruder* as his favourite EP of 1998. The first signings on Greg Haver and Ceri Collier's Big Noise label, Derrero's early magic culminated in a typically quirky, self-titled debut album, from which 'Dipstick' was selected here.

Dial M for Merthyr wasn't quite *the* ultimate time capsule of Welsh '90s music: the Furries and Gorky's dropped out at the last minute, while The Crocketts and Topper were missing and no Welsh-language music was included. That didn't go unnoticed by *NME*'s Mark Sutherland: 'The "Welshness" of these bands is derived purely from an accident of birth rather than any particular sonic and cultural similarity, [so] this turns out to be a hit-and-miss collection of the great and the gruesome.'[318]

Regardless, the compilation should be fondly remembered for capturing that magic moment when the Welsh scene edged into the mainstream, as Sutherland himself admits (even if he couldn't resist signing off with a cliché):

> A few years ago, a compilation of twenty-one 'hot' Welsh acts would have had most people running for anywhere but the valleys.
>
> Nowadays, the Manics win BRITs rather than brick-bats, Wales has its own hip *Trainspotting*-style movie *Twin Town*, and MPs gleefully acclaim Newport as the 'new Seattle'...For those about to Llanfairpwllgwyngyllgogerychwyrndrobwllllantysiliogogogoch, we salute you. Sort of.[319]

Dylan Moore of *Wales Arts Review* concluded: 'With every year that goes by, *Dial M for Merthyr* becomes an ever more important historical artefact. Devolution on a disc? Not quite. "Welsh Bands Suck"? Hardly. See, we could even do irony now.'[320]

The following month saw several of the compilation's featured artists performing at two notable festivals.

On 10 May 1997, the Manics and Stereophonics performed at Anfield as part of the Hillsborough Justice Concert with headliners Lightning Seeds, plus The Beautiful South, Space, Dodgy, Smaller and The Bootleg Beatles.

All participants gave their time for free in aid of the Hillsborough Family Support Group. The event raised awareness for the fight for justice for the ninety-seven victims who died in the crush at Liverpool's match against Nottingham Forest in April 1989.

Nicky Wire had been particularly affected by the disaster, and went on to write about it twice with the Manics on 'South Yorkshire Mass Murderer' in 1998 and 'Liverpool Revisited' in 2018.

'A Design for Life' was inspired by an episode of Scouse screenwriter Jimmy McGovern's *Cracker*, starring Robert Carlyle, in the aftermath of Hillsborough. Coincidentally, the song was released seven years to the day after the disaster.

It was a special day for drummers and fellow Liverpool fans Sean Moore and Stuart Cable. The latter played with Stereophonics as they showcased several tunes off their forthcoming debut, *Word Gets Around*.

Kelly Jones found the event particularly memorable for one hair-raising moment, as Pier Reid at V2 Records explained: 'It was pouring down with rain and he touched the microphone, and literally flew back and got electrocuted! I thought, "We're going to kill the artist!" You could see on the big screens, he'd obviously had a shock.'[321]

The following day, The Big Noise festival took place in Cardiff Bay. Hosted by Dannii Minogue, it celebrated the centenary of the world's first radio broadcast, sent by Guglielmo Marconi from Lavernock Point to Flat Holm Island in the Bristol Channel.

For Catatonia's slot, Cerys Matthews channelled her inner Peter Schmeichel, wearing a Manchester United goalie away shirt (before gatecrashing Space's set).

Not to be outdone, Kelly Jones wore the furry coat he nicked from the props cupboard at Aberdare's Coliseum Theatre throughout a wonderfully bass-heavy mix from Stereophonics, while 60 Ft. Dolls delivered a typically raucous performance.

Also on the bill were Gene (led by Cardiff-born frontman Martin Rossiter) and headliner Paul Weller, but it was a strange day for the 10,000 in attendance with all the acts marooned on a specially assembled floating stage at Scott Harbour.

Catatonia's Owen Powell said: 'That was a weird gig. The crowd were twenty-five yards away from you before you'd even started and in between songs you couldn't hear people clapping. All you could hear was just the hum of your amp behind you.'[322]

———

'People in Wales sit in pubs all day saying, "Let's go off and have a revolution." Tystion is about actually getting up and doing something,'[323] said Steffan Cravos in his band's mission statement.

A thrilling mix of samples and social commentary, Tystion ('Witnesses') brought hip-hop to Wales in the mid-'90s. Contrary to Cravos's grumble about fellow musicians endlessly waffling in pubs, he ironically formed Tystion in an Aberystwyth bar in 1996 after bumping into Gruff Meredith. A devotee of hip-hop and punk, Cravos (MC Sleifar) first met Meredith (MC Gruff) at an Eisteddfod in the early '90s, and quickly found this fellow DIY musician, with a peculiar love for kazoos and harmonicas, to be magnetic company.

Cravos had recently relocated to Cardiff (some distance from Meredith's north Wales home), but the pair bounced around ideas by mailing each other tapes. For a while, Cravos lent his sampling skills to Meredith's band of psychedelic indie rockers, Datsyn, before the latter moved to the Welsh capital. Hailed as the first Welsh-language hip-hop group in the pages of *Golwg* and *Y Cymro*, Tystion was born.

As Sarah Hill highlights in '*Blerwytirhwng?*', although Welsh rap was something of a novelty when Tystion formed, rap and hip-hop in general were starting to become mainstream. Nonetheless, while some Welsh groups 'had dabbled in rap as a type of fictitious identity (Diffiniad, Hanner Pei)...there had not been a group solely devoted to creating, as Tystion put it, "hip-hop poetry in motion in the mother tongue"'.[324]

Like Llwybr Llaethog and Datblygu, Tystion set about creating a new version of Welshness, but this time within an urban soundscape that mixed Afrocentric hip-hop with Anglo-American rap. The Welsh-language hip-hop revolution wasn't instantaneous though. An early demo tape was met with indifference, so Cravos decided to bypass the music industry altogether by setting up his own label, Fitamin Un. *Dyma'r Dystiolaeth* ('This Is the Evidence') in 1995 and *Tystion vs Alffa* the following year were rough, lo-fi cassette-only releases that further nailed their anti-mainstream colours to the flag.

When their self-released debut album did arrive, it certainly didn't disappoint. BBC Wales said that *Rhaid i Rhywbeth Ddigwydd* 'took a spray can to the grey-slate drudgery of small-town Welsh life with Cravos and Meredith rapping about pulling handbrakes in Tesco car park and smoking themselves senseless in a hedge.'[325]

Recorded with future Murry the Hump member Curig Huws across fifteen tracks, *Rhaid i Rhywbeth Ddigwydd* ('Something's Got to Happen') combined carefree youthful abandon in a hip-hop group ('Ffristyle' – ['Freestyle'] and 'MG yn y Ty' – ['MG in the House']) with a frustration at their surroundings ('Dal Yma a Dal i Frwydro' – ['Still Here and Still Fighting'], and 'Ailsgrifennu'r Cynllun' – ['Rewriting the Plan']). 'Euro '96' was a light-hearted piss-take that was never going to feature on any official soundtrack, especially with Wales so far from a major football tournament at the time.

Tystion's radical spirit caught the attention of Ankst, who released the *Brewer Spinks* EP in 1998. National acclaim followed with a *Melody Maker* Single of the Week and airplay from John Peel.

Regardless of the plaudits and additional exposure via slots on BBC Radio Cymru's *Ram Jam* and *Gang Bangor*, Tystion continued to revel in their outsiderdom. In a 1997 performance of 'Gwyddbwyll' ('Chess') for S4C, the band mimicked the Manics' early, punk-inspired aesthetic by wearing clothing emblazoned with slogans like 'Media Whore' and 'Career Move', albeit with a knowing wink.

Another parallel with the Manics was Tystion's aptitude for highlighting a moment in history to negotiate a sense of contemporary Welshness. Like 'Ready for Drowning' on *This Is My Truth Tell Me Yours*, Tystion referenced Capel Celyn on the track 'Tryweryn' from their second album, *Shrug Off Ya Complex*, in 1999 ('I remember a small town in '62 / Remember Tryweryn, resistance from the people').

The song also mentioned another radical moment in Welsh political history when three leading members of Plaid Cymru – Saunders Lewis, Reverend Lewis Valentine and D. J. Williams – set fire to an RAF bombing school in the Llŷn Peninsula. Despite public protest that the school harmed local farming, it was constructed nevertheless. The subsequent trial was held at the Old Bailey (and not in Wales) and all three were handed nine-month prison sentences.

Sprawled across sixteen tracks, *Shrug Off Ya Complex* was as equally ambitious as their debut. But it was a patchy affair that perhaps suffered from too many cooks spoiling the broth.

It mixed references to Wales's past with irony about their Welsh identity ('Taffi Triog' – ['Toffee Taffy'] and 'Meddwi Dros Gymru' – ['Drunk Over Wales']), while hinting at brighter days ahead with devolution ('Crefydd Newydd' – ['A New Religion'] and 'Cân Rhyddid' – ['Freedom Song']).

The titular 'complex' revolved around centuries of English rule and the forced assimilation into that culture combined with the gradual decline of the Welsh language. Devolution may have been achieved in 1997, but that didn't mean that every Welsh person was suddenly self-confident. Only 50.22 per cent of registered voters turned out in the referendum, and the result hinged on the narrowest of margins.

As Sarah Hill said: 'Tystion are inciting the Welsh people to seize the opportunity to create a modern Wales in the new century, and to meet the challenges of her political future with confidence.'[326]

With an overt bilingualism on *Shrug Off Ya Complex*, there were suggestions that Tystion would be the next Welsh-language act to switch to English. If they did so, critics feared that the marketability of Wales's own indigenous brand of hip-hop would become diluted.

Tystion later delved into this dilemma on their 2000 track 'Y Byd Hip Hop vs Y Byd Cymraeg' ('The Hip Hop World vs The Welsh World') and concluded that there is a place for Welsh hip-hop regardless of the language it's delivered in:

Dwi'n byw ar y Blaned Hip-Hop, ond paid galw fi'n boyo...Er mwyn cynnal unrhyw iaith, rhaid cyfoethogi ac ychwanegu at eu diwylliant. Dim jyst côrau, oedfa'r bore a Cerdd Dant.

I'm living on Planet Hip-Hop, but don't call me boyo...In order to support any language, you must enrich and add to their culture. Not just choirs, morning meetings and *Cerdd Dant*.[327]

Cerdd Dant (meaning 'String Music') is a form of vocal improvisation often performed in competitions at Eisteddfodau where a singer or small choir sings a counter-melody over a traditional Welsh-language melody usually played on a harp.

Either way, the ingenious collaboration between Cravos and Meredith remained Tystion's trump card. BBC Wales said:

> [*Shrug Off Ya Complex*] was most notable for the juxtaposition of Cravos's and Meredith's rapidly diverging rapping styles…As Cravos's purist rhymes took on a politically charged dimension inspired by an interest in Welsh independence and his past in Cymdeithas yr Iaith Gymraeg, Meredith continued to indulge his whimsical, often surrealist muse.[328]

Yet, the partnership was severed at its peak when Meredith left the band in 1999 and pursued a solo career under the name MC Mabon. Undeterred and with Cravos at the reins, Tystion returned in the new millennium with *Hen Gelwydd Prydain Newydd* ('New Britain's Old Lie').

Their most explosively political work, the sleeve featured the band hoisting placards with slogans inspired by the track titles within ('*Un Bobl, Dwy Iaith, Un Genedl*' ['One People, Two Languages, One Nation']; 'Wales Is Over – If You Want It'; and '*Ddoe o ni'n Brotestwr, Heddiw Dwi'n Derfysgwr*' ['Yesterday I Was a Protester, Today I'm a Terrorist']).

Tystion continued to recruit exciting fresh blood from across the Welsh music scene including Gareth Williams (MC Chef) and ex-Catatonia keyboardist Clancy Pegg. Despite breaking away from Ankst and reverting to their own label, tracks from their prospective fourth album, *Y Meistri* ('The Masters'), appeared very promising.

Playlisted by Public Enemy's Chuck D on his Bring the Noise internet radio station and several underground channels across Europe, it introduced Tystion's 'hip-hop poetry in motion in the mother tongue'[329] to an international audience.

Sadly, *Y Meistri* was never released and Cravos called time on the band from the Maes B stage at the Eisteddfod in August 2000.

———

'We aren't post-grunge…'

That was a response Grant Nicholas expressed ad nauseam throughout the late '90s to journalists keen to pigeonhole his band.

On their 1997 debut, *Polythene*, Feeder matched huge overdriven riffs with sugary melodies that saw them likened to Smashing Pumpkins, while their quiet/LOUD dynamics often drew comparisons with Nirvana. Nicholas was always keen to point out there was more nuance to their oeuvre.

'It does upset me when I hear that,' he told *NME*. 'It's frustrating that we've been seen as this heavy guitar band all the time. People have to put some form of a label on us, and it just happens to be "post-grunge".'[330]

A US tour with Everclear further lumped them in with the post-Cobain crowd. Even today, Nicholas insists that Feeder's sound is best described as 'mid-Atlantic', combining the best of both British and American influences.

After years of ignoring Welsh bands, the fact that they were suddenly the in thing was perhaps getting up the nose of the London press, especially if said bands were proud of their Welshness. The intro to Stuart Bailie's above *NME* piece read: 'They quaff Jägermeister by the neck, hail the booty-shaking power of Van Halen and are that rarest of items – a predominantly Welsh band that don't want to talk about it much.'[331]

Born in Newport in November 1967, Grant Nicholas played trumpet in the school orchestra before writing his first song aged twelve. His earliest influences included ABBA, the Sex Pistols and The Beatles before branching into heavier stuff like Led Zeppelin and Judas Priest as a teenager. At school, his first group was named Sweet Leaf after a song by Black Sabbath.

'I'm a big fan of bands that may not seem cool, like Boston and ELO,' said Nicholas. 'I love all of that stuff…U2, the Carpenters and American acts like Tom Petty.'[332]

Gifted his first guitar by his parents for passing his school exams, Nicholas then worked as a courier in London while honing his craft as a songwriter with local group Silent Partner. He was then recruited by prog-rockers Multi-Story, with whom he released an album before they disbanded

There were bands closer to home too. Cardiff-based Temper Temper were a sprawling nine-piece hair-metal outfit featuring Tim Lewis and Greg Haver. Nicholas credits Lewis's early support of his singing as a key inspiration behind him becoming a frontman, and described Temper Temper's sound as ''80s avant-garde muso rock – like Frank Zappa meets Van Halen meets indie-goth.'[333]

When Haver left to play with Canadian artist Corey Hart, he was replaced on drums by close friend Jon Lee. The duo was also in Newport/Chepstow acoustic-rock outfit Raindancer.

Repackaged initially as Hum before becoming Reel in 1992, Nicholas and Lee went through several bassists before Taka Hirose answered an ad in *Loot* magazine. Bringing his fandom of funk and soul to the table, Hirose helped fuse his love of Van Halen with Nicholas and Lee's passion for The Police. Back in London and signed to Echo in mid-1995, there was one last name change as the trio became Feeder after Nicholas's goldfish.

Their limited release debut EP, *Two Colours*, won them support slots with Terrorvision and Reef before their first album in May 1997. With a working title of *Here in the Bubble*, *Polythene* arrived amid widespread critical acclaim. Alongside 4/5 scores in *Q* and *Kerrang*, *Metal Hammer* gave a glowing 10/10 rating before awarding it Album of the Year ahead of Metallica, Foo Fighters and Faith No More. Despite this, *Polythene* didn't bother The Chemical Brothers and The Charlatans in the upper reaches of the UK charts, and stalled at No. 65. None of the album's initial four singles reached the Top 40 either.

In a twenty-fifth anniversary revisit, *Metal Hammer* said:

It remains baffling that *Polythene* didn't go on to sell millions. Everything about it screams blockbuster, pop-rock perfection and marks Grant Nicholas out as one of his generation's finest songwriters…

Awe-inspiring in its beauty, yet modest in its delivery, *Polythene* is a genuine lost classic from an underrated band. They may have got bigger, but Feeder never got better than how they sound here.[334]

One thing that did make Feeder's popularity eventually skyrocket was the ingenious use of their music in the classic PlayStation racing game *Gran Turismo*. Five songs including the single 'Tangerine' (and cuts from the *Two Colours* and *Swim* EPs) were featured. When their later song 'Just a Day' was included in *Grand Turismo 3* in 2001, it transformed the former B-side into a Top 20 single and provided Feeder with their trademark set-closer.

Polythene's slow-burn success added Feeder to the main stage of the 1997 Reading Festival, and Nicholas had an inadvertent master stroke up his sleeve. Picking out a fuzzy arpeggio, he began playing a song left over from the album sessions. In its electric form, 'High' was already enough of a singalong to have the front rows bouncing.

In early October 1997, it was slowed down to an acoustic strum for a stand-alone single release. Added to a reissued and rejigged version of the album a few weeks later, it provided *Polythene*'s breakthrough. *Metal Hammer* said:

> Some songs are just too universal to fail. So evocative of British summer was it that you can almost smell the freshly cut grass, crisp, ice-cold cans of cider and the perfume of that girl you had a secret crush on. It was a clear and obvious, platinum-plated anthem from the very first listen.[335]

Featured in American teen romcom *Can't Hardly Wait* and reaching No. 24, its hazy chorus brought to mind John Lennon on 'I'm Only Sleeping'. Nicholas told *Kerrang* in 2008:

> When I first wrote it, I drunkenly played it to my girlfriend on an acoustic. She started crying because she liked it so much. I thought that was probably a good sign!
>
> It's a really simple song. There are only three chords in it, but the lyrics 'I'm going out for a while so I can get high with my friends' seemed to connect with people. [336]

Tragically, Jon Lee died by suicide at his Miami home in January 2002 aged thirty-three.

The last song Feeder recorded with him was a poignant cover of 'Can't Stand Losing You' by The Police, a B-side to their single 'Just a Day' (which reached No. 12 in December 2001). Lee's death came at a time when Feeder were finally enjoying the success that their incredible work rate deserved.

Even more heartbreaking was that 'High' was played at his funeral. One thousand mourners attended an open service at St Mary's Church in Newport including family, friends and fans.

In October 2002, Feeder returned with a touching collection of songs called *Comfort in Sound*, dedicated to Jon Lee.

Likewise, Stereophonics lost their hugely charismatic drummer, Stuart Cable, at the age of forty in June 2010.

Thousands lined the streets in Aberdare to pay their respects as Cable's horse-drawn carriage to St Elvan's Church was accompanied by 'Back in Black' by his beloved AC/DC.

In 2017, Stereophonics paid tribute to their late friend on the piano ballad 'Before Anyone Knew Our Name'.

––––

Since 1992, Ankst had been the perfect home for Gorky's in nurturing their quirkiness. Across three albums, the band progressed from ragged, off-kilter lo-fi on *Patio* to vibrant improvisational homages of the '60s Canterbury scene on *Tatay* to enchanting medievalism on *Bwyd Time*.

By 1996, Gorky's harboured ambitions to be heard outside of Wales, and, like Catatonia and the Furries, this meant changing from a majority of Welsh-language songs to a minority.

In June that year, the band released the brilliant *Amber Gambler* EP. Not only was it their last output on Ankst, but also their last release where the Welsh language was predominant.

'Sdim yr Adar yn Canu' ('The Birds Don't Sing') was arguably its best track, but *Melody Maker* implied that including a song in their mother tongue was stubbornness to conform:

You start to suspect that when they start singing in Welsh, it's really just down to the same bloody-mindedness they apply to their songs. If they'd only relax into their own rather lovely sense of sound and melody, and drop the pointless Faust-iness, they could be genuinely special.[337]

Following *Amber Gambler*, Gorky's signed to Fontana Records, which included distribution with Mercury in the US.

John Lawrence said:

Cool Cymru was more a case of good timing really. We had always been true to ourselves, and coming from a bilingual background, we had always written songs in both Welsh and English. We were always trying to conform with Radio Cymru and with any Eisteddfod gigs in that we would make a creative compromise to sing in Welsh.

In particular, we leaned towards Welsh songs during our time with Ankst. For the major labels, we went more with the English-language songs. We cynically moulded our language policy to the market.[338]

In his *Sunday Times* column, Stewart Lee suggested that this most peculiar of bands could've signed to Sony:

On the train back to London, Megan talks about playing the pedal-steel-guitar-led 'Heart of Kentucky' to bewildered Epic Records [a subsidiary of Sony] executives suddenly afraid that Gorky's might transmute into an unmarketable Welsh country and western band. But that is Gorky's prerogative, so they signed with Fontana.[339]

Conveniently, Gorky's next release was their biggest hit and proved they could still reach a mainstream audience bilingually. Although the band were less experimental now, they poured their energies into crafting vibrant pop tunes – and they don't come much better than 'Patio Song'.

Awarded BBC Radio 1 Single of the Week, it reached No. 8 in John Peel's Festive Fifty and the band were soon singing about a patio on fire on *Jools Holland*.

Not only does 'Patio Song' change language, mood and melody, but there's also a turn in the weather! In Wales, it pours down all year with only a few good weeks of summer weather (if we're lucky). Hence, it's very apt that 'Isn't it a lovely day' transforms into '*Mae'n bwrw glaw*' ('It's raining').

Despite unglamorous images of concrete in its title, 'Patio Song' is somehow one of the sweetest love songs ever written. Elis James said: 'It's absolutely lovely, and every time someone tells me they walked down the aisle to it (which happens more often than you'd imagine), I think, "Yes, of course!"'[340]

It also came agonisingly close to giving Gorky's their first Top 40 hit, but stalled at No. 41. Therefore, from 'Patio Song' to 'Stood on Gold' in 2001, Gorky's held the record for having the most Top 75 singles in the charts without ever hitting the Top 40.

Likewise, 'Patio Song's parent album, *Barafundle*, reached No. 46 in the UK, and was their first album stateside, although the band claimed they only secured thirty-four first-week sales there. As *Record Collector* said: 'They didn't exactly go overground, but people outside of the valleys pricked up their ears.'[341]

Regardless, *Barafundle* was Gorky's most accessible album to date. Named after the beach adjacent to Euros Childs's home, it was their first record without any 'cheapo guitars'. Inspired by Euros's father's medieval band, it featured sixteen songs of simple folk-pop played on obscure instruments like the bodhran, hurdy-gurdy and jaw harp.

There were instances of John Lawrence's trademark experimentation too. His masterpiece here was 'Starmoonsun', which alternated between contemporary Welsh pop music and traditional Welsh folk including a middle eight played on the shawm, a medieval ancestor of the oboe with a loud, trumpet-like resonance.

Elsewhere, there were deviations from the folk-pop template like on the off-kilter heavy-metal riffing of 'Meirion Wyllt', but even then their juvenile humour shone through. The title means 'Mad Meirion' as Euros Childs explained to *NME*: 'We had this mad chemistry teacher called Meirion, who said we were all wasters and wouldn't amount to anything.'[342]

Their typical playfulness remained including a sub-two-minute semi-instrumental called 'Bola Bola' ('Belly Belly'), while 'The Barafundle Bumbler' revolved around a peeping tom at the beach. As ever in Gorky's canon, though, darkness is never far away – as *God Is in the TV* explained:

The inquisitive and morbid nature of children's minds and imaginations provides the album's dark corners…'Diamond Dew' best encapsulates this, contrasting its memories of an idyllic home life ('room is warm, organ plays') with a disconcerting line about the 'uncovering of the bodies'.

This is possibly a reference to medieval burial sites being found along the Pembrokeshire coast – catnip to imaginative young minds. 'Dark Night' marries another wonderfully hummable melody to lyrics concerning the death of two young girls on Halloween. It's a story that you can imagine children embellishing for years on local schoolyards.[343]

Conversely, their between-song chatter was nowhere near as prevalent on *Barafundle*, but there was a funny moment at the end of 'Heywood Lane' – an audible cry of pain as a piano lid slams shut on fingers. A reworking of one of their earliest songs, it sounds like 'Hey Jude'.

While Paul McCartney packed 'Penny Lane' with memories of his childhood, 'Heywood Lane' referenced the school bus journey past the Tenby street where John Lawrence's great-aunt lived. It's a simple melody that even kids can hum, as Euros Childs said to *Melody Maker*:

> We were going to have a children's section on the album. There is such a thing as a song a kid can latch onto. Some of our friends have children, who sing along to our songs…If you can do that, that's really special – like 'Yellow Submarine'.[344]

A lovingly crafted time capsule, *Barafundle* harked back to more innocent times of campfires, warm weather and visiting family in Pembrokeshire. Its pinboard artwork – featuring an assortment of postcards and dusty bric-a-brac – evokes half-forgotten, fond memories of holidays. In an age of instantaneous, albeit fleeting, social media, that era seems more distant than ever, but no less romantic.

Ranked at No. 11 in their list of the '100 Greatest Welsh Albums of All Time', *Wales Arts Review* wrote:

> *Barafundle* sees Gorky's embracing of Welsh folk and psychedelic rock and delivering it to us with the sweetly melodic weirdness we love them for.

There are shades of the medieval especially in 'Cursed, Coined and Crucified', 'Pen Gwag Glas' and 'Starmoonsun' edging the record into prog territory, but we don't mind that one bit, do we? Pass the harpsichord please![345]

─────

If Creation indulged the Furries' strangeness by buying them a tank for *Fuzzy Logic*, then they wanted something bigger and better for its follow-up, *Radiator* – namely giant bears.

Thankfully, they were of the inflatable variety, and two would be made depicting Good and Evil. Ric Rawlins described the moment the cuddly and cunning bears of the album's artwork became blown-up beasts:

Pete Fowler was driving through the car park of a Bethesda music festival where SFA were due to headline. It was a sunny afternoon, and he smiled as he drove. Then he hit the brakes.

The car skidded. He blinked a few times and got out of the vehicle, walking carefully sideways with his head tilted towards the sky. Up there, from behind some tall trees, a fifty-foot monster was slowly moving into view: a huge red bear with demonic eyes strapped behind a Zorro mask, its polyester belly gently but powerfully breathing in the sun.

The monster's creator took a few moments to take this in – then paused for a quiet laugh. His painting had travelled further than just the album cover; it had morphed into reality.[346]

Fowler's illustration for the Furries' second album in August 1997 featured a bear strolling down the street amid a futuristic cityscape. As he glances at his reflection in a shop window, his devil-horned alter ego glares back at him. Now synonymous with the Furries' artwork, the *Radiator* campaign started Pete Fowler's collaboration with the band. He had been contributing to *GQ* and creating flyers for psychedelic all-nighters when Cardiff-based writer (and future BBC Radio Wales presenter) Bethan Elfyn noticed his work and asked for an interview. The Furries were fans straight away too.

'I love the landscape of *Mario*,' Fowler said. 'The little hills, and the way that you might see a mountain with eyes in the far distance. I love the idea of everything being alive and a bit weird.'[347]

With Creation literally having money to burn thanks to Oasis, they could bring Fowler's fantasy to life like Frankenstein's monster – as Ben Thompson pointed out in *Mojo*: 'Looking at the frenzied public reaction – the queues of people lining up to fondle, photograph, and urinate on them – Super Furry Animals have clearly got value for money.'[348]

At a gig with The Fall at Cooper's Field in Cardiff, Evil actually overcame Good. Ric Rawlins continued:

> The Good bear started hissing air from its knee. Within an hour, the fifty-foot beast had limped over sideways like a malfunctioning King Kong. By the time SFA's largely teenage audience began to flock out of the tent, it had collapsed entirely, prompting a mass cheering.[349]

According to *Guardian* writer Tom Cox, the Good and Evil bears are a metaphor for the Furries' contrasting sides:

> At their best, they sound like two bands performing at the same time. One writing radiant, immensely pretty pop songs. The other, attempting to sabotage them with a selection of looped bleeping, burping and blooping noises, mind-bending melodies colliding with mutant electronica and demented lyricism.[350]

Gruff agreed: 'Sometimes it's nice to write pompous, cliché-ridden pop songs and then puncture that pomposity with an evil coda or wall of techno.'[351]

Reaching No. 8, *Radiator* was more adventurous musically than *Fuzzy Logic* as the band dabbled with Gorwel Owen's Atari computers and banks of vintage synths.

Inspired by Datblygu, Happy Mondays and The Beach Boys, its lead single, 'Hermann Loves Pauline', was named after Albert Einstein's parents. Marie Curie and Ernesto 'Che' Guevara also crop up in the lyrics, which stemmed from biographies Gruff saw in motorway service stations. *Melody Maker* wrote: '"Hermann Loves Pauline" shows that while the band may be a bit unusual as people, they're currently making some of the most intelligent pop music anywhere in the world.'[352]

Second single 'The International Language of Screaming' was even more memorable. It harked back to their more anarchic days when the internationalist Furries steamrollered a tank into the National Eisteddfod. Although now singing predominantly in English, the band hadn't forgotten their roots – *'Teg Edrych Tuag Adref'* proclaimed the sleeve (meaning 'Home Sweet Home'). Starting with a simple strum, the song evolved into a cacophony of electronic bleeps, buzzsaws and wailing, which zoomed by in two minutes. Whether they were singing in English or Welsh, screaming proved to be an international language.

Like their B-side 'Blerwytirhwng?' ('Whereareyoubetween?'), the song examined the 'in-between' nature of Wales ('It's not where you're from…It's not where you've been, it's where you're between'). Sarah Hill said:

> The type of compromise implied here is that no language is being privileged. Screaming – whether for ease of communication or out of sheer frustration – is not a coded linguistic signifier of either Welsh or English, or of either culture…
>
> Politically, Wales has taken tentative steps from centralised British power to devolution. Culturally, Wales is home to two unrelated languages, Welsh and English…Wales is a concertina of cultures and languages wondering what kinds of sounds it can, or should make in the world.[353]

Third single 'Play It Cool' was accompanied by a promo video featuring digitised versions of the band beating Brazil in the PlayStation game *Actua Soccer 2*. The Furries were fans of the game and by inputting a code, you could play as them. Believing their teammates would consist of their heroes, the band were in for a shock when their emailed list of requested teammates went AWOL. Resplendent in his trusty orange cagoule and jeans, Gruff suddenly found himself up front with mass murderer Genghis Khan. Another teammate, Al Capone, had 'shooting' stats of 82/100.

'[The developers] thought we just wanted anyone with a strange name,' Gruff told *Select*. 'They picked Stalin and Churchill, and I hate both passionately. We asked for Bob Marley, Fidel Castro, Bill Hicks, Muhammad Ali. We want to distance ourselves from the line-up they picked…I like *FIFA '98* better anyway.'[354]

Radiator's fourth and final single, 'Demons', is one of their greatest-ever songs. Described by *Wales Arts Review* as a 'swooping, mariachi-flavoured ballad and a mordant cousin of "If You Don't Want Me to Destroy You"',[355] its lyric revolved around a relationship breakdown and not letting inner demons consume you.

Simon Price can pinpoint the exact moment when he realised he was witnessing a very special band – Saturday, 23 August 1997 at the Reading Festival. The Furries were halfway between openers Stereophonics and headliners the Manics on the Main Stage. This, along with Gorky's on the Melody Maker Stage and Catatonia the previous day, amounted to something of a Welsh takeover.

Price said:

> I was half watching, my expectations moderate-to-low when Gruff Rhys stepped up to the mic and began singing 'Demons'…
>
> That voice, oh that voice; so rich with warmth, humanity, vulnerability, empathy. It held me transfixed. Super Furry Animals quickly became my new favourite band.[356]

All four singles deserved to be hits, but each proved to be a little bit too odd to breach the Top 20. That suited the band just fine though. Their set of unwritten rules included despising celebrity, always recording quality B-sides and never allowing multiple format releases.

Other *Radiator* highlights included 'Torra Fy Ngwallt yn Hir' ('Cut My Hair Long' – the sole Welsh-language track) and 'She's Got Spies' (a Thatcher-baiting slice of Cold War paranoia). Elsewhere, there was a meandering, metaphorical journey on 'Down a Different River', which suggested the shedding of old ideas and the embracing of new ones at a time of devolution.

A more obvious rumination of Welsh identity came via 'Mountain People', which reviewer Everett True hilariously thought was about abominable snowmen.

Perfectly placed as the album's epic finale, it gradually gathered momentum over six minutes and morphed into an elongated techno juggernaut live like 'The Man Don't Give a Fuck'. The lyric delved into Wales's oppressed history and examined how it's viewed from the outside, especially in rural areas.

The song suggests a Wales–England divide wherein isolated

communities are ignored by the establishment. It also juxtaposes the 'mountain people' who live beyond mainstream society and those who reside in the more refined leafy suburbs of 'tree-lined streets' (an image met with a defiant 'not for us'). The lyric also hints at affluent outsiders (who 'own the milk and runny honey') sneering and exploiting the mountain people when required, and gatecrashing their communities buying second homes.

When the Furries took *Melody Maker* on a tour through the mountains of north Wales in May 1997, Daf revealed:

> Gruff and Cian grew up in places like this. No matter how many times you go to the city, you realise that you'll always be a country bumpkin.
>
> Yet, there's also a unwavering self-sufficiency and resilient pride in the mountain people that they're happy living on the edges of society and won't be assimilated into 'hand-me-down' culture.[357]

Reflecting with *The Guardian* in 2011 on one of his finest poetic lyrics, Gruff said:

> For some reason, plays are quite conducive to songwriting…I picked up Harold Pinter's *Mountain Language*, quite randomly, when we were recording *Radiator*.
>
> It's about a group of people living in isolation, persecuted, on a kind of hillside. I grew up in a mountain village, so it really resonated with me. That had a direct influence on the song 'Mountain People' – I almost credited Pinter on the sleeve.[358]

Fellow Pinter fan Nicky Wire described 'Mountain People' as 'the best exploration of Welshness ever written in a song'.[359]

Gruff Rhys should be recognised as one our finest wordsmiths of the last quarter century. Like a wise old sage, he's often slow in interviews with concentration etched across his face as he ponders the correct word, and yet he always chooses the right one. This whimsical quality extends to his lyricism where he can succinctly nail a subject, or, like Gorky's, unearth magic from the mundane.

Simon Price continued:

Gruff's words acknowledge the earthy reality and take you by your hand to lead you along the path to a better place. Gruff is a thoughtful and underrated lyricist, ever capable of coming up with unconventional lines. For Nicky Wire, an early champion of the band, it was the bleak poignancy of 'You and I, united by itemised bills'.[360]

Who else could summarise marriage like those seven words found in 'Gathering Moss'? Not many bands would name an album after a household appliance either, but as the *Melody Maker* headline said: '*Radiator*: Every Bedroom Should Have One!'[361]

———

While the Furries were anthropomorphising inflatable bears, a young songwriter from Cwmaman was bringing to life stories of his humble hometown.

Stereophonics may have been a tight trio, but their classic debut album was very much the brainchild of Kelly Jones. Released on the same day as *Radiator*, *Word Gets Around* gestated from his childhood bedroom where he wrote a remarkable collection of anecdotes depicting the characters, camaraderie, drama and daydreams of the Cynon valley. Sat on the floor of this makeshift studio armed with an acoustic guitar, his notebook scribbles transformed into some of the biggest anthems of the '90s.

Few had heard of Cwmaman until Stereophonics put it on the map. Home to just 1,500 people with only one road in and out, it's a tiny place only three miles away from Aberdare – but tell the Phonics they're from the latter at your peril.

With a string of accolades to their name by the end of the decade, Stereophonics may have seemed like an overnight sensation. Yet their success stemmed from slogging it. One of Kelly's first idols was his father, Arwyn, who fronted Oscar and the Kingfishers – one of the top turns on the south Wales valleys scene of the early '70s. He secured a record deal with Polydor, who rebranded him as 'Arwyn Davidson' as they felt there were already too many Joneses in the music industry to keep up with.

Mesmerised by his father's cover of Graham Nash's 'Simple Man' on the pub jukebox, Kelly sat quietly sipping a Coke while absorbing his dad's stagecraft. By the age of twelve, Kelly had just enough education to perform his first gig. In between renditions of 'Bad Moon Rising', 'Jump', 'Hotel California' and 'All Right Now', he slipped in his own tunes.

Aged sixteen, Kelly embarked on college courses in film-making and scriptwriting. His tutor introduced him to the BBC, who commissioned one of his kitchen-sink drama scripts before his music career took off. Kelly credited Jimmy McGovern's *Hearts and Minds*, Peter Flannery's *Our Friends in the North*, and John Sullivan's *Only Fools and Horses* as just as much an influence on his songwriting as any lyricist.

Another influence was Roald Dahl, and the themes splashed across the twelve tracks on *Word Gets Around* could easily have sprung from *Tales of the Unexpected* – fate ('Not Up to You'), infidelity ('Same Size Feet') and boozing ('Check My Eyelids for Holes', 'Last of the Big Time Drinkers' and 'Too Many Sandwiches'). A potential title for the album was *Goldfish Bowl* (named after one of its songs), and it certainly felt we were the gawping voyeurs looking in on these people's lives.

A decade after Kelly's first live performance, Stereophonics became the first band signed to Richard Branson's new V2 label in May 1996. 'We rehearsed every Thursday and every Sunday for ten years,' said Kelly. 'Fuck knows why, but something was driving us to continue.'[362]

Living a few doors away from Kelly on Glanaman Road was the larger-than-life Stuart Cable, and the duo went through several guises in bands including Zephyr, Silent Runner, The Stillborn Lambs and The Applejacks. Recruiting Richard Jones, they briefly even considered calling themselves The Mabel Cables after Stuart's mother. 'We thought it made us sound like Lynyrd Skynyrd,' laughed Kelly.[363]

One name that had a bit more of a shelf life was Tragic Love Company (combining three of their favourite groups in The Tragically Hip, Mother Love Bone and Bad Company). That would all change one historic night in March 1996 – ironically, just down the road in Aberdare.

Catatonia were due to headline this leg of the Splash tour at the town's 600-capacity Coliseum Theatre with a support bill of unsigned local bands including The Pocket Devils (fronted by Merthyr Tydfil film-maker and radio personality Jonny Owen). Tragic Love Company were also due to appear, but there was a last-minute ultimatum. The promoter, Wayne Coleman, hated their name and said unless they changed it, they wouldn't be playing.

With sign-off of the gig poster imminent, the band were stumped for inspiration, until Stuart Cable glanced across his living room and saw the brand name 'Falcon Stereophonic' etched into the side of his parents' gramophone. Stereophonics were born.

A & R men were out in force in Aberdare to assess the hype of The Pocket Devils with their 'Noelrock' aesthetic and early promise supporting INXS in Cardiff. But it was the Phonics who stormed the Coliseum. Even a slightly worse-for-wear Catatonia were able to admit the Phonics stole the show: 'They did a brilliant gig and we were ruddy awful,' said Cerys.[364] 'They blew us offstage.'

Suitably impressed, John Brand ventured backstage and offered his services to the band. As a producer and engineer, he made his name working with the likes of Elton John, George Harrison, Kiss and The Cult before moving into management. Luckily, he was at the Coliseum having participated in a seminar earlier that day. Helped by a raw demo of 'A Thousand Trees', Brand ignited a bidding war featuring over thirty labels.

EMI were apparently out of the bidding after their rep asked Kelly if 'A Thousand Trees' was a song for Greenpeace!

A very famous entrepreneur changed their lives. There was a slight hitch though, as Kelly told Radio X:

He called my mother's house and said, 'It's Richard Branson… Can I speak to Kelly, Richard or Stuart?' like we were The Monkees all living in one house! And my mother said, 'Yeah right, and I'm Elizabeth Taylor,' and put the phone down![365]

Their first output for V2 was a strangely low-key one in November 1996. Limited to just 500 copies and ineligible to chart, 'Looks Like Chaplin' provided a fascinating first glimpse of Kelly's songwriting style, and it's now a rare collector's item.

By March 1997, V2 were ready to officially release Stereophonics' first single proper. 'Local Boy in the Photograph' reached No. 51, but soared all the way up to No. 15 on its rerelease in February 1998.

Backed by a chiming guitar riff, Kelly penned his poignant lyric aged eighteen in tribute to Paul Boggis, who died by suicide. Paul had asked Kelly's friend for train times, and then jumped in front of one travelling between Cwmbach and Aberdare.

Speaking to 'Whispering' Bob Harris at the 2010 Hay Festival, Kelly said:

> I used to play county football and there was a kid that played right-back. I got to know him pretty well. He was a really cool and good-looking kid. He was one of those that you looked at and thought, 'He's got it all.'
>
> A few years later, we found out he jumped in front of a train. We were all a bit shocked and read about it in the local paper. There was a picture of him smoking – it was the local boy in the photograph. The song was more a celebration of his life than about his death really.

'Local Boy' wasn't the only song inspired by real-life tragedy. 'Billy Davey's Daughter' brought the album to a heartbreaking conclusion. Speaking in Danny O'Connor's biography, *Stereophonics: Just Enough Evidence to Print*, Kelly said:

> I remember us being in Stuart's yellow van…We were going across the Severn Bridge and Stuart mentioned that it was there that Billy Davey's daughter had jumped.
>
> Someone had told me the story vaguely before…Some people say she jumped, some people say she was pushed off. That's why at the end, there's the line 'word gets around' because it's like Chinese whispers…
>
> We were finishing off the record, I didn't want to put it on. We tried a version where we changed the name. We changed it to 'Millie Davey' and all these different things, and then we thought, this isn't right. We went to see Billy Davey and said, 'Look, we've got this song,' and he said it was alright.[366]

Talking of Chinese whispers, there's no finer example of how quickly rumours spread than the album's opening track, 'A Thousand Trees'. As a child, Kelly saw a slogan on the back of a pack of England's

Glory matches that stuck with him: 'It only takes one tree to make a thousand matches / It only takes one match to burn a thousand trees.' Kelly explains:

> The story is about a football coach, who coached us when we were kids. He was well respected within the community. I was in his under-12s team, we were called 'Billy's Babes'.
>
> One day a couple of girls complained that he'd been messing with them in the changing rooms. They told their parents and then it all got blown up in a court case and he went down. I don't think he served the full sentence…
>
> I just remember being in the club, I think it was Christmas morning, and he came in and everybody shook his hand, welcoming him home…If it had been anyone our age, the guy wouldn't have been given the time of day…The village was completely split – half believed it, the other half didn't.
>
> The song is more about how rumours in a small town can change people's perspectives about somebody else…and the metaphor sums it up.[367]

Elsewhere, Kelly's first-person, observational wit shone through on 'More Life in a Tramp's Vest'. Originally called 'Last Minute Shoppers', it was inspired by his time working on a fruit and veg stall at Aberdare market:

> You could be sitting there till five o' clock and you could guarantee you'd be dead for the two hours before that, but as soon as you're just about to close up, twenty people would walk in and I'd want to kill them!
>
> It was a great phrase from Malcolm, one of the boys I worked with on the market. He was known as 'Mac the Knife' and when it got quiet, he'd always say, 'There's more life in a tramp's vest.'[368]

Kelly Jones's songwriting has occasionally been inspired by Britpop's front runners like Pulp.
In fact, he revisited Jarvis Cocker's conversational

lyricism on 'Common People' as inspiration for 'Dakota'. Throughout Stereophonics' 2005 No. 1 single, there are lines that clarify and confirm the previous ones. Instances like 'Summertime, think it was June / Yeah, I think it was June' are akin to 'I don't know why, but I had to start it somewhere / So it started there' from 'Common People'.

Like many of Kelly's '90s contemporaries, the influence of The Beatles was also inescapable. Back and better than ever following the release of their *Anthology* compilations, it was sacrilege to be anything other than gushing about the Fab Four by the mid-'90s.

Kelly said to *Melody Maker*: 'I always loved The Beatles for doing "When I'm Sixty-Four", "A Day in the Life" and "I Am the Walrus" – you've got a rock 'n' roll song, a story song and a cabaret piece. I always liked that about them.'[369]

While Kelly loved Cwmaman, 'Tramp's Vest' also expressed his frustration with small-town mentality – a theme further explored on 'Traffic' and its lyric 'Is anyone going anywhere?' Awarded Single of the Week by guest reviewer David Baddiel in *Melody Maker*, the BBC filmed a performance of it for *Top of the Pops* outside Kelly and Stuart's childhood homes.

Influenced by the storytelling style of 'That's Entertainment' by The Jam, the song evolved from Kelly's car journey home and his imaginings of the lives of other commuters caught in the congestion. Of all his lyrics, 'Traffic' is one of the most closely linked to the human condition, as Paul Elliott explained in *Q* in 2003:

Two years ago, Kelly was troubled by the effect that one of his songs had on another person's life. He got a letter from a young woman, who had become pregnant by rape.

While in the waiting room at an abortion clinic, she heard 'Traffic' playing on the radio. One line acted as a trigger inside her: 'To kill an unborn scare'. She decided to have the child, and walked out. She named her son Kelly.

'Stuff like that blows your head up,' said the Stereophonics frontman.[370]

Charting at No. 6, *Word Gets Around* helped the band secure the British Breakthrough Act at the 1998 BRIT Awards. Receiving the accolade, Kelly said: 'It's about fucking time we got some recognition.'

One person unimpressed by his swearing on national TV was his mother, Beryl: 'My God, I could've killed him! I said, "You're like those bloody Oasis boys…"'[371]

———

The peak of the *Word Gets Around* era came at Cardiff Castle in June 1998. Billed as Cwmaman Feel the Noize, it was the first gig at the venue since Queen in 1976.

It hadn't been long since the band were playing to dwindling crowds as Tragic Love Company, and now here they were in front of 10,000. The gig was only announced ten weeks in advance, but tickets sold out in ten days.

'Two years ago, we couldn't sell out the pub across the road,' said Kelly. 'When we were playing Sam's Bar, we had to take the money on the door and then go and do the gig.'[372]

After supports from Subcircus and Warm Jets, Stereophonics delivered a varied set including fan-favourite B-sides 'Carrot Cake and Wine' and 'Raymond's Shop', plus five cuts from their forthcoming second album.

Given the strength of Kelly's songwriting, it's no surprise that Stereophonics broke through, but it was the foundations laid by other '90s Welsh acts that helped them go huge – an acknowledgement he didn't forget on the night. Concluding the set, Kelly paid tribute to Catatonia, the Furries, the Manics, the cast from *Twin Town*, Welsh-language soap opera *Pobol y Cwm* and 'anybody who's doing anything for Wales'.

But what did he think of *Word Gets Around* making Cwmaman common property?

The lyrics are observational, rather than judgemental. 'Last of the Big Time Drinkers', for instance, is a celebration of where we come from. It's not a put-down. People work all year and they're happy having two weeks' holiday. If you don't want that, you can get out.

People always thought we wanted to get out of Cwmaman. We didn't really, we just didn't want to work in a factory.[373]

Stereophonics dedicated *Word Gets Around* to their hometown with a well-known local phrase that later became the title of one of their chart-topping albums: 'Keep the Village Alive!'

EVERY DAY WHEN I WAKE UP, I THANK THE LORD I'M WELSH!

THE NATION'S EMBRACING OF WELSHNESS

'*Deffrwch Cymry cysglyd, Gwlad y Gân...*'[374]
There was definitely something rumbling in Wales by 1998 if a song could be released into the British mainstream with a first line even non-Welsh speakers could sing along to.

The rest of the Welsh-language lyrics may have been less easy to latch onto, but that opening salvo sung in Cerys's alluring lilt was so irresistible that Catatonia hooked in fans from all nations. As the song's title, 'International Velvet', suggested, Wales was now exporting great music to the world.

It's indicative of the change in national mood that the band were happy to release a song with a chorus that boomed, 'Every day when I wake up, I thank the Lord I'm Welsh'. The narrow devolution victory may have ushered in feelings of quiet optimism, but there was no such caution amongst Welsh musicians. Brimming with confidence, they took the baton and ran with it.

Stereophonics proudly presented stories of a tiny village in the south Wales valleys on *Word Gets Around*, while the Furries examined Welshness on songs like 'Mountain People'. They also tempted monoglots into the joys of bilingualism on 'The International Language of Screaming', which was tellingly offered in English for a mainstream, English-language audience. In addition to the Welsh takeover of the 1997 Reading Festival, the Manics returned from the BRIT Award-winning success of *Everything Must Go* with *This Is My Truth Tell Me Yours* in 1998 – a No. 1 album inspired by Wales like no other in their catalogue.

The most overt expression of Welsh pride came via Catatonia though, even if it was intended as tongue-in-cheek. Translated as 'Wake up, sleepy Wales, Land of Song', it's interesting that this line opened and closed 'International Velvet', as if this sleeping giant had awoken, realised its potential within the bombast of the chorus, and then ironically returned to its slumber at the song's conclusion.

'It's very innocent,' said Cerys, referring to the sarcasm of the lyric. 'It's just questioning the good things people say about Wales (*'Darganfyddais gwir baradwys Rhyl'* ['I discovered the true paradise of Rhyl'], but then saying it's not that good, is it? And then coming along in English and saying, "Every day when I wake up, I thank the Lord I'm Welsh".'[375]

On the album of the same name, released in February 1998, the sleeve notes offered no translation or explanation of its title track's Welsh-language lyrics. Elsewhere, there were further bold nods to the band's national identity with Cerys's accent shining through, from her elongated vowel sounds on 'Mulder and Scully' to the rolled r's of 'Road Rage'.

Debuting at No. 11, there was little sign of the album's huge success ahead. Their New Year tour around Wales's lesser-known locations was a subdued affair including an opening show at Tenby's 400-capacity De Valence Pavilion. *NME*'s David Quantick observed that not even the premiere of the album's title track roused the Welsh audience: 'The crowd do not go wild. [They are] not ready to rock, spending most of the show shuffling about chatting. And, despite a rump of wild enthusiasts in front of the stage, "International Velvet" goes generally unremarked.'[376]

Yet, bolstered by the popularity of 'Mulder and Scully' and 'Road Rage', the album topped the charts in May 1998 – three months on from its release. It may have only stayed at the top of the charts for a week, but that wasn't going to stop Cerys living up to her media reputation on holiday.

Returning home with a bloodstream largely consisting of alcohol, she said: 'I got a letter from the bank saying, "Miss Matthews, due to the unnatural abuse of your card, we're writing to you to warn you that someone may have stolen your card."'

Like Gorky's 'Patio Song', (the album track) 'International Velvet' could easily have been released as a bilingual UK single – and you can't help thinking Catatonia missed a trick by not doing so. *Welsh Bands Weekly* certainly felt it was the right time to promote the Welsh language beyond the borders:

> The record-buying public would be aware that there's another language every day on this island and they'd have the guts to go out and spend their money on records that are sung in it.
>
> You'd get some of the brilliant Welsh-language bands like Nâr, Pic Nic, Tystion, Big Leaves, Topper and Melys getting a bite of the apple, and not being written off as strange mushroom-munching sheep-shaggers. People would learn Welsh so they could understand the songs.[377]

Some of those learners were living beyond Wales, which demonstrated a remarkable shift.

It's doubtful Warner would've risked alienating a huge chunk of the fanbase. As Barbara Ellen indicated in *The Observer*: 'The fact remains that if an English band had sung such a song, it would've led to PC Armageddon, and quite right too.'[378]

A song featuring the Welsh language was always going to be treated with suspicion by the English media, especially if there was hidden irony. There was hypocrisy in this reaction in that a ubiquitous song released not long before proudly proclaimed the heroism of wearing 'three lions on a shirt'. Mark said to *NME*: 'It's in strict Welsh poetic meter and if we'd entered it into an Eisteddfod about 100 years ago, we'd have got the chair. And anyway, what the fuck does "Swing Low, Sweet Chariot" mean?'[379]

Cerys added: 'The English have never had anywhere near the same amount of crap that Welsh people get…If you translated the Welsh bits, you would see that it's trying to tear down stereotypes. It's not a song about Welsh nationalism. It's a song about *internationalism*.'[380]

Far from being anti-English, 'International Velvet' was about celebrating your own nation rather than hating another. It's also possible to honour (and question) another nation, while still being patriotic.

EVERY DAY WHEN I WAKE UP, I THANK THE LORD I'M WELSH!

Caroline Sullivan at *The Guardian* hit the nail on the head: 'Cerys and her Catablokes deliver a rock show that translates into any language…Welsh by birth, *international* by inclination.'[381]

Not every Cool Cymru group was thanking the Lord they were Welsh every time they woke up. Some of them found fame thanks to unlikely influences from much further afield.

Named after an American folk hero who fought at the Battle of the Alamo, The Crocketts made waves in Aberystwyth as labelmates of Stereophonics on V2.

Fronted by Davey 'Crockett' MacManus and recorded with Cure producer David M. Allen, their 1998 debut album, *We May Be Skinny & Wirey*, remains a lost Welsh classic. Melding styles of country and punk, The Crocketts created their own thrilling brand of 'cowpunk' – imagine The Pogues, Violent Femmes and The Clash in a blender!

———

'I put horses' heads in people's beds'[382] was one of the unlikeliest opening lines of a Top 40 hit ever, let alone the lead single from a chart-topping album.

Yet, that's exactly what Catatonia did with 'I Am the Mob' in October 1997. Its chart position was all the more impressive given it was banned from daytime airplay on BBC Radio 1 due to its *Godfather*-inspired lyrics including 'That Luca Brasi, he sleeps with the fishes'.

The irony of the radio blackout didn't go unnoticed amongst critics. Biographer Brian Wright said: 'When it comes to double standards, England are world champions. While Catatonia faced a ban, "Smack My Bitch Up" by The Prodigy was allowed full airplay.'[383]

The song's intro sample was also deemed too violent by the Beeb. It was from an American chat show, *Jenny Jones*, where a bullied girl finally confronts her tormentor.

Far from the band glorifying violence, it was actually the band's reply to the bullying tactics they felt from Warner Brothers. Mark Roberts said to *Melody Maker*:

181

We're constantly faced with people in places higher than ourselves. They're telling us, 'Why don't you do it this way or that way?' Making excuses that it's all for our sake, in our best interests. What they mean is, 'We can make more money out of you if you do it like this.'[384]

Catatonia thought 1997 would be their breakthrough year after the critical acclaim of *Way Beyond Blue*, but they weren't making waves beyond Wales. There were vocal problems for Cerys, a cancelled Glastonbury set and fighting with a record label based thousands of miles away. The genuine threat of being dropped was a sword of Damocles too.

Warner probably would've been relieved with the lack of airplay for 'I Am the Mob' given its barely veiled references to the label's profit-making. Catatonia's second album, *International Velvet*, was originally scheduled for release in October 1997. Yet Warner delayed its release until February 1998, negating the impact of its lead single (which the label insisted should be 'I Am the Mob', and not 'Mulder and Scully').

The band even wondered if the delay had been purposely implemented so the single would flop and the label could discard Catatonia without issuing an album. Plans to release 'Lost Cat' stateside were abandoned in 1996, so *International Velvet* would be the first output in the US (via Neil Young's Vapor label) if plans got that far.

That was a big 'if', considering the final track Catatonia included on promo copies of the album. With a title borrowed from Bugs Bunny and Porky Pig, the Warner-baiting 'That's All Folks' offered no subtlety in its lyrics, which referred to the tension of working with a label that was never satisfied: when Cerys sang, 'Did no one warn us', it sounded suspiciously like 'Warner's'.

David Owens said:

> The way she screams 'That's all folks' in such a distressed manner makes your spine spasm as you wonder just where her mindset was when this was recorded…The sound of anguish, frustration and bitterness…
>
> They believed it would be a fitting epitaph – the curtain-closer, the final track on the final album, the final nail in the coffin of their career.[385]

Incredibly, Warner didn't even notice until an executive deigned to listen to the album. Once the cat was out of the bag, they ordered the song's removal. Previously a B-side on 'I Am the Mob', the Richard Dawkins-inspired 'My Selfish Gene' got promoted in its place (surprisingly, 'That's All Folks' was still released in July 1998 on the flip side of 'Strange Glue').

After their skirmishes with Warner, their next brush would be with the law. Named after the FBI special agents in *The X-Files*, 'Mulder and Scully' launched Catatonia to No. 3 – thirty-two places higher than their previous best, and almost ousted Oasis's 'All Around the World' from No. 1.

Awarding it Single of the Week, *Melody Maker* commented: 'It pisses a glorious shower of contempt on Catatonia's contemporaries (Sleeper/Echobelly/any other young guitar band) or indeed any other single this week from a great height.'

The initial idea for the artwork was a spaceship hovering ominously over London Bridge, but the band asked for an ingenious change of location. After buying a picture of Cardiff from the Welsh tourist board and a plastic spaceship from Forbidden Planet, the image was transformed into an atmospheric night shot of a UFO zapping City Hall.

Surprisingly, the band weren't regular viewers of the TV show, so it wasn't a cynical cash-in. The band believed in the song's quality regardless of its association with the huge sci-fi series, but that link certainly didn't harm either.

Rather than an examination of all things extraterrestrial, it was a metaphor asking Mulder and Scully to solve the riddle of romance. Talking closer to home than you might initially think, Cerys added: 'I like the idea of two people going round the planet investigating odd phenomena – in this case love.'

It was actually a case of 'The Ex-Files' after Mark and Cerys had split up during the *Way Beyond Blue* campaign. With Cerys lamenting about her lonely bed and the dilemma of moving on to other lovers, the lyrics lay bare the heartache of their relationship, especially when you consider the song's working titles were 'I Can't Sleep Alone' and 'Stop Doing What You Keep Doing'.

Cerys also claimed their new material was better *because* of the split: '*International Velvet* worked because it was getting more and more difficult to stay together, so we had a lot at stake…We just poured it into the music, and when we're onstage. It has to mean something to put up with that shit.'[386]

Brian Wright added:

> The close songwriting collaboration effectively ended with the relationship. There is a distinct difference between the songs written before and after the split. Many found it sad that they would no longer write songs in the vein of their earlier material, but it doesn't mean that the quality of the output has been affected.[387]

The band weren't averse to a bit of gallows humour either, with Paul Jones's remix titled 'Mulder and Scully (The Ex-Files)'. Cerys even referred to the alternative title herself and took another swing at Warner: 'We had a single called "A Case for Mulder and Scully (The Ex-Files)", but the record company didn't want to release it until the album comes out. I think Bugs Bunny has run out of money!'[388]

Linking up again with Kevin Allen (who directed the promo for 'I Am the Mob'), the video for 'Mulder and Scully' was shot at TJ's as 60 Ft. Dolls waited to soundcheck.

Starring Rhys Ifans, a stage-diving Cerys and two FBI special agents hot on their tails, it still wasn't deemed good enough for the American market.

Much to the relief of the band, 'Mulder and Scully' was their first US single (albeit delayed since May 1997), but Warner insisted on a different video for across the Atlantic, weirdly featuring Cerys running from a city full of sentient filing cabinets!

'Mulder and Scully' was the perfect appetiser for *International Velvet*, which was released on 2 February 1998. Sharing its name with a 1978 movie starring Anthony Hopkins, its stunning artwork of gleaming white horses dashing through water against a backdrop of baby-blue sky was equally filmic.

The songs were first written while on the road with the Manics in late 1996 and demo sessions started early the following year. While at Big Noise, Mark even had time to try his hand at production, working with Greg Haver on Topper's mini-album *Something to Tell Her*.

If 'Mulder and Scully' penetrated the mainstream, Catatonia's next single, 'Road Rage', skyrocketed their fame. Featuring brilliant artwork – a yellow spacecraft zooming through a futuristic cityscape – the promo video transplanted the band straight into this environment. Cerys commented: 'Videos cost ten times as much as it does to make an album – just for a three-minute bit of footage!'[389] Once on set though, Cerys was every bit the star in an emerald-green designer suit.

Nominated for a BRIT and an Ivor Novello, the anthemic 'Road Rage' reached No. 5. The dark origins of its title come from the December 1996 murder of Lee Harvey by his girlfriend, Tracie Andrews, who stabbed him more than thirty times. She later claimed it had been committed by a stranger in a road rage attack.

Speaking to the *Birmingham Post* of the song's release, Lee's mother, Maureen, said: 'It's disgusting that people are trying to make money from such a tragedy. My son did not die in a road rage attack, he was killed by Tracie Andrews. We simply do need songs like this.'[390]

Cerys responded that while the title was inspired by the case, the lyrics were about advances in technology. In her book *Pure Evil*, Maureen Harvey said: 'At least Cerys Matthews had the decency to return my call and explain that she hadn't intended to cause any offence.'[391]

Warner finally recognised they were onto a good thing and ended up releasing five singles in total, adding the Owen Powell-penned 'Strange Glue', and 'Game On' (another rumination on Mark and Cerys's troubled relationship). In December 1998, *Melody Maker* awarded *International Velvet* Album of the Year.

Elsewhere, 'Don't Need the Sunshine' offered a gorgeous campfire singalong, while the ghostly 'Johnny Come Lately' was Cerys at her ethereal best. The version used was actually the demo recorded at Big Noise as the band felt they couldn't better the vocal.

John Harris said:

> This was pop music free of rock's macho piety and endowed with a biting intelligence – love, loss, life and death viewed through lenses that seemed to flip between cynicism, innocence and a

very penetrating kind of existential insight when the zeitgeist seems divided between Butlin's Redcoats and cripplingly earnest young rock musicians.[392]

'Who doesn't want to be compared to Dusty Springfield?'[393]

Andrea Adams (née Parker) beamed at *The Guardian*'s description of Melys as 'Dusty Springfield backed by Saint Etienne'. It's nice, but it only tells half of the story.

'I always thought there was more bite to us than Saint Etienne. We were darker,' interjected her husband and Melys guitarist, Paul Adams.

Watching the couple sitting together in their Seagrass beach café in Llanfairfechan opposite Puffin Island, it was easy to see how they had been together for so long. Often they finished one another's sentences, nodded in unison or qualified what the other was saying. Their partnership has survived the Chinese whispers of living in a tiny community, and was at the heart of one of Wales's best bands of the '90s.

First meeting in 1996 in Betws-y-Coed, they began dating and soon formed the group with keyboardist Carys Jones and Paul's brother, Gary Husband, who could barely play the drums at the time. After recording their first demo, 'Cysur', in a mate's squat, Gorwel Owen recommended them to Ankst, who released the *Fragile* and *Cuckoo* EPs.

Meaning 'sweet' in Welsh, 'Melys' perfectly encapsulated Andrea's angelic vocal delivery. While their contemporaries committed themselves to recreating The-Beatles-by-numbers, Melys juxtaposed that vocal sweetness with crystalline guitar lines, brooding beats and sinister, Depeche Mode synths.

Their modus operandi was weaving tales of torment, bitter break-ups and betrayal. Like Suede, Melys depicted the gloomy underbelly of society, albeit in a small north Wales village where everyone knows everybody else's business. Hence, their aptly titled 1998 debut, *Rumours and Curses*, released via Pinnacle Records in June 1998. *Melody Maker* wrote:

Small towns breed paranoia: lonely people twitch uncomfortably behind soiled shop windows, little kids make gestures behind your back near the lake and disappear three days later never to resurface. The unexplained is best left that way; claustrophobia is a way of life.[394]

Opening track 'Achilles Heel' delved into a deceitful character with a 'barbed wire heart',[395] while 'Fade Away (For the Last Time)' was a bleak song about the way people act around a dying relative. 'Hatshepsut' was inspired by the female Egyptian pharaoh's presumed love affair with her servant, while the identity of the 'Acid Queen' is the question the band have been asked most. 'When You Put Leonard Cohen On' summoned that feeling of post-argument sadness, complete with melancholic music in tribute to the man who mastered the form. 'Painfully Thin' dealt not just with an unhealthy relationship, but also obsession with body image.

'Growing up, Andrea, myself and Carys got constantly asked about why we were so skinny,' said Paul.

The 'rumours' of the album title were amply covered by tales of local tittle-tattle throughout, including 'Hope You Cry Yourself to Sleep', while the 'curses' referred to the strange goings on during recording.

'Everything went tits up at Parr Street Studio,' said Paul. 'That's why we thought it was cursed. The tape machines started self-operating and there were crashes from empty rooms.'

Regardless of the mysterious occurrences, producer Gorwel Owen remained a strict taskmaster. His oft-repeated phrases included, 'Yes, it's getting there', and, 'No, we're not sampling that.'

'My favourite was when I thought I'd nailed a vocal and Gorwel would say, "Now try it in the Western harmonic scale" – meaning "in tune"', laughed Andrea.

'We've known Gorwel for years and still work with him to this day,' said Paul. 'It wouldn't be Melys without that continuity. He knows the way we work, and vice versa.'

Described by Gary Husband as a 'human metronome',[396] Gorwel's production brought grandeur to 'Diwifr'. Like 'Patio Song', 'Diwifr' ('Wireless') was a bilingual tune that received national airplay from the likes of Mark and Lard at BBC Radio 1.

Andrea said:

It's one of my favourite Melys songs; I love singing it live. 'Diwifr' also makes me sad that two of my favourite tracks didn't get on the album. One of the problems with signing to a big label is that they also have a say because they've paid for it. I'll always argue that 'In Love with Danielle Steele' and 'Paper, Stone, Scissors' should've been album tracks – not B-sides for 'Diwifr'.[397]

Paul wasn't a fan of the third and final song Pinnacle released from *Rumours and Curses*: '"Ambulance Chaser" is the one I'm not sure about; I didn't want it on the album. The label was going to release it as is, but we persuaded them to let us rerecord it.'

In between 'Diwifr' and 'Ambulance Chaser', 'Lemming' was also released as an EP accompanied by a video filmed at an abandoned hospital in east London with scalpels left everywhere. 'We turned down a trip to Spain in a VW camper-van to record in a freezing cold hospital,' said Paul. 'What dicks!'

The album closed with 'Matryoshka', which borrowed its name from the 'little matron' wooden Russian dolls and featured Llanrwst Male Voice Choir.

'We bussed the choir up from north Wales to Liverpool for the mix,' said Paul. 'They got pissed in the green room of Parr Street, and it took a while for Gorwel to put them right.'

Rumours and Curses received promising critical acclaim, with Everett True declaring it 'a most disquieting, unsettling and pleasurable experience'. Big things were expected, but then Pinnacle went bust just one album into a five-record deal. The band was in transition too, with Carys leaving to join John Lawrence's solo project, Infinity Chimps, while tour manager Rich Eardley was drafted in on bass.

Regardless, Andrea and Paul set up their own studio and label, Sylem ('Melys' spelled backwards) and self-released their second album, *Kamikaze*, in 2000. Their biggest career highlight was still to come though.

After first meeting him at a TV show recording, the band gave John Peel a lift home and it was the start of a lasting friendship. Melys went on to record several of the DJ's legendary Peel Sessions. One evening he was planning to broadcast a repeat when the band surprised him with an impromptu set at his Peel Acres home. Their rendition of 'Happy Birthday' had him in tears.

At another session, they sang 'You'll Never Walk Alone' with the London Welsh Male Voice Choir for the lifelong Liverpool fan. Peel even went as far as to call Melys 'part of the family', and he officially opened their studio.

In December 2001, John Peel ranked 'Chinese Whispers' at No. 1 in his Festive Fifty, calling it one of the best songs ever written. After his passing in October 2004, Melys dedicated their album *Life's Too Short* to Peel.

'I hated Britpop...'[398]

Paul Adams winced at the very mention of the word. With its legacy of oafish laddism and misogyny, it's a movement that in some respects hasn't aged as well as others. The weeklies often commented on the physical attractiveness of the singers in female-fronted bands before even a note of music had been analysed. Take for instance this *NME* coverage of Catatonia from February 1998:

OK, let's be honest, we're all 'lads', right? What you really want to know is – this singer, Cerys, is she fit? Yes, she is. But she's still not even half as fit as The Voice. No mere human could be.

The Voice is sex on a stick dipped in sex with added sex sprinkled on top minus the stick. And, um, are the songs any good? Well, yes they are, some of them.[399]

Andrea Adams was the subject of one such quote that found its way onto the cover of *Melody Maker*. Blur were the issue's guest reviewers, and bassist Alex James remarked he would give Melys's single an extra star 'if the singer had big tits'.

Andrea said:

It was disgraceful. For me, Britpop also represented the death of indie music. Oasis and Blur have a lot to answer for in killing off a scene where suddenly any

*indie band with guitars became the best thing since
sliced bread, whereas now it's very difficult to find
pockets of good independent music.*[400]

Noel Gallagher was always quick to acknowledge that Oasis
moved the goalposts and made releasing records a compet-
itive sport. A chart entry outside the Top 40 was no longer
accepted; it was all about the upper reaches of the Top 10
now. For the Britpop years, success was gauged
entirely in chart positions and units shifted as A & R men
sold their souls for spreadsheets.

This led to intense competition between bands, which
could quickly descend from playground insults to vile
remarks. Who can forget Noel's wish that Blur's Damon
Albarn and Alex James die of AIDS?

While not quite as vitriolic, fierce competition extended
to Welsh groups. They may all have seemed like mates, but
they were still vying for the same magazine covers, festival
slots and TV spots. In particular, a rivalry developed
between the Manics and Stereophonics.

Filming a Phonics documentary titled *The Great Escape*,
a BBC Wales camera crew captured Kelly Jones and band
manager John Brand complaining about the Manics.
Bottom of a bill headlined by the Manics at the Manchester
Apollo in December 1996 (also featuring indie rockers
Tiger), Brand commented on the apparent lack of time
given to Stereophonics for a soundcheck:

*The main band do not leave until their equipment is
perfect and then the second band don't want to leave
until they've got the best sound. Unfortunately, the
band that is opening gets whatever is left.*[401]

Kelly added:

We came here at four o'clock, and we didn't even get chance to do one song. Don't tell me they couldn't have held the doors for five more minutes?...What difference does it make? They're only here to see one band anyway.[402]

The barbs didn't stop there. Speaking to *NME* in March 1999, Kelly said:

I listened to The Holy Bible *once and I thought it was the most depressing record I'd ever heard in my life... Nicky [Wire] takes all his lyrics from books because he never goes out, and I take all mine from life because I never stay in.*[403]

———

It's often said that bands produce their best work while under the influence. This could certainly be said for the Furries, whose mind-bending intake allowed them to indulge in their beloved psychedelia.

In May 1998, they returned with their first EP since their Ankst days. Its lead track was nearly as old. Ric Rawlins said:

By the time the band recorded 'Ice Hockey Hair', the song had already been through as many incarnations as *Doctor Who*. Starting life as a simple piano melody during the *Fuzzy Logic* sessions, by 1997 it had acquired a temporary name – 'The Naff Song'.[404]

Gruff elaborated to *NME*: 'We got the title off this Swedish Third Division footballer we met, who said that a really naff thing is "ice hockey hair" – whatever that means.'[405]

Elsewhere, the band said the title referred to a mullet hairstyle.

Recorded at London's Orinoco Studios with Gorwel Owen, the band expressed frustration that they could've recorded an entire album in the time it took to make it. Mixed several times to a flawless production sheen, it's certainly not naff regardless of what the band think. Gruff's guitar hook evoked memories of '70s heroes Badfinger, ELO and Queen, while the slew of samples and synths came straight out of a sci-fi score. Although *Melody Maker* acknowledged its 'kitschy grace', it also revelled in a tune 'so syrupy and '70s that you can imagine it sipping martini in a beige cocktail lounge'.[406]

There's a gloriously DIY feel to its lyric too. Gruff acknowledged that although he sometimes 'empties his emotional state'[407] into songs, 'Ice Hockey Hair' was written spontaneously in the 'instant pop' tradition. Therefore, when he finds himself short of a sentence in the bridge, he just wails, 'Take me to a chorus now!' Another of its lines was seemingly addressed directly to the Furries' army of followers: 'Now that you're here, tell me you're a non-believer.' Thankfully, they were preaching to the converted.

Sandwiched between *Radiator* and *Guerrilla*, *Ice Hockey Hair* is a unique artefact that possessed a sound unbefitting of either. Reaching No. 12, it was awarded *NME* Single of the Week and ranked No. 2 in the magazine's end-of-year list, while Nicky Wire voted for it as his favourite EP. *The Guardian* commended *Ice Hockey Hair* to be as 'gleeful and excessive a record as these impurists have made yet'.[408]

The EP was bookended by two tunes that fed into the band's media representation as stoners. The first track, 'Smokin'', was commissioned by Channel 4 for a series about the seven deadly sins, and in this case an episode presented by Howard Marks on sloth. It was recorded at Grassroots in Cardiff in June 1997, and the band improvised around a looped sample of Black Uhuru's 'I Love King Selassie' before building to a wild crescendo. When Ted Kessler asked if the song was intended to be subversive like The Shamen singing 'E's are good', Gruff replied: 'Jesus Christ, I hope not!…It's too obvious to be subversive…

'I think people patronise their audience too much by insulting their intelligence. We do feel a moral and social responsibility…This song is just saying, "We just want to smoke it" – that's *us* in the band.'[409]

Perhaps anticipating the furore, a conciliatory remix called 'Let's Quit Smoking' closed the EP. Smoking is bad, kids…

———

Just like their Creation labelmates Oasis, the Furries also released a B-sides compilation in November 1998. *The Masterplan* and *Out*

Spaced not only stand up as outstanding albums in their own right, but you're unlikely to find two better rarity collections.

Rather than being an exhaustive set like Suede's *Sci-Fi Lullabies*, *Out Spaced* was a concise collection (meaning there wasn't room for deep cuts like 'Calimero' and 'Waiting to Happen'). The thirteen songs spanning 1993–8 that made the grade were painstakingly chosen to capture the other (and no less essential) side of the Furries. With its diverse styles encapsulating techno, punk and classic rock, Bunf has even called it his favourite album of theirs.

Pete Fowler's artwork featured another classic character – this time a dazed-looking bear with its head in a vice. He said:

> The original idea was just to take quite a cute, Nookie-style bear and put a G-clamp on its head. I always thought he was doing it himself as some sort of pleasurable thing. Maybe he's gone mad, or he's just trying to crank it up to see what happens. It was just a playful idea about sadomasochism.[410]

In early 1998, Fowler pitched to Creation for an edible sleeve using rice paper. That concept was vetoed, but he was given free rein over *Out Spaced*, including a bizarre brief for the special edition – its rubber casing should be able to withstand an intergalactic journey.

While Fowler worked on a design that could survive re-entry to Earth from outer space, he inadvertently made the package resemble something else:

> Someone described the result as a novelty CD cover with a nipple. I was like, 'Whaaat?!'
> Gruff Rhys added: 'It wasn't actually meant to be in the shape of a breast!…The teat was there so that you could hold it and pull out the CD. The design made it into the V&A Museum!'[411]

Starting non-chronologically with 'The Man Don't Give a Fuck', the compilation included four gems from the early Ankst EPs as well as 'Dim Brys, Dim Chwys', which was on the *Triskedekaphilia* compilation.

Never a group to tuck away their most experimental material on B-sides, *Out Spaced* gave much-needed recognition to cult classics like 'Arnofio/Glô in the Dark' (a track that bridged the gap between *Fuzzy Logic* and *Radiator*). Daf said: 'None of the songs were made to be B-sides. It's more that we try to design our albums, so they're coherent. Sometimes a bunch of songs fit into that, but we can't always agree.'[412]

Closing track 'Blerwytirhwng?' ('Where Are You Between?') certainly fit into the experimental category, clocking in at eleven minutes with a repeated riff and extended outro of *Space Invaders*-style sound effects. Sarah Hill said:

> 'Blerwytirhwng' is a question posed as much to the Super Furry Animals' Welsh audience as to Wales itself…Super Furry Animals, a Welsh band signed to the global Sony label (via Creation), represent the most recent phase in a multi-layered cultural process…
>
> Over the past fifty years, Welsh musicians have appropriated a variety of Anglo-American musical styles to expedite the Welsh quest for national self-definition. This process is by no means unique to Wales, but as a peripheral culture, Wales has often lagged behind the mainstream – cultural change has only shadowed, not instigated, political upheaval.[413]

Meanwhile, 'Guacamole' recalled the band's experience of recording at Rockfield. Yet in typically left-field fashion, the Furries preferred to sing about the studio's catering. 'You get loads of free food there,' said bassist Guto Pryce. 'And for some reason, they're obsessed with guacamole…They give it to you constantly. And carrots…But carrots haven't made it into any of our songs yet.'[414]

Fast-forward to 2001, and this would become reality thanks to a legendary cameo buried deep within the layers of 'Receptacle for the Respectable'. A stunning centrepiece to their fifth album, *Rings Around the World*, it featured Paul McCartney chewing carrots and celery – a role he reprised from an appearance on The Beach Boys' track 'Vegetables' in 1967.

McCartney took the unusual request in good humour. Gruff said: 'When we phoned him up, he said, "You're fucking mad, you are! You mad bastards!"'[415]

———

Gorky's output had been prolific even before signing with a major label, but by 1998 the prodigious group was at last showing signs of strain.

After all, they had issued four albums and two EPs, plus a string of singles and rarities over the last six years, and now there was pressure to replicate the brilliance of *Barafundle*.

The unimaginative title of their fifth album, *Gorky 5*, could've suggested it was rush-released by Mercury Records at a time when the burned-out band was running low in ideas. But it's their most underrated work in that it straddles the label's need for commercialism and the group's idiosyncratic streak, while retaining those gorgeous melodies. It still didn't translate into chart success though.

This was certainly the case for 'Let's Get Together (In Our Minds)', which continued their frustrating trend of landing just outside the Top 40 – this time at No. 43. Speaking of this psych-folk, bittersweet tearjerker, Elis James said: 'How this wasn't a huge hit is beyond me. The string arrangement makes me want to try to jump into the music. A triumph.'[416]

The fact that it was their third-highest-charting single didn't appease the label. *Gorky 5*'s other single, 'Sweet Johnny', stiffed at No. 60 and, despite its critical acclaim, the album reached No. 67.

On *Gorky 5*, the band largely jettisoned the wild psychedelia of *Bwyd Time* and further mined the serene sweetness of *Barafundle*. Released in April 1998 and wonderfully arranged by Gorwel Owen at Monnow Valley Studio, there was the wistful warmth of 'Dyle Fi' and the lush strings of 'Tsunami', while closing track 'Catrin' was up there with Gorky's melancholic best. 'Softly' did exactly what it said on the tin, and 'Only the Sea Makes Sense' is one of the most beautiful songs they ever wrote.

There were still moments of trademark whimsy like the heavy wig-out sections of 'The Tidal Wave' and the Cossack-dancing cabaret of 'Theme from Gorky 5 (Russian Song)'. Much like the Furries' knack for evoking strange images, Gorky's do likewise here: 'From an Alaskan river to a Pavlova mountain / You can suck on a sunset, you can bask in the lava'. John Lawrence said: '*Gorky 5* was much darker, but still stuck in that major-label mentality.'[417]

More serious than its predecessors and sandwiched between the more popular *Barafundle* and *Spanish Dance Troupe*, *Gorky 5* is an overlooked album that requires re-examination. It's the favourite Gorky's record of former Coral guitarist and solo artist Bill Ryder-Jones:

> It has a feel of the sea somehow. The songs roll into each other so brilliantly. It's very easy to get lost in…
>
> The melody and sentiment of 'Only the Sea Makes Sense' belong to each other and that's so hard to do… 'Let's Get Together (In Our Minds)' features one of my favourite lines ever: 'I fell in love with you, or was it your picture?'
>
> Gorky's songs are about universal things – love and loss… *Gorky 5* can be heard and loved by anyone…It doesn't speak of a certain time, it doesn't cash in on any current zeitgeist, it's just real, moving, honest songwriting.[418]

While the Furries were boldly releasing a B-sides collection, Gorky's were showing similar self-belief in writing music in English that was every bit as magical as in their mother tongue. The end result was their most mature record to date.

Bill Ryder-Jones's love for Gorky's runs so deep that the Merseysider called his 2024 album *Iechyd Da* after a classic song off *Bwyd Time*.

The Welsh inspirations didn't stop there as its final track was titled 'Nos Da'.

––––––

'MANIC STREET PREACHERS WILL ALWAYS MATTER.'

Unfurled on a massive banner at their gig at Cork Opera House in August 1998, those words rendered Nicky Wire speechless and he temporarily forgot what he was playing.

That summer, the Manics were on top of the world. 'If You Tolerate This Your Children Will Be Next' was their newly crowned first No. 1 single, having sold 156,000 copies in its first week (on its way to eventually achieving platinum status with over 600,000 sales in the UK alone).

Initially neck and neck with Steps' 'One for Sorrow', the Manics won the battle for top spot and slotted in between Boyzone and All Saints for one week only. Likewise, each song's parent album was released within days of each other the following month, but the result was the same. *Step One* peaked at No. 2, while *This Is My Truth Tell Me Yours* secured top spot with 136,000 first-week sales and a massive margin of 95,000.

While the Manics won 'the Double', they had found themselves enemies – Steps fans! Bradfield said to *Q*:

> Playing it on *Top of the Pops* brought me back down to Earth because I realised that all those kids in the studio were really wishing that Steps had beaten us…They were staring up at us thinking, 'Why the fuck are these old blokes No. 1?'[419]

Almost twenty-three years to the day later, the Manics beat Steps to No. 1 in another chart battle – this time with their fourteenth album, *The Ultra Vivid Lament*, going head-to-head with *What the Future Holds Pt. 2*.

This Is My Truth remains the Manics' most successful record with an enormous 5 million sales (including 1 million in Wales alone), leading to a string of accolades including two BRITs and four *NME* Awards, 'Best Act in the World Today' from *Q* and a headline slot at Glastonbury 1999.

Featuring thirteen songs written late at night amid the Welsh rain, the Manics' fifth album was unveiled after a free gig at Cooper's Field in Cardiff as late additions to a line-up including Robbie Williams and Ash. The occasion was memorable for James Dean Bradfield rebranding their Top 10 hit 'Bobby Gould Must Go' after the ex-Wimbledon manager had presided over a bizarre tenure with the Welsh football team. Hours later, the Manics held a midnight signing at Virgin Megastore, which went on till 3.30 a.m. to accommodate 5,000 fans.

Incredibly though, its lead single, 'If You Tolerate This', was originally only deemed B-side status. With the album pretty much in the bag, the band were far more excited by 'Be Natural' (briefly touted as its first release). A great venture into sonic experimentation it may have been, with its sitar-like riffs, Hammond organ and melody horn, but 'Be Natural' certainly didn't have 'hit' written all over it.

It's only when Sony reps visited the studio that they pointed out the obvious potential of the song that had been cast aside. Thankfully, the band changed their mind.

It was Rob Stringer who recognised the greatness of 'Tolerate' and 'A Design for Life', and, having previously saved the Manics from being dropped by Sony, it was fitting that he broke the news:

> Running the record company meant I had access to the chart information. At first, I didn't tell them and I said, 'No news yet.' They were all sitting there waiting to get on the bus and looking really edgy. Then the hotel manager brought out three bottles of champagne with loads of glasses and I just smiled and said, 'It's No. 1,' and it was very, very emotional.[420]

In 1976, ABBA topped the charts with 'Fernando', a song about the Spanish Civil War, and now the Manics had achieved the same sixty years after the end of the conflict. In doing so, they also became the first Welsh act to have a No. 1 single since Shakin' Stevens with 'Merry Christmas Everyone' in 1985.

James Dean Bradfield said:

> I didn't recognise the weight or the prescience of the lyrics. Perhaps that took the pressure off trying to write the tune...I sat there one morning, absent-mindedly playing my J-45 acoustic guitar and it seemed like a really simple song – five or six chords.[421]

The band still weren't convinced though and Sean Moore in particular couldn't have been less enthused: 'It was one of the last things we recorded...I can remember saying, "I'll do three takes. I'm going to leave my car running, and when I'm finished, I'm going to get in my car and fuck off." And I did!'[422]

Bradfield felt there was an elusive magic element missing, and set a strange task at Rockfield for producer Dave Eringa: 'James just said to me, "It needs something like a comet flying through the sky." Then he went to dinner and left me and [keyboardist] Nick Naysmyth to try and come up with something.'[423]

The 'comet' was just one component in a long line that converged – the inspiration, lyric, video and delivery of 'Tolerate' couldn't have been better. Influenced by George Orwell's *Homage to Catalonia* and 'Spanish Bombs' by The Clash, and aptly written in Barcelona, its title came from a Republican poster of a child killed by Nationalist bomber planes. Plus, the line 'If I can shoot rabbits, then I can shoot fascists' derives from a comment made by a Welsh farmer. Like hundreds of Welshmen, he signed up to the International Brigades to aid Republican fighters in combat against Franco's military rebels.

'Tolerate' was both an instruction and a warning – to learn the lessons of the past and ensure that apathy never allows such horrors to happen again. Wire said to BBC Radio 2: 'The point I was making was directed at myself as well. I wouldn't have gone and joined an international brigade to fight in Bosnia…It's just the malaise of young people. I think we're more interested in our trainers than we are real issues.'[424]

One of Wire's most remarkable lyrics, it's also one of his proudest moments:

I genuinely fall in love with that song every time I hear it. Playing it in Barcelona on the Ramblas with 5,000 Spanish people singing that song was just truly an amazing moment.

It was Manic Street Preachers, *This Is My Truth Tell Me Yours* and 'If You Tolerate This Your Children Will Be Next.' In a world where words have been reduced, it was glorious to hear so many letters and vowels pronounced.[425]

The fact that 'Tolerate' was the longest titled No. 1 since Scott McKenzie's 'San Francisco (Be Sure to Wear Flowers in Your Hair)' in 1967 probably delighted Wire.

The promo video, directed by W.I.Z., is arguably the Manics' best ever, and included a snippet of the socialist anthem 'The Internationale', a popular Republican song during the war. Within a futuristic, sealed-off glass room, a prosthetic family without ears, eyes or mouths reflect the 'hear no evil, see no evil, speak no evil' oppression of living in a dictatorship.

One common misconception about 'Tolerate' is that it's about pacifism. Wire's persona may be a 'gutless wonder' ('I've walked Las Ramblas, but not with real intent') who couldn't shoot a rabbit, let alone a fascist. However, the song is actually saying that sometimes going to war is the only answer to stopping evil – quite simply, if you tolerate this (fascism), your children will be next. Somehow the far-right-leaning British National Party misconstrued this in March 2009. Without permission, they used it to soundtrack an article describing the 'violence, hatred, fragmentation and despair' wrought on London by the 'great multicultural experiment'.[426] Sony swiftly ordered them to take it down.

The BNP claimed the song had been mistakenly streamed and you could 'interpret the lyrics any way you want'. An exasperated Nicky Wire said: 'That's some kind of surrealist joke, just absolutely fucking baffling.'[427]

Along with its themes of Welshmen fighting Franco, 'Tolerate' wasn't the only reference to the band's homeland. In fact, *This Is My Truth* is the Manics' most quintessentially Welsh album, starting with its title.

One rainy Friday evening in 1998, Wire stood atop a mountain near his home at a service to commemorate the fiftieth anniversary of the National Health Service. Booming up from the hillside came quotes from its creator, Aneurin Bevan, and one phrase lodged in Wire's mind: 'This is my truth, tell me yours.'

'It was one of those moments,' he said. 'One of those epiphanies when things connect.'[428] Momentarily, he had an out-of-body experience: 'There's no way any other band in Britain would be doing anything remotely like this, no way in a fucking million years.'

One thing immediately noticeable from *This Is My Truth* is that it felt sombre and bruised. It has that Welsh air of the underdog, reflected in the Manics' heroes. As Keith Cameron said: 'But what of the inheritors of Bevan's torch? Today sees Benn, Scargill, even Kinnock, all marginalised; irritants and mavericks rather than major players. Good men one and all, but not winners.'[429]

At this point, Richey Edwards had been missing for three and a half years and this was their first album without any input from him. Yet, his 1994 quote to *Melody Maker* resonated: 'Where we come from, there's a natural melancholy in the air. Everybody, ever since you could comprehend it, felt pretty much defeated.'[430]

EVERY DAY WHEN I WAKE UP, I THANK THE LORD I'M WELSH!

It may have been harder in their earlier career to hear that the Manics were Welsh, but their surroundings definitely had an impact. Wire said to *The Guardian*:

> There's a lovely Welsh word, '*cynefin*', which means 'habitat'. It's the idea that there are factors in your environment that have an influence on you even if you don't realise it – your art, your language, even your religion. The Manic Street Preachers have been very influenced by our environment.[431]

The band's increasing comfort in their national identity wasn't an overnight process. As well as embracing '*Y Ddraig Goch*', Wire rediscovered his love of Wales during *Everything Must Go*. From his new house in Wattsville, he rejoiced in the poetry of R. S. Thomas and Dylan Thomas, plus the landscape art of Kyffin Williams.

Furthermore, David Evans claims that *The Holy Bible* was 'drenched in Welsh drizzle':

> Richey's lyrics allude to economic ruin, social decay and cultural loss. The Welsh have a word for this sort of compulsion to look back – '*hiraeth*'. [It] encompasses a sombre palette of emotions including 'grief or sadness after the lost or departed, longing, yearning, nostalgia', as well as wistful homesickness.
>
> There's another Welsh word – '*hwyl*', which denotes inspiration and energy…Richey's melancholy, reflective lyrics are punctuated by others that thrum with *hwyl*, in which he is alive to possibility, flexing his lyrical muscles and using his command of language to create anew.[432]

Still so anguished by their friend's disappearance, the Manics adopted another 'non-image' artwork for *This Is My Truth*. Borrowing the bareness of a Welsh beach from Echo and the Bunnymen's *Heaven Up Here* (shot at Porthcawl), the Manics opted for Black Rock Sands near Porthmadog.

The Welsh references came thick and fast thereon. Opening track 'The Everlasting' recalled choral singing of hymns like 'The Old Rugged Cross'. 'You Stole the Sun from My Heart' referenced R. S. Thomas's collection *No Truce with the Furies*, and one of his poems,

'Reflections', was included on the album's sleeve. The song's theme of homesickness while on tour once again captured feelings of *hiraeth*.

'Tsunami' was about the 'Silent Twins', June and Jennifer Gibbons of Haverfordwest, who only communicated with each other and were later admitted to Broadmoor psychiatric hospital. A poem about their lives, 'We Two Made One', was featured line by line in its video. In 'Nobody Loved You', Wire even referenced Spillers and the carrier bags of records he and Richey would return home with after trips to Cardiff.

Like Tystion, the Manics also wrote about the 1965 Tryweryn flooding of Capel Celyn on 'Ready for Drowning'. Families lost their homes, and had to decide whether to have bodies of dead relatives disinterred from the local cemetery or abandon them. When the reservoir dried up due to droughts in the 1980s and early '90s, the village became visible again. Inspired by R. S. Thomas's 'Reservoirs', the song's echoey chapel organ motif sounds both funereal and submerged in water. Wire said: 'It's that idea of the serenity of the reservoir, but underneath you have all this decay and loss of culture.'[433]

There's also a metaphorical meaning to 'drowning' relating to the destructive alcoholism of Welsh stars like Dylan Thomas, Rachel Roberts and Richard Burton (whose voice is sampled from the 1978 film *The Medusa Touch* in the song). Coincidentally, Burton's first movie role in 1949, *The Last Days of Dolwyn*, revolved around the flooding of a Welsh village. Lastly, the song mentions Patagonia, where over 2,500 Welsh people emigrated in the late nineteenth century to protect their native language and culture, which they felt was threatened in their homeland.

Away from all the Welshness was 'You're Tender and You're Tired', which included arguably Bradfield's best vocal of the album before finishing with an unexpected whistling solo. Meanwhile, 'South Yorkshire Mass Murderer' could've been one of Wire's bravest lyrics with its criticism of the police in its handling of the Hillsborough disaster. Yet with its vague conclusion, it ends up pulling its punches. The title was abbreviated to 'S.Y.M.M.' on the sleeve too – presumably for fear of legal action.

Elsewhere, there were three of Wire's most personal, introspective lyrics. With a title borrowed from a Winston Churchill quote, 'Black Dog on My Shoulder' juxtaposed an upbeat, jaunty rhythm against his travails with depression. 'My Little Empire' was Wire's ode to domestication, while 'Born a Girl' examined his gender confusion:

> I have in my time, loved dressing up in women's clothes. I can't say I'm desperate to be a woman, but sometimes I feel it would've been a bit easier if I'd been born one…And let's be honest, a large percentage of our fans prefer to see me in a dress.'[434]

Over a sparse arrangement akin to Jeff Buckley's 'Hallelujah', the masculine Bradfield was tasked with singing Wire's words, which he accepted without any qualms. That didn't stop oafish laddism rearing its ugly head though, as he told *Classic Rock* in 2018:

> Success really propositioned Nicky intellectually. He would be onstage in his skirt, socks and eyeliner…Suddenly having a more general populace in front of him sometimes shouting, 'Who's the queer on the bass?'…He'd never had that before because he'd had the faithful in front of him.
>
> On *This Is My Truth*, a lot more casual record buyers were bedded into our audience and they were like, 'Why are you wearing that skirt, you big poofter?' And he's looking into the crowd going, 'How dare you say that to me? That's not what one of our crowd says.'[435]

Mining the same seam of late twentieth-century melancholia/ 'millenncholia' as *Urban Hymns* and *OK Computer*, it's surprising how many reviewers misunderstood the glacial, alienated bleakness *This Is My Truth* set out to achieve, and used it as a criticism.

NME said: 'If it had a posture, it would be shoulders hunched forward, head slumped, the body language of the vanquished… resigned, insecure, lacking confidence.'[436]

Uncut remarked how 'Bradfield has reined in his usual strained bellowing, sounding ever more like Freddie Mercury clothed in designer despair'.[437]

Simon Price joked: '"Tolerate" may have seemed a strangely muted choice for a single, but in the context of *This Is My Truth*, it was practically "Wake Me Up Before You Go-Go"'.[438]

Yes, the album is top-heavy and the second half is too midtempo, but *This Is My Truth* has moments of sheer elation up there with any Manics record. 'You Stole the Sun from My Heart' may be a bit 'Marmite' amongst the faithful, but to this day it is an unashamedly anthemic live staple. The rising repetition of 'in between' on 'Tsunami' is trademark Manics euphoria, while the goosebump-inducing outro to 'Tolerate' is utterly breathtaking (with a multitracked vocal delivery akin to a Welsh male choir).

In less than a year, the optimism of New Labour had started to dissipate. Tony Blair adorned the cover of *NME* in March 1998 next to a Johnny Rotten-inspired headline: 'Welfare to Work, Student Tuition Fees, No Debate on Drugs, Curfews…EVER HAD THE FEELING YOU'VE BEEN CHEATED?'

Uncut applauded the Manics' dignity in the face of such disappointment:

> *This Is My Truth* feels like a work of fierce intelligence and principle…The first Manics opus of our education-slashing Blairite era sounds more than ever like a hymn to old Labour values: moralistic, class-conscious and in its own way, conservative.
>
> For a guitar band to bring such topics to rock's increasingly bare ideological table without making arses of themselves is justification enough for their existence.[439]

Now reaching the heady heights of being one of the biggest bands in the country, the Manics were quick to bat aside accusations of selling out. This was the same band who always wanted to be huge and signed to Sony in 1991 before their debut album was released. Bradfield said:

> Since Richey has gone missing, it's ridiculous that people don't actually spot that a lot of what we've achieved since then is what he stood for. A song like 'If You Tolerate This' – a song that got to No. 1, a song that used the past to illuminate what was missing in the present.[440]

Who could begrudge the Manics this success after all they had been through? The fact they had been originally ridiculed for coming from

Wales, and now topped the charts with an album so inspired by their homeland, made the success all the sweeter.

It also allowed them to release 2013's *Rewind the Film,* which could be considered a sister album to *This Is My Truth.* A collection of earthy folk songs with titles like 'This Sullen Welsh Heart' and 'Manorbier', it included the lead single 'Show Me the Wonder', where the band addressed the Welsh language for the first time on a record.

Richey Edwards's negative views of the Welsh language were well documented, but the Manics are from the generation who came of age during a *Cymraeg* resurgence. Speaking the mother tongue represented authority and authenticity, which perhaps prompted feelings of inadequacy in non-Welsh speakers.

If that was the case with the Manics, they certainly didn't show it – escaping a nation seemingly without a future before ultimately crafting their own. As Alun Hamnett wrote in *Record Collector,* their music 'slapped an oxygen mask on an alternative form of national pride – one that is complex and fractured, but no less profound… They may write in English, but their *truth* remains in Wales'.[441]

LEAVING THE TWENTIETH CENTURY

WALES AT THE DAWN OF THE NEW MILLENNIUM

If 1997 represented devolution at long last, 1999 marked the miraculous peak of the nation's growth and confidence across the decade.

Two years prior, Ron Davies may have announced the 'very good morning in Wales', but at the dawn of the new millennium it's no exaggeration to say that the eyes of the world were on Wales.

For the first time in over 600 years, Wales had its own parliament with the National Assembly in Cardiff. The Welsh capital was also proving to be a cosmopolitan capital city that was the envy of Europe, and where prestigious events like the Rugby World Cup were staged (and the FA Cup Final from 2001–6).

Not since the 1960s had Wales been such a thriving tourist attraction. Previously popular for dodgems and donkey rides at Trecco Bay or Butlin's at Barry Island, Wales' first five-star getaway opened in January 1999 at St David's Hotel. It was based within the newly renamed Cardiff Bay (after Tiger Bay had fallen on hard times). A multimillion-pound makeover saw the introduction of bars, restaurants and entertainment complexes, giving the area a European vibe. The fact that visitors were now prepared to spend upwards of £400 a night highlighted Wales's transformation.

The lure of Wales was irresistible even amid the glitz and glamour of Hollywood. That same year The Big Sleep, a 'designer budget hotel' part-owned by John Malkovich, opened on the edge of the city centre opposite Cardiff International Arena.

Simultaneously, home-grown stars were making waves in Tinseltown. Rhys Ifans is most fondly remembered in his homeland for the eternally quotable cult classic *Twin Town* from 1997. Directed in Port Talbot and Swansea by Kevin Allen (brother and uncle to Keith and Lily Allen respectively), the dark comedy revolved around the notorious Lewis twins portrayed by Ifans and his actual younger sibling, Llŷr. Yet it was Ifans's 1999 role in *Notting Hill* that made him a household name, albeit in his Y-fronts.

Likewise, Catherine Zeta-Jones starred in *The Mask of Zorro*, alongside onscreen father Anthony Hopkins, before dipping between lasers in the crime caper *Entrapment*. The Swansea-born star closed out the millennium by getting engaged to Michael Douglas on New Year's Eve. She later acknowledged her Welsh roots when winning a BAFTA for Best Supporting Actress for her role in 2002's *Chicago*: 'To my mam and dad in Swansea, south Wales – oggy oggy oggy, oi oi oi!'

Meanwhile, Ioan Gruffudd secured himself a cameo in *Titanic* and starred in Paul Morrison's Oscar-nominated *Solomon & Gaenor*. Plus, Justin Kerrigan's 1999 coming-of-age comedy drama, *Human Traffic*, captured the hedonistic thrills of a drug-fuelled weekend in Cardiff.

There was a further trio of renowned Welsh movies made during the '90s starting with the 1992 anti-war biopic *Hedd Wyn*, which was nominated for an Oscar.

Set in a Welsh mining village, Marc Evans's 1997 *House of America* won Best Directorial Debut at the Stockholm International Film Festival. Also released that year was Julian Richards's *Darklands* – a foreboding horror flick hailed by WalesOnline as a 'Welsh *Wicker Man*'.[442]

The Welsh accent was also becoming ubiquitous as a familiar part of Britain's daily teatime TV viewing via Bridgend-born broadcaster Huw Edwards on the *BBC Six O'Clock News*. Plus, Merthyr Tydfil fashion designer Julien Macdonald was dominating catwalks with his showstopping dresses worn by the likes of Naomi Campbell and Jodie Kidd.

In sport, Cardiff sprinter Colin Jackson won a host of gold medals throughout the decade including two World Championships. He responded to anti-Welsh discrimination by draping himself in '*Y Ddraig Goch*' after races. Known as 'The Pride of Wales', Newbridge boxer Joe Calzaghe amassed an impressive 27–0 win–loss record by the end of the '90s – including an upset victory over Chris Eubank – on his way to an incredible fifteen-year 46–0 undefeated career.

Featuring Morriston-born England international spin bowler Robert Croft, Glamorgan County Cricket Club won the County Championship in 1997, while 'The Welsh Dragon' Matthew Stevens went on to win the snooker Masters in 2000 and the UK Championship in 2003. The less said about Welsh football, the better, even if the '90s squad did feature a world-class quartet of Ian Rush, Ryan Giggs, Neville Southall and Mark Hughes, plus the late, great Gary Speed.

Then there was rugby union. Wales had an indifferent decade with a sole Five Nations Championship in 1994 sandwiched between 'wooden spoon' campaigns in 1990 and 1995. The opening line to 'Cwm Rhondda' asked for guidance from a 'Great Redeemer' and one arrived in the form of Graham Henry, who masterminded a ten-game winning streak in 1999 including victories over France and South Africa.

Most memorable was an April 1999 'home' encounter with 'The Old Enemy' at Wembley while the £121 million Millennium Stadium was being built. The mere mention of *that* last-minute winning try by Scott Gibbs against England still makes many a Welsh rugby fan go doe-eyed – a moment of jinking genius up there with Gareth Edwards's best. Wales's 32–31 victory not only gave Scotland the Five Nations Championship, but also denied England a twelfth grand slam.

Welsh music continued to thrive with No. 1 albums for Catatonia, Stereophonics and Tom Jones, while the Manics headlined Glastonbury. In 1999, the trio staged three of the biggest gigs of their career on home soil, with a combined attendance figure of nearly 140,000.

The 'Cool Cymru' tag may not have been for everyone, but Wales was now in control of its own destiny in terms of music, culture, sport, language and politics.

———

After hours of torrential rain, sludgy mud and trench-like toilets, the wait at Margam Park in May 1999 was finally over. Cerys Matthews, overwhelmed and ecstatic, sauntered onstage in a silver-sequinned crop top and skirt. 'When I was a little girl, I dreamed I would come back and haunt this place…It's nice to do it before I've died.'

The Guardian later observed: 'It was the sort of Twentieth Century Fox entrance at which Matthews excels.'[443]

Their biggest-ever gig, it was the third and final leg of Catatonia's Home Internationals, which had also seen them conquer the Llangollen International Pavilion on consecutive nights the previous weekend. Furthermore, the band were back at No. 1 with their third album, *Equally Cursed and Blessed*.

Compered by comedian Phill Jupitus, the Margam support bill featured Richard Parfitt, Big Leaves, Scouse indie icons Shack, ABBA tribute Björn Again and Ian Brown.

In 1990, Brown's band had staged their era-defining Spike Island gig, while Catatonia later promised a debut album as good as *The Stone Roses*. Now here they were hosting a massive show with the Roses' frontman supporting *them*. As John Harris said: 'Back in 1994 they'd meant it, and in a roundabout way, they'd pulled it off. In Welsh, that's called *"cyfiawnhad"* (vindication).'[444] Even English journalists were using the formerly much-maligned Welsh language.

Unfortunately, the early glorious sunshine gave way to a biblical downpour that descended two hours before the gates opened and churned the ground into a swamp.

Nothing could dampen the spirits of the band though, who had chosen Margam Park for sentimental reasons, being regular visitors with family and friends. In the run-up, Cerys referred to the town's smouldering skyline of steelworks and smoking chimneys, which apparently inspired Ridley Scott's sci-fi classic *Blade Runner*: 'Port Talbot's got one of the most beautiful sights at night because it's got a huge oil refinery. It looks futuristic with lots of lights and tall buildings and flames. We're playing opposite. It's got a kind of natural amphitheatre kind of thing.'[445]

Across ninety minutes, Catatonia reeled off a greatest-hits set with aplomb. The most spine-tingling moment came when the old and new worlds of Welsh music meshed seamlessly. Brian Wright described it in *To Hell and Back with Catatonia*:

> The Pontarddulais Male Voice Choir sang a haunting, un-accompanied introduction to 'Mulder and Scully'. There was a slight pause – Aled drummed in, the guitars ripped the evening air apart and Cerys cruised in from backstage. She was like a

Spanish galleon in full rigging cutting through the sparkling ocean, bringing home the spoils of battle.

She smiled in sheer delight as she neared the front of the stage, to be met by a wall of sound as the crowd sang as one, 'I'd rather be liberated'. It happened in seconds, but that moment will last my lifetime.[446]

As tears rolled down her cheeks, Cerys was given another almighty accompaniment for the rousing finale of 'International Velvet' – the 30,000-voice Margam Park Choir.

Select said:

Maybe it's the way the screens, lights and crowd allow Catatonia to look – for the first time in their history – genuinely heroic. Perhaps it's the fact that you would be hard pushed to find a group who've played a gig this big after mid-career chapters involving such crushing frustration as theirs.[447]

David Owens added:

Cerys was personality personified playing up to the crowd with her cheeky chit-chat and matey bonhomie…That she swigged from a wine bottle, drunkenly danced like you or I would after a few too many only heightened the human aspects of her personality and the everyman – and woman – appeal of the band.[448]

Catatonia's profile had never been bigger, and in Cerys they had a megastar gracing front covers from *NME* to *FHM*. Previously wearing tracksuits and known as the 'Queen of the Council Estates' (much to her chagrin), Cerys was now a Welsh national treasure decked in designer dresses.

If any further confirmation was needed that Cerys and Catatonia were massive, it was that they got the *French and Saunders* parody treatment. While highlights of the Margam gig were broadcast in Wales over the late May bank holiday weekend, there was also a bit of national TV velvet as Dawn French sang 'Cymru Pride'. Aided by an ample supply of lager, wine, whisky and ciggies, its chorus went:

'Don't mess with me, I'm a working-class Taffy'. At the start of the decade, such a piss-take would've rankled the Welsh population. Now it was recognition of how far Catatonia (and the country) had come.

Like Madonna, Cerys no longer required a surname. Her aim was to become a 'dirtier version of Celine Dion',[449] and such was her crossover appeal that the media, from women's weeklies and teenager mags to tabloid gossip columns and broadsheets, were falling over themselves to accurately describe her. *Select* hailed her as a 'rasping Janis Joplin gone pop',[450] while *The Edge* fanzine called Cerys 'a tight-trousered Minnie Mouse on helium'.[451]

The Guardian claimed she was the most engaging singer to hit the charts since Blondie, while *The Independent* labelled her 'Debbie Harry without the discipline'.[452] Plus, there was the ever-inimitable Steven Wells in *NME*: 'Cerys' voice sounds exactly like Shirley Bassey puking five pints of Jack Daniel's (with snakebite chasers) into the Grand Canyon through a megaphone during an earthquake.'[453]

———

By the time of their Margam Park triumph, Catatonia fans were already well versed in the new songs. With the nation still in an elated (and inebriated) state after Wales's last-gasp win over England, the band unveiled their third album the following morning.

Those able to shake off their hangovers and head to the shops didn't regret it. Considering their relentless release schedule and twenty-two months of constant touring, a knackered band could've been forgiven for chucking out something half-hearted. The fact that *Equally Cursed and Blessed* sold 300,000 compared to the 1 million of *International Velvet* perhaps suggested they were oversaturating the mainstream and could've benefited from a break.

But while it was less consistently brilliant than its predecessor, Catatonia's third record was a more varied release. David Owens said:

> While *International Velvet* was angst and turmoil painted in bright pop colours, *Equally Cursed and Blessed* has a more thoughtful, pared-down approach in equal parts wistful and elegant, downbeat and reflective…Far warmer, sunnier and humorous than past efforts.[454]

Regardless of the drop-off in sales, the album reached No. 1 – their second chart-topper in less than a year. Even more impressive was that they held off stiff competition from one of the biggest-selling albums ever to do so: a reissued *ABBA Gold*.

Such was Catatonia's popularity that all three of their albums were in the Top 40. Woolworths allowed fans a copy of *Way Beyond Blue* for a fiver when buying the new record, which catapulted it to No. 32. Plus, *International Velvet* was still so alluring for music fans, it sprang to No. 36.

The majestic lead single, 'Dead from the Waist Down', also topped the midweek charts before eventually settling at No. 7. Placed as the album's opening track, the lushness of its Bacharach-like orchestral sweep was aided by a great video. Despite demoing the album while touring the States, Catatonia weren't in Kansas anymore (more like a west London studio). Yet that didn't stop Cerys hamming it up as a less innocent Dorothy in homage to *The Wizard of Oz*. It had more serious notes too: at a time of the Kosovo conflict, its chorus line of 'make hay, not war' resonated more than ever.

The song reflected the album's overall theme of hope over adversity. Its artwork depicted a fight of Good versus Evil as an unknowing chicken is stalked by a fox. Plus, the album's title was lifted from a lyric in 'She's a Millionaire', which explored the joys and perils of fame and fortune.

Regardless of all the success, problems persisted with Warner. The band's choice of second single was the straightforward pop of 'Karaoke Queen' (eventually released in November 1999). Yet, the label insisted it should be 'Londinium', which writ large Mark's disdain for the English capital – a strange choice considering it risked alienating London-based fans.

Elsewhere, 'Bulimic Beats' addressed eating disorders and the media obsession with body image (a juxtaposition with 'I'd rather stay single and thin' on 'Mulder and Scully'). Plus, there was the rabble-rousing, royalty-baiting 'Storm the Palace', which had provided an edgy opener to their recent gigs. Producer TommyD pinned pics of the Queen Mother onto the walls at Monnow Valley while recording it, to conjure the requisite amount of rage after it was leaked that she had a £1 million overdraft.

Like the Manics, Catatonia refused to play at the National Assembly for Wales's inaugural Voices of a Nation concert due to the Queen being in attendance. It would've been worth the price of admission alone to hear them singing 'Repeat' and 'Storm the Palace' respectively (ironically, Cerys accepted an MBE in 2014 for services to music).

Fortunately, the reaction to *Equally Cursed and Blessed* wasn't equally positive and negative. In fact, Mark Beaumont at *NME* was the lone voice of dissent (at one point even referring to the group as the 'Disneyland house band'):

> There are no road rages here, no dead gangsters, no pregnancy scares. No real pain to speak of at all…Around half of *Equally Cursed and Blessed* is insipid orchestral indie-pop fluff…The overwhelming stench is of money…A few more hits, you fear, and Catatonia could be dead from the bank balance up.[455]

Such criticism was lost amid a deluge of positivity. *Welsh Bands Weekly* awarded it 11/10. *Melody Maker* described it as sounding 'like nobody else matters',[456] while *Maxim* said: 'This album is more blessed than cursed.'[457]

———

The promotional campaign for Stereophonics' *Performance and Cocktails* started with a bumpy boat ride – not aboard a scenic cruise ship as the album's swanky title might suggest.

Instead, the band were bombarded with explosions as they sailed along the River Kwai – this really was *Apocalypse Now!*

Inspired by Kelly Jones's love of scriptwriting, the songs on Stereophonics' second album followed a more cinematic direction. The videos for *Word Gets Around* hadn't really caught MTV's eye, so the promos to accompany the new singles would be tributes to Kelly's favourite films.

Therefore, the shoot for 'The Bartender and the Thief' was a tribute to Francis Ford Coppola's 1979 war epic. The video's director, Pinko, recalled:

> The track had this really American rock feel and for some reason, I just thought of the scene in *Apocalypse Now* where the Playboy Bunnies arrive on floating pontoons in the jungle to play to the troops.

> There's a quick performance, then the crowd goes mental and they have to make their escape on a helicopter and disappear…As fate would have it, the band were in Thailand on a promotional tour.[458]

Filmed over twenty-four hours of mosquitos and monsoon rain, the director even risked life and limb:

> We go up to do our helicopter shots of the band below…We're flying around and suddenly the helicopter goes out of control. The engine splutters and all we can see is the fire…Then the helicopter flips the other way, but I wasn't on a harness…
>
> I was literally thinking of jumping and hoping I landed in the river, but something in the back of my head told me that helicopter blades go round quite fast. We finally landed in this bit of wasteland in total darkness.[459]

Kelly added:

> We're sitting there playing cards hoping that the aerial shots are working out when suddenly it sounds like Armageddon…These three explosions go off and it was like, 'Fucking hell,' and all your hair gets singed. In the video, you see the three of us just turning around in a state of shock. We thought it was fucking Vietnam![460]

Another reason for the shift into a more filmic songwriting style was that Kelly couldn't continue reeling off tales of tittle-tattle in Cwmaman once he had become a star. Quite simply, he was no longer 'standing at the bus stop with his shopping in his hands overhearing elderly ladies as the rumours start to fly'.

He said in 1998:

> We've matured a lot as a band and as musicians, writing-wise and lyrically, it's not so much all small-town stories anymore. It's more like 'Not Up to You' and 'Traffic' – that sort of train-of-thought writing, rather than having a beginning, middle and end…
>
> The new record is obviously about different people, different places, different countries, different situations, but it's still all about things we've experienced.[461]

The new approach certainly worked. *Performance and Cocktails* surged to No. 1 in March 1999 and went on to sell over 2.5 million copies. It was nominated for the Mercury Prize and a BRIT Award, and all five of its singles were Top 20 with three landing in the Top 5. Its film-poster-like cover photo of a disinterested woman kissing her boyfriend was taken by Scarlet Page (daughter of Led Zeppelin's Jimmy Page), and was inspired by Annie Leibovitz's shot of lovers outside a prison.

Written in an Amsterdam hotel room and previously called 'The List', 'Just Looking' contemplated fulfilling life's expectations and chasing dreams. Featuring a slowed-down version of the riff recycled from 'Goldfish Bowl', it was an anomaly in that its video wasn't inspired by film. Instead, the cinematic theme continued on the next single, 'Pick a Part That's New', with a nod to *The Italian Job*.

Originally intended as a 'cheesy B-side with a big brass section',[462] the title for 'I Wouldn't Believe Your Radio' came via Ringo Starr singing it to Kelly in a dream. In keeping with the drummer theme, Kelly wanted Stuart on vocals (this version ended up as a B-side). The chosen film this time was *Easy Rider* as the band swept through the sweltering desert on motorcycles. Another Beatles influence came via the *Magical Mystery Tour*-inspired title of 'Roll Up and Shine'. Kelly's elongated pronunciation of 'shine' also echoed those Fab Four copyists Oasis in Liam's vocal delivery on 'Cigarettes & Alcohol'.

Completing the filmed-themed promo videos was 'Hurry Up and Wait', which saw the boys parodying the war comedy drama *M*A*S*H*. Featuring a title coined by Kelly's brother Kevin, it was a lyrical counterpart to 'Just Looking' in its ruminations of life's anxieties. 'When you see everyone around you having kids, buying houses and settling down, you wonder how long you have to wait,' said Kelly. 'It's that idea of what life should be that seems to be drummed into everybody.'[463]

Elsewhere, 'She Takes Her Clothes Off' stemmed from one of the Phonics' earliest punky demos before evolving into a more mellow tune following an acoustic radio session. Like 'Last of the Big Time Drinkers', 'T-Shirt Sun Tan' captured that typically British vibe of boozing outdoors as soon as summer arrives.

The most cinematic lyric was saved for last on 'I Stopped to Fill My Car Up', accompanied by an unsettling 'Imagine' piano riff played backwards. Devouring a diet of Kubrick, Hitchcock and Tarantino on tour, Kelly's lyrics for the album's finale featured a homicidal hitchhiker. The character was inspired by a college acquaintance's experience of a petrol station carjacking, and Kelly's fears of similar happening to him while driving on the unlit A470 at Abercynon.

Performance and Cocktails garnered slightly mixed reviews including the perennial 'meat and potatoes' criticism. *Pitchfork* took aim at its anthems moulded for mass singalongs, while *Rolling Stone* suggested Stereophonics were inferior versions of their contemporaries, describing them as 'a dumbed-down Radiohead with Oasis bravado'.[464]

Regardless, the album was an overwhelming success. On its first day alone, *Performance and Cocktails* sold 45,000 copies. By the end of the week, it was outselling Robbie Williams and The Corrs on its way to a total of 120,000.

Johnny Cigarettes of *NME* said:

> Kelly Jones dares to tell stories, which is something his impressionistic contemporaries could learn from. He deals in the beauty, sadness and bad craziness of commonplace things everyone else thinks aren't worth a second glance.[465]

Melody Maker added that the album had tunes 'so rich and deep that even the hardest of men will be weeping openly into their beer'.[466]

Such was the popularity of *Performance and Cocktails* that it re-entered the UK charts five years later, reaching No. 25 in January 2004.

In two short years from 1996–8, Stereophonics had gone from performing their first headline gig as a signed band to 400 people at Cardiff University to playing in front of 10,000 fans at Cardiff Castle.

What they had planned next was even more astounding. In fact, it was five times the size. With 50,000 crammed into Morfa Stadium, the event on 31 July 1999 was the biggest outdoor summer party south Wales had ever seen. It was also the final farewell to the Landore-based athletics ground, which was demolished soon after. The announcement for the gig also highlighted that the stadium, built on the former site of a steelworks, had been chosen for its links to the south Walian working classes that so often featured in their music.

A month prior to Morfa, the Phonics tested their match fitness at Wembley Stadium. At the Toxic Twin Towers Ball, the band formed part of a support line-up for headliners Aerosmith, alongside The Black Crowes, Lenny Kravitz and 3 Colours Red.

The event proved to be a baptism of fire. Reeling from their surreal surroundings, an ashen-faced and nauseous Kelly Jones couldn't settle all night – from meeting Noel Gallagher side-stage to being too nervous to ask Chris Robinson to sign his records. Not so long ago, Kelly had been performing Black Crowes covers in The Ivy Bush.

The band remained in shock weeks later, but this time it was with astonishment at their transformation in fortunes. Arriving backstage at Morfa, Kelly said: 'The one thing I noticed on the way here is that all the digital road signs are saying, "Diverted traffic due to pop concert". I was thinking, "We're doing all this."'[467]

When the promoter first suggested it could be a sell-out, Kelly's only response was to laugh with disbelief. 'As we were waiting by the side of the stage to go on, this thought came into my head – "Everyone here knows my name. That's a lot of people!" Then I went, "Right, I need a vodka!"'[468]

Manic Street Preachers may have espoused culture, alienation, boredom and despair, but it was the Blackwood boys Stuart Cable and Richard Jones turned to for some pre-gig relaxation. The night before the big day, they only wanted to get drunk watching a Manics tribute act.

Unlike Catatonia at Margam Park, the weather gods offered idyllic sunshine and scorching heat. A carnival atmosphere included a funfair, bike shows, tattooists and tug-of-war contests, plus football and rugby tournaments, all for under £20 a ticket!

The jovial mood was shared by the band, who at one point amazed the hordes when Kelly and keyboardist Tony Kirkham dashed through the crowd with Stuart spreadeagled on a stretcher. Thankfully, the trio were all sporting Cheshire-cat grins and there was nothing wrong with the drummer.

With the temperature ratcheting into the nineties, support sets from The Crocketts, Gay Dad, Reef and AC/DC tribute act AB/CD warmed the crowd up even further.

When the band emerged, Kelly was resplendent in the same white shirt he'd worn at the Coliseum Theatre gig three years previously when the band didn't even have management, let alone a record deal.

With the sun finally setting, the band chose to ease themselves into proceedings. Reminiscing with WalesOnline in 2018, Kelly said: 'I remember opening up the show with "Hurry Up and Wait". We decided on a mid tempo number because had we kicked off with something fast like "Bartender and the Thief", it would've all gone off the rails very early on.'[469]

'Bartender' came up next anyway with Stuart Cable launching his flat cap into the audience and drumming maniacally – equal parts Keith Moon and Animal from *The Muppets*. The setlist covered most of *Word Gets Around* and *Performance and Cocktails*, and the crowd hung on Kelly's every word. Here was a small-town storyteller that could relate to the masses.

The gig's understated beginning was echoed in set-closer 'I Stopped to Fill My Car Up' – a strangely subdued choice, which nevertheless progressed into an extended wig-out as fireworks exploded.

Morfa wasn't just a key moment in Welsh music history, but a major milestone for Stereophonics, consolidating the success of *Performance and Cocktails* and setting them on a run of five consecutive No. 1 albums between 1999 and 2007.

Kelly continued to WalesOnline: 'A lot of the people who came to our gigs back then are still turning up now, except they're bringing their kids with them too. It's quite possible some of them were conceived the weekend of that Morfa show!'[470]

———

Much of the subsequent media coverage of Morfa didn't focus on its success, but what happened during the encore.

The uproar started on 21 August 1999 when *NME* asked the ludicrous question 'Is Wales the new Germany?'[471] An English reader wrote into the magazine's letters page stating that the nationalist fervour surrounding the gig 'bordered on fascism'.[472] He also accused Stereophonics of inciting the partisan crowd into hating the English.

As the band wrapped up their set, Kelly returned with an acoustic guitar to sing 'As Long as We Beat the English' (later omitted from the VHS and DVD). Behind him was a montage of Wales's greatest rugby tries including Scott Gibbs's recent match-winner. Not all the clips were against England – there was Gareth Edwards's lung-busting effort against Scotland in 1972, and '*that* try' the following year for the Barbarians against the All Blacks.

Regardless, the footage sent the fans into a frenzy including Edwards himself, who was in attendance with other Welsh sporting greats like Ieuan Evans, Ian Rush and Joe Calzaghe.

The controversial song dated back to April 1999 when Kelly was filmed for a BBC Wales advert promoting the forthcoming Wales–England Five Nations clash. He wasn't impressed by the subsequent accusations flung his way by the *NME*, especially given the lyrics' origins.

> That song was commissioned by an English guy at the BBC. He said, 'Will you write a song called "As Long as We Beat the English"?' I said, 'You've got to be joking...'
>
> I went home and left it at that...I had this B-side tune on the go. I woke up one morning and eight lines came onto this piece of paper...I wanted to make it a chant sort of thing. I thought, 'Shall I? Shan't I?' So, I ended up recording it.[473]

The cartoon version of the ad featured (Graham) Henry's Heroes bumping into the band busking on the street as Kelly launches into his new enemy-baiting tune. But Kelly didn't have his cartoon alter ego to hide behind for the real-life version. Politely declining the request to sing it outside Twickenham, he agreed to record the clip in Chiswick.

Kelly said:

> That went on the telly, and we did beat England for the first time in I don't know how long! I was in the workingmen's club and the advert came on after and everybody just went mental.
>
> So, when it comes to Morfa, Gareth Edwards was there and we were doing this celebration rugby thing at the end...It was a celebration of people that we felt had done something for the country...I said, 'We'll do that song just for the craic.' Looking back now, I shouldn't have done it really. I played the song and the crowd went barmy. There were probably 49,800 Welsh people![474]

Presiding over the *NME* letters page was James Oldham, who responded: 'There's a thin line between patriotism and nationalism, and the moment you start waving a national flag around you're in danger of tripping over it.'[475]

Oldham also pointed out that race-related attacks in south Wales had risen significantly of late, so inciting such agitation wasn't wise. After years of anti-Welsh headlines, though, it seemed *NME* didn't like it now the shoe was on the other foot. Kelly lamented that it felt like manufactured outrage, and the first line of the song is even 'We don't want to be your enemy'.

> It did put a dampener on the ending really because it was in all the Welsh papers as well, especially the headline saying 'Nazis'.[476]

As the *Western Mail* boomed: 'Apparently it's not OK for the Welsh to be too vocal about their Welshness…And we should rise above the fact that verbal Taffy-bashing is still such a popular pastime over the bridge.'[477]

In the immediate aftermath, the Phonics refused to comment, so *NME* reached out to other Welsh musicians. Megan Childs said she didn't believe their celebration of Welshness had spilled into nationalism, while Tom Jones voiced concern that Welsh pride could be misconstrued as xenophobia.

Daf Ieuan didn't have time for any kind of tub-thumping: '[This thing of] "We're Welsh, we're so great" – it's no different from that Britpop attitude. It's not good *because* it's Welsh.'[478]

Cerys Matthews couldn't understand what all the fuss was about. At Catatonia's headline set at Pilton Village Fete, she randomly linked the furore with the '90s outbreak of 'mad cow disease': 'So, what's all this about Welsh nationalism? I'm no nationalist. I just say eat British beef and you'll be OK!'

A war of words between the band and *NME* followed. When Stereophonics finally released a statement rebuking the magazine's attitude towards the gig in September 1999, it included cheeky digs highlighting their pride in being one of *Britain's* most successful new bands and global exports. In response, *NME* editor Steve Sutherland said they had always enthusiastically supported Stereophonics and that they had never claimed that the band were racist. They did at least seem to thank the band for clarifying that they had not been intentionally stirring up anti-English sentiment.

———

Ever pushing the boundaries of their sound, the Furries returned in June 1999 with their most experimental work yet, *Guerrilla*.

A pun on the band's name, the album's title encapsulated their rebel spirit and resonated in the wake of the recent NATO bombing of Yugoslavia. The Furries also reiterated their stance of non-violent direct action to ensure nobody read any crass, militaristic statements into their intentions.

At the demo sessions in north Wales, the band embraced serendipity by tinkering with an array of electronic gadgets and allowed the music to dictate itself. As they rode their 'new, multicoloured synth foot pedals like jet skis',[479] the sound of one song came to them by fluke. Ric Rawlins explained:

> During a tea break, Bunf slipped and crashed into his guitars, knocking over an amp in the process. By chance, Cian's microphone had not only recorded this commotion, but fed it automatically into his sampler.
>
> Listening back, the band were impressed by its weird, clanging qualities, and after Cian looped the sample, Daf kicked in with a breakbeat. Suddenly, the bare bones of an anthemic rhythm were in place. 'We'll keep that,' nodded the drummer, as Gruff wrote down a provisional title of 'Mobile Phone'.[480]

Parodying a title of a Paul Young chart-topper from 1983, the song morphed into 'Wherever I Lay My Phone (That's My Home)'. With a techno sound akin to Daft Punk, *Pitchfork* loved its 'floor-slapping LSD-infused electronica',[481] while *Spin* called it 'a psycho ward of tweaked noises'.[482] The Furries fancied the idea of a novelty hit single that captured the late '90s obsession with mobile phone radiation melting your brain. Yet, their plans were scuppered when Jimmy Cauty and Guy Pratt, under the name Solid Gold Chartbusters, released 'I Wanna 1-2-1 With You', which heavily sampled the Nokia ringtone.

For the main recording sessions, the band decamped to rural Wiltshire and Real World Studios, owned by Peter Gabriel. Housed within a spaceship-style glass building, its spacious surroundings included a lake with swans serenely gliding by. Rather than being Genesis fans, its idyllic location was chosen for its proximity to their homes in Wales, and because they could bring along their pets. 'I had a dog at the time and one day he came to visit,' said Cian. 'He shat in the control room, but the studio was so big that no one noticed for a couple of days.'[483]

The 1998 FIFA World Cup was kicking off and there was a well-stocked wine cellar waiting to be emptied. With glorious sunshine added to the mix, it seemed a perfect scenario. However, there was a problem: Gorwel Owen pulled out, exhausted from eighteen months of non-stop producing. Undeterred, the Furries chose to produce themselves.

Deliberately conceived as commercial-sounding pop, a 'jukebox album where every song is different',[484] *Guerrilla* would be an immediate, forty-five-minute record formed by picking the most upbeat tunes from the twenty-five recorded.

With more weird and wonderful equipment at their fingertips than ever, the band went crazy with samplers. *NME* labelled it 'nu-psychedelia'[485] in their attempts to generate yet another new movement. It was a tag Gruff wasn't comfortable with:

> We thought we'd made a really conventional sort of pop album, and then everybody goes, 'Wow, that's really psychedelic!' I can think of bands that are so much more psychedelic than us. Psychedelia to me is all about improvisation, and our album was almost entirely preconceived.[486]

Cian – the band's technical guru – went down a rabbit hole, with his gear-laden workstation becoming a makeshift 'NASA control room'. 'Some Things Come from Nothing' and 'The Sound of Life Today' evolved from dabbling in acid house, while he described the more elaborate arrangement on 'Chewing Chewing Gum' as like 'trying to pour custard backwards'.[487] Plus, 'The Door to This House Remains Open' gestated from a half-hour jam of Rod Stewart's 'Da Ya Think I'm Sexy?'

Further improvisation from Cian resulted in *Guerrilla*'s lead single. Dabbling with steel drums he found unattended in the corridor, the calypso rhythms he conjured up became the main motif of 'Northern Lites'.

Released a month prior to the album and reaching No. 11, its gorgeous Burt Bacharach lilt and Herb Alpert Tijuana brass landed the Single of the Week in *NME* and *Melody Maker*. The track's title referred to the stunning natural light display usually seen in polar regions, and it was almost called 'Aurora Borealis' after its Latin name. Gruff's lyric imagined the unpredictable El Niño weather phenomenon from the tropical ocean as a metaphor for a demanding lover. In thrall to the power of nature, he recorded his vocal in the open air.

Warmer vibes were the order of the day for the next single, 'Fire in My Heart', even if the band were performing on Mars in the video. Originally called 'Heartburn' before opting for the more romantic title, it started out as a sparse acoustic arrangement before bursting into a full-blooded country and western campfire singalong. *Melody Maker* guest reviewer Caprice likened the song to Carole King and Rickie Lee Jones, while lauding it as the sort of music that 'never goes out of fashion'.[488]

A couple of weeks into 2000, 'Do or Die' was *Guerrilla*'s third single. Referencing oceans, camels, tornadoes and tomatoes in under two minutes, it reached No. 20 and became the shortest song to be performed on *Top of the Pops*. Devised as a 'dumb pop song that five-year-olds can jump up and down to',[489] its title stemmed from a 1942 Mahatma Gandhi speech.

Gruff said:

> We don't claim to write poetry, [but] I define myself against bloated rock wankers like Jim Morrison – humourless and self-important. He thought he was a poet, but he was rubbish. And Robert Plant, another really pompous fool. He thought he was sexy, writing horrible songs about ladies…I've never had a pair of leather trousers in my life![490]

Creation's wish had actually been to release 'Night Vision'. Sounding like The Stooges playing 'She's Lost Control' by Joy Division, the band turned down a bumper advertising deal from Levi's for its use. The most aggressive song on *Guerrilla*, it was inspired by the band getting chucked out of Cardiff nightclubs. Likewise, 'Keep the Cosmic Trigger Happy' revelled in their jaunts to the Hippo Club 'feeling bulletproof and unstoppable'.[491]

In a departure from his cartoons, Pete Fowler worked in 3D for *Guerrilla*'s cover, moulding a mysterious Cyclops-like creature dubbed the 'God of Communications'. Continuing the album's obsession with mobile phones, this monster had one embedded in his forehead as it presided over the 'control panel of the universe'[492] within a nuclear reactor.

Another form of communication the group explored was the coded language featured on 'The Citizen's Band', a secret track that could be found by rewinding the CD from the start of the first song. As the tune didn't fit in with *Guerrilla*'s overall sound, the Furries decided to hide it along with its lyrics, which were only accessible by breaking into the album's artwork. The original idea was to conceal the song on a vinyl single within the cardboard sleeve, but Creation refused due to escalating costs.

After several minutes of silence, *Guerrilla* closed with a reprise of 'Keep the Cosmic Trigger Happy'. In bookending the album with two little surprises, the band realised their aim of making it seem like discovering new levels of a computer game. Their boldest project thus far, *Guerrilla* stormed to No. 10.

Melody Maker's Neil Kulkarni concluded: 'You love this band, you don't want them to ever stop, everything they do is wonderful, you're happier to be alive because they exist…Just say yes.'[493]

As well as endorsing Robin Friday and appearing as players in *Actua Soccer 2*, the Furries made a further foray into the football world in 1999.

In September, they became the first band in history to sponsor a Football League team when they backed Cardiff City. For FAW Premier Cup clashes in the 1999/2000 season, 'Super Furry Animals' was emblazoned across the Bluebirds' shirts.

At the kit launch at Ninian Park, Gruff – looking very much like he had been unveiled as City's new star striker – said: 'Hopefully, they will go through to Europe.' Guto added: 'We're very proud to be associated with arguably the greatest football side in the world – even though some of the group support Bangor City!'

The wonderfully retro strip received a mixed reaction from the players though. Midfielder Willie Boland said: 'You cannot get much trendier than that, can you?' Somewhat less impressed was Kevin Nugent: 'Once you get the shirt on, you tend to forget about it.'[494]

Chairman Steve Borley added: 'I believe the partnership of Cardiff City and the Super Furry Animals will be beneficial for both parties.'[495]

That didn't quite prove to be the case as the Bluebirds were beaten 2–0 by Wrexham in the cup final.

After an extended hiatus, the Furries made one final venture into football with 'Bing Bong' – the unofficial anthem for Wales's Euro 2016 campaign, and to date their last song recorded together.

Already living in London when Newport became the 'new Seattle', by the time Cool Cymru reached its zenith Feeder were thousands of miles away trying to conquer America.

Their combination of heavy guitars and bubblegum-pop choruses better fitted the zeitgeist stateside, so they spent nine gruelling months touring there throughout 1998. The band's American label, Elektra, sold 25,000 copies of *Polythene*, and 'High' topped local alternative charts, but securing radio airplay was a constant grind. After pouring so much heart and soul into the American dream, agonisingly, Feeder's second album wasn't released in the States.

Nevertheless, *Yesterday Went Too Soon* fared well on British shores in August 1999. Charting at No. 8 and securing *Melody Maker*'s Album of the Week, it received widespread rave reviews. *Kerrang* said:

> The music that accompanies Nicholas's soul-bearing is a suitable mix of grand gestures and heart-tugging melancholy. Like a rock equivalent of Radiohead's *OK Computer*, *Yesterday Went Too Soon* is a record charged with emotion and driven by turmoil and rage, and one that manages to be both giddily insistent and genuinely moving.[496]

NME added:

> Their first album *Polythene* was never a classic, but *Yesterday Went Too Soon* has lots of big tunes, vitality and compassion You know that tune you keep humming, but you never know who recorded it? That'll be one of the new Feeder songs.[497]

The second album ushered in a stylistic makeover too. Out were the grunge haircuts and pale faces, and in were spiky, bleached blond highlights and bronzed complexions from the American sun. Written mostly on the tour bus and self-produced by Nicholas, the collection signalled a more introspective songwriting style with themes including failed relationships ('Dry'), music industry frustrations ('Hole in My Head') and homesickness ('You're My Evergreen').

The album's working title was *A Life Through Headphones*, but Robbie Williams had already released his chart-topping solo debut, *Life Thru a Lens*, in 1997. With such a similar title, Feeder risked drawing comparisons with the mega-selling pop star. Instead, they opted for the more pensive *Yesterday Went Too Soon*.

While the initial singles released from *Polythene* hadn't made much difference to the album's success, the opposite proved to be the case with *Yesterday*. First up was 'Day In Day Out' in March 1999, which revolved around an employee wanting to escape menial daily tasks. Nicholas said he wanted the vocal to sound like 'someone recounting their life experiences through a tannoy for everyone to hear – like it's over the tannoy in Sainsbury's'.[498]

Feeder's next single, 'Insomnia', led to their first appearance on *Top of the Pops*. With lyrics inspired by Nicholas's trouble sleeping, the song also referenced the fatigue caused by the band's never-ending schedule: 'It's all about how difficult it is to switch off. We'd come offstage and be buzzing, then get straight onto the bus and there was nowhere for our energy to go.'[499]

'Insomnia' also gave Feeder their debut on *TFI Friday*, and they were invited back to perform 'Paperfaces'. However, fierce competition intruded again. Stereophonics were on the same show playing 'Hurry Up and Wait', but instead of capitalising on two top Welsh bands playing their new singles, the producers gave the Cwmaman boys a second slot. To add insult to injury, it wasn't even an original song from the Phonics, but a cover of The Kinks' 'Sunny Afternoon'.

Most crucial to the album and the band's future sound, though, was the title track. Thanks to regular rotation on *MTV2* and a *Melody Maker* Single of the Week, 'Yesterday Went Too Soon' secured their highest single ranking at the time of No. 20. Nicholas said:

> This is one of the last tracks I wrote for the album and it came really quickly to me. It's about relationships when you want to be with someone, but with time things have got a bit stale.
>
> You want to put life back into the relationship, and make it as exciting as when you first met. I think the person I wrote it about felt happy and sad at the same time when she heard it.[500]

———

Despite all the magical melodies, there was a darkness growing at the heart of Gorky's Zygotic Mynci heading into the new millennium.

Tensions simmered during the recording of *Gorky 5*, and a fortnight after its release the band were dropped by Fontana.

Halfway through the sessions for its follow-up, *Spanish Dance Troupe*, the band's mercurial, psychedelic genius, John Lawrence, departed. As Gorky's focused on the gentler and more accessible side to their music, he grew frustrated at their dwindling experimentation. Their eccentricities had previously been their calling card, and the single, 'Poodle Rockin'', was one pop song too many for Lawrence, who left the band while they were recording it.

A daft earworm it may be, but it still had that quintessentially Gorky's idiosyncratic stamp. Written in tribute to Gorwel Owen's dog, the song possessed a Furries-style surrealism. 'We're prone to making stupid animal noises when we've got a bit of cabin fever,' said Euros Childs. 'I don't know why animals feature quite so heavily in our humour, but that's the most important thing – to not take yourself so seriously.'[501]

'Poodle Rockin'' may have been the breaking point, but there were underlying issues: a seeming power struggle between band members. 'There was a personal and group dynamic darkness,' said Lawrence. 'It doesn't matter how glamorous it is, how exciting it all is – going on *Jools Holland*, getting in the charts – I'm getting off.'

'By then I was on the outside of it all and could see through all the bullshit. You lose enthusiasm, you get pushed out of it, or you push yourself out of it.'[502]

Richard James took over Lawrence's duties as main guitarist, and Rhodri Puw was recruited as an additional multi-instrumentalist. Without a label and missing a vital cog in their machine, Gorky's fortunes were looking grim. As *Shindig!* summarised: '"Patio Song" may have extolled "Isn't it a lovely day?" but now the thunder clouds had not just appeared, but erupted too.'[503]

The recordings for *Spanish Dance Troupe* were self-financed. Ironically, it became their first album not to feature a Welsh-language song at a time when they were free of record company pressure.

Euros told the *Washington Post*:

> We never planned that at all. We just went every couple of weeks to record tracks. At the end, we realised there's no Welsh songs on it, but sitting down to write Welsh songs to go on the album was against the whole idea of the record…We haven't got any policy. It just felt right for us.[504]

Regardless of the language issue, when *Spanish Dance Troupe* was released in October 1999 via Mantra Recordings, there was no sign of the band easing their quality control. *NME* hailed Gorky's for 'returning from their season in the abyss with their best work yet'.

A sublime fifteen-track collection of earthy melancholia, *Spanish Dance Troupe* may have been fixated with death, but it also signalled rebirth. *NME* continued:

> Their efforts stand as testimony to a pop life after metaphorical death. Sure enough, death crops up from the opening bereavement hymn 'Hallway' through the barbed 'Desolation Blues' and the eerie 'Murder Ballad', but it's an innocuous presence…
>
> The grim reaper holds no fear for Gorky's because, with the whole Mercury debacle, they've been through that palaver already. What's important is life.[505]

Hence, wonderful moments are sprinkled throughout, from when the horns kick in on 'She Lives on a Mountain' to the beautiful brevity of instrumentals like 'Drws' ('Doors') and 'The Fool'. At the album's halfway point, there's the double-header of 'Don't You Worry' and 'Faraway Eyes' – a violin-led heartbreaker followed by a sunny slice of Americana. That's not to mention the Nick Drake-like semi-instrumental 'Christmas Eve', which captures that warm-hearted festive feeling like no other.

With *Spanish Dance Troupe*, Gorky's survived their darkest days teetering on the precipice and breathed new life into their future.

———

Charlotte Church was an ordinary Cardiff schoolgirl, but with one exception – her incredible singing voice.

Little did she know that singing Andrew Lloyd Webber's 'Pie Jesu' over the telephone on *This Morning* in 1997 would turn her into an overnight sensation. Another performance on ITV's *Big Big Talent Show* sealed her place in the nation's hearts, and led to a contract with Sony Music.

The bumper record deal proved life-changing, and the cherubic twelve-year-old soprano's 1998 debut album, *Voice of Angel*, made her the youngest artist in history with a No. 1 album on the British classical crossover charts. Most impressively, it also topped the classical charts in the States.

Born in Llandaff in February 1986, Church's love of singing came at a very early age: 'When I was three and a half, I sang "Ghostbusters" with my cousin at a seaside holiday camp in Caernarfon. When we'd finished, she left the stage, but I refused to go. They had to drag me off!'[506]

Less than a decade later, her audience grew much bigger. From audiences with the Pope, the Queen and Bill Clinton, to concerts at Cardiff Arms Park and the Royal Albert Hall, to supporting Dame Shirley Bassey and an acting cameo in *Heartbeat*, the world was her oyster.

Sony were quick to capitalise on her success, rushing out her second, self-titled album in time for Christmas 1999. Mixing operatic masterpieces with Welsh choral classics like 'Cwm Rhondda' and 'Men of Harlech', it went platinum on both sides of the Atlantic.

Church was reportedly unhappy with her musical direction and cited The Corrs, Puff Daddy and Gloria Estefan as her preferred listening. 'I never wanted to be famous,' she said. 'I just wanted to sing. But at the same time, I didn't want to be just another pop star. I love so many different styles of music.'[507]

Nevertheless, Sony dug their heels in and stuck to what sold. Although it was her first foray into a more pop-oriented genre, the Christmas carol collection *Dream a Dream* delighted her core audience and became the biggest-selling holiday album of 2000 in the States. Its follow-up, *Enchantment*, again topped the US Classical Billboard.

It would take another four years before Church made the full crossover. Following a Top 10 hit with Jurgen Vries on 'The Opera Song', she introduced the world to her bold new image on 2005's *Tissues and Issues*. With tunes like 'Crazy Chick' and 'Call My Name', the Voice of an Angel at last became the Pop Princess – a reputation that has sustained into recent years with her popular Late Night Pop Dungeon shows.

────

With so much great Welsh music being created in the late '90s, it was understandable that competition developed between artists. Many still came together to celebrate each other's work.

The dawn of a new millennium signalled three memorable collaborations starting with Patrick Jones's *Commemoration and Amnesia*. Released in July 1999 on Big Noise Recordings, it was a powerful collection of twenty-two poems accompanied by a who's who of the Welsh scene.

James Dean Bradfield played on the title track and 'The Guerilla Tapestry', while Jones's brother, Nicky Wire, provided the sleeve photography and the spoken-word section about Welsh identity on 'Hiraeth'. Catatonia's Paul Jones also contributed keyboards and programming to that track, while 'The Dead Bloom' and 'Interface, Interface' included collaborations with Gruff Rhys and Cian Ciarán respectively. There were also cameos from Derrero, Topper, Pink Assassin, Curveside and its producer, Greg Haver.

'Their Life on Their Heads', and 'Democratis' were written for the people of Kosovo, while the album was dedicated to anyone who has ever been bullied, and the family of Stephen Lawrence.

Arguably its most resonant poem was 'The Eloquence in the Screaming', which featured John Lawrence of Gorky's. A sample of it had preceded the Manics' single 'Love's Sweet Exile'. In his foreword to Jones's 2001 collection, *Fuse*, Nicky Wire said:

Back in 1990, we were playing Salisbury Arts Centre supporting The Levellers. As always in those days, we lasted about fifteen minutes, alienating 1,000 people and being bottled off. Travelling back in a cold transit van my brother Patrick, who had come along for moral support, began reciting – or better, ranting – a poem.

Suddenly, everything made sense. Alienation felt comforting. The poem was 'The Eloquence in the Screaming', which still inspires me. The moment crystalised, froze and stayed with me ever since. Patrick had become a poet, we weren't alone. He had realised himself. Our voices had become one.[508]

Dating back to their membership of an Andy Warhol-esque art collective called The Blue Generation, Patrick Jones was one of the Manics' biggest early influences; holding them transfixed with passages of Jack Kerouac.

Nicky Wire has often cherry-picked from his older sibling's poems including the 'neon loneliness' refrain of 'Motorcycle Emptiness'. He borrowed the title of *Everything Must Go* too after seeing a photo of Jones's son outside a shop window displaying the slogan. It also shared its name with Jones's play, which premiered at Cardiff's Sherman Theatre in 1999.

Manics biographer Mick Middles described it as:

A bleak block of polemic, bitterness and hurt…It proves to be a work which revolves furiously around the generation of the lost Welsh, of the unhinged valley clusters, of the vibrant young talent of Wales drifting sadly away into bitterness and despair…

This concept is rather ironic, given the context. As the play itself, as its esteemed author and as the gaggle of bands who gather in the soundtrack serve to testify, young Welsh culture had risen to unprecedented heights by the start of 1999.[509]

Director Phil Clark added:

Very few Welsh plays are ever produced outside Wales, but the way is much more open to us now. What's liberated Wales is rock music. It's done more for us than any politician in giving us an international identity. If we'd done this ten years ago, we'd have just had Shirley Bassey on the soundtrack.[510]

The Manics and the new breed of Welsh music may all have featured prominently, but that's not to say that *Everything Must Go* was a wholesale celebration of all things Welsh. It railed against the 'so-called Cool Cymru and the idea that Wales is suddenly sexy'.[511] As Martin Chapman said in the *Socialist Review*:

> It would be a great mistake to see this play as a glorification of Welshness. To Catatonia's song 'International Velvet', a scene showed how the praising of all things Welsh was just another way of disguising and deflecting from the grim reality of everyday life.[512]

In *Brittle with Relics*, Patrick Jones said:

> Big pieces were written about the valleys and how they were a cauldron of despair. We had this slight nudge of Cool Cymru, and I was thinking, 'This isn't cool here.'
> Blackwood High Street was like the Wild West in 1995–6: drug-addled, pissed up, souped-up cars and violence, male testosterone and unemployment.[513]

The south Wales valleys communities like the one in which Jones lived were the most affected by the aftershocks and deprivation of coal mine closures. Therefore, he felt like Cool Cymru was like living in a 'fragmented reality'. His experience was closer to 'Uncool Cymru'.

Speaking to *The Guardian* in 1999, Jones elaborated: 'We're so apathetic, so used to accepting second best...I don't want to romanticise the mines, but they did stitch communities together, and factories fracture them, but passion and creativity come out of hard times.'[514]

The Manics were certainly creative by-products of Thatcherism and the miners' strike. When they swept the board with four gongs at the 1999 *NME* Awards, they didn't forget their early muse. On his voting form, James Dean Bradfield had only one name in mind for Best New Band: Patrick Jones.

In *The '90s: What the Fuck Was That All About?*, punk icon John Robb summarised:

> Post-Manics, there's a rumbling volcano of Welsh bands of all different shapes and sizes. Far from being uncool, some bands even flaunt their Welshness – a delicious V-sign to the years of being considered a backwards pop region…Fuck, even Tom Jones and the divine Shirley Bassey – two of the greatest voices to ever come out of the UK – were hip again![515]

Indeed, with his tight-trousered, snake-like swivel of hips, ample chest hair, gold medallion and Cuban heels, there was a time when Tom Jones was (pardon the pun) tragically unhip.

He was positioned alongside not just Shirley Bassey, but Bonnie Tyler and Shakin' Stevens when alternative music fans pushed back against pop. Wales had so much more to offer, and Cool Cymru proved it. Yet, by the end of the '90s, the foursome were re-evaluated as a major part of the Welsh music story, and on the brink of his sixtieth birthday Tom Jones was back in vogue.

Finding himself without a label after his union with Interscope came to an end, Jones was approached by Gut Records. Formed in 1991 by former Island Records Head of Promotions Guy Holmes, the Maida Vale-based indie label had a worldwide hit and a US No. 1 with its first release, 'I'm Too Sexy' by Right Said Fred.

The original idea was for an album of duets – Tom Jones's hits reworked and potentially featuring the likes of Rod Stewart, Elton John, Cher, Sting and Shania Twain. Jones, however, recognised that he needed to attract a younger audience and set about drawing up a more imaginative wish list than the usual showbiz veterans.

Each of these cool contemporary artists would suggest a song then record it in their studio with their own producer and musicians. Jones would come to them and give a classic hit the cover treatment – something he had previously pulled off with aplomb.

Back in 1988, Jones joined forces with London synth-poppers the Art of Noise for a dance-floor remake of 'Kiss' by Prince, and it surged to No. 5. Jones then hooked up with Van Morrison on 'Carrying a Torch', and with New Model Army for a rendition of the Rolling Stones' 'Gimme Shelter'. He even made his first expedition into rap in

'94 with 'If I Only Knew' – a dance/rock crossover reworking of the 1992 hip-hop song by Rise Robots Rise.

> Tom Jones's renaissance was more than just collaborations.
> Throughout the '90s, the Treforest-born singer appealed to a newfound younger demographic thanks to appearances in *The Fresh Prince of Bel-Air*, *The Simpsons* and *Mars Attacks!* He even had his own TV series, *The Right Time*, interviewing the likes of Stevie Wonder and Cyndi Lauper.

George Michael revealed he was raised on Jones's music, while the box office bonanza *The Full Monty* featured Tom singing Randy Newman's 'You Can Leave Your Hat On'. He subsequently reprised the song at the 1998 BRIT Awards with Robbie Williams.

Another Randy Newman composition featured prominently on *Reload* – 'Mama Told Me Not to Come', selected by Stereophonics. Tom described the session in his 2015 autobiography, *Over the Top and Back*:

> Kelly was in one booth and I was in the other, and we were looking at each other as we were singing it. I loved it because I felt as if I was singing with somebody who was like me when I was young. It seemed that nothing had really changed in south Wales…
>
> They'd cut their teeth in the workingmen's clubs, the same as I did. It turned out they had even rehearsed in the same pub that I'd rehearsed in with The Senators [Tom Jones' first group] – the Thorn Hotel in Abercynon.[516]

Also high up on Jones's list was James Dean Bradfield with whom he tackled Elvis Presley's 1955 skiffle single 'I'm Left, You're Right, She's Gone' – not the easiest song to sing, but the duo rose to the challenge with aplomb.

Jones arrived in the studio sweating and feeling the effects of a boozy night before. Regardless, he laid down a vocal so loud it's actually distorted on the final edit. On the Manics podcast *Do You Love Us?*, producer Dave Eringa said the duo were the loudest pair of voices he had ever recorded:

Tom came in and we played the backing track to try to work out who would sing what bit…Tom was holding back, and James was like, 'Ah, fuck this,' and he just went for it.

And then Tom was thinking, 'Well, I'm not going to let this little prick outdo me,' and he just started going for it too…I was just sat there with these two incredible Welsh voices, and it was *so* loud![517]

Speaking on the BBC Wales special *Tom Jones at 70* in 2010, James Dean Bradfield said:

He still gave the impression of being a hard-working, hard-living singer…So many people tried to relaunch their careers by being a bit more contemporary and getting younger people around them, but *Reload* really worked.

[He was] really, really impressive…He nailed it in two takes. We asked for a third take and he was like, 'I don't think you'll need that…'

Then he insisted that we go out in the evening…I didn't take much encouraging. We got to a private members' bar. He ate a massive burger, started drinking brandy, started smoking cigars…And lo and behold, there was a piano in the next room and everybody in the place was around him. He lent on the piano with a brandy and sang all night. Quite a force of nature…[518]

Completing the Welsh contingent on *Reload* was Cerys Matthews, who had always wanted to sing a big-band swing number. Therefore, they revisited 'Baby, It's Cold Outside', which they had first sung together on *Jools' Annual Hootenanny* the previous year. When the pair shared a snog at the album's launch party it started all manner of tabloid rumours. Over 10 million viewers watched the pair reunite for another performance of the song on *An Audience with Tom Jones* in December 1999 as they vied for Christmas No. 1.

The song was originally penned in 1944 by Broadway songwriter Frank Loesser for his house-warming party, and he sung it with his wife as a hint to their guests that the night was over. It later won an Academy Award for Best Original Song after featuring in *Neptune's Daughter* (1949) and has been performed by countless duos ever since.

The alleged implication of its lyric has caused controversy, especially the female singer's repeated line 'I really can't stay' and her question of 'Say, what's in this drink?' In the promo video though, Cerys's angelic persona gets her own back on Jones's devilish character by trapping him at the finale.

Coincidentally, Cerys had a No. 4 hit in February 1998 duetting with Space on 'The Ballad of Tom Jones'.

An even bigger coincidence is that Space's singer is called Tommy Scott, which was Tom Jones's original stage name on his debut single, 'Chills and Fever', in 1964!

Reload was preceded by the single 'Burning Down the House', which reached No. 7 and led to a performance of the Talking Heads song on *Top of the Pops*. Accompanied by The Cardigans and their vocalist Nina Persson (who Jones described as 'just about the coolest and most self-possessed singer on the planet at that moment'[519]), it was a clear message to everyone that he was trying something new.

The old ways still persisted, including the omnipresent underwear that followed Jones around, and the show's floor manager handed out knickers to the audience to throw at the singer. Consequently, he stopped the song mid-performance to say they didn't want that kind of audience participation.

Jones already had enough songs for the album, but was alerted to one more possible inclusion – a demo of a song called 'Sex Bomb' by German DJ Mousse T.

It was being sung by a girl, but it was jumping out as an instant hit song…It reminded me of one of those tongue-in-cheek, filthy, innuendo-laden blues classics – a late-twentieth-century Howlin' Wolf number…

The only problem was the lyric. The way the girl was doing it, the chorus went, 'Sex bomb, sex bomb, I'm your sex bomb…' Did I really want to be going around saying, 'I'm your sex bomb' knocking on sixty?

So [we] thought what if we flip it to 'You're my sex bomb'.

Address it to someone else rather than swagger around making a boast out of it. Right away it sat more comfortably.[520]

With a stellar line-up already in place, Gut Records were unsure of whether another collaboration was required, or if it really fit. Jones disagreed as the album was 'deliberately, gloriously all over the place'. He was proved right – 'Sex Bomb' became a huge international hit, reaching No. 3 in the UK and topping the charts in France and Switzerland.

While not ungrateful for his long career, Tom Jones also admitted that the versatility he showed with albums such as *Reload* caused challenges. At live shows, older fans expected the classics, while the younger audience wanted new songs like 'Sex Bomb'. 'But that's always been something I've had to face, right back to the days of the workingmen's clubs,' he told biographer Peter Doggett.

Jones also told him how singing was in his bones:

> If 'It's Not Unusual' had flopped back in 1965, and that had been the end of my professional career, I would've kept on singing, no question. I'd be in Wales right now, probably still singing in the clubs…And that's what I'll always do. Forget retirement, I'll be singing until I drop.[521]

Associating himself with the cream of the '90s crop from Cool Cymru to Britpop was a master stroke. Guy Holmes had been so confident in the recording sessions, he remortgaged his Hampstead house to support the venture. He promised to take all his staff to Ibiza if the album shifted 1 million copies. His colleagues were soon working on their tans in the Mediterranean as *Reload* sold six times that.

In conjunction with V2 Records, Jones's thirty-fourth album reached No. 1 in September 1999 and became the biggest seller of his career. That stat is all the more extraordinary considering *Reload* wasn't released in the States. The album spent sixty-nine weeks on the UK charts with an initial three weeks at the top before returning to the summit again in 2000.

Entering his fourth decade in the business, Tom Jones was as popular as ever.

Sir Tom Jones wasn't the only Welsh legend enjoying a '90s renaissance.

Dame Shirley Bassey celebrated her sixtieth birthday in 1997 with a No. 1 UK Dance Chart single alongside electronic duo Propellerheads on 'History Repeating'. She continued her revival into the new millennium by teaming up with them again for *Diamonds Are Forever* (an album featuring remixes of her hits from the likes of Groove Armada), before collaborating with the Manics on 'The Girl from Tiger Bay' in 2009.

———

While some viewed Tom Jones's collaborations with mainstream contemporary artists as a cynical ploy to become relevant again, the same couldn't quite be said of John Cale.

In his exciting new project, Cale joined forces with the leading names of the Welsh scene, but he also painted a vibrant portrait of the nation's musical landscape via collaborations with some lesser-known talents.

Throughout 1999, Cale worked on an atmospheric score at New York's TMF Studios to soundtrack 'a snapshot of Cardiff in the year 2000'.[522] Linking up with *House of America* director Marc Evans, he then spent ten days in the Welsh capital recording performances at the Coal Exchange and The Point. Premiered at the Cardiff International Film Festival in November 2000, *Camgymeriad Gwych* ('Beautiful Mistake') encapsulated Wales's evolving position on the world stage at the turn of the millennium.

In his Cale biography, *Sedition and Alchemy*, Tim Mitchell said: '[The project was] Cale's most substantial contact with the culture of his homeland since his youth, and significantly concerned itself with new life and creativity.'[523]

With Cale moving between rooms as a 'musical janitor', each collaboration often gave exposure to one of the guest artist's compositions rather than his own.

Spliced between songs were artful sequences illustrating Cardiff's modernisation including burning furnaces and factory machinery, stop-motion cityscapes and the muddy banks of the barrage, plus St David's Hotel and the Millennium Stadium. Narrated by Cale in Welsh, *Camgymeriad Gwych* was all the more culturally significant in that it wasn't subtitled, and an English-language version was never released.

Its soundtrack featured Catatonia's track 'Whispering Room', which hasn't been released anywhere else, along with a preview of 'Presidential Suite', which featured on the Furries' fifth album, *Rings Around the World*, in 2001. Cale once listed *Patio* as his favourite album, but it was 'O, Caroline II' from Gorky's follow-up, *Tatay*, that proved to be another spellbinding highlight.

There were also appearances from folk group Fernhill, flautist Ceri Rhys Matthews, harpist Llio Rhydderch and Cardiff-based techno/punk outfit Manchild. Ash Cooke worked a double shift as part of Cale's backing band and playing with Derrero on 'Buffalo Ballet'. Plus, there were showcases for the era's best albums with Big Leaves ('Synfyfyrio' from *Pwy Sy'n Galw?*), Tystion ('Gwyddbwyll' from *Rhaid i Rhywbeth Ddigwydd*) and Patrick Jones featuring Pink Assassin ('Scalpel and Heart' and 'Of Temazepam and Petroleum' from *Commemoration and Amnesia*).

The initial plan was for the Furries to accompany Cale over the end credits with a new song called 'Things', which he had written in his hotel room a couple of days prior. This was vetoed in favour of a jam fronted by Tystion alongside several of the performers.

Ever the workaholic, Cale contributed to several soundtracks and scores throughout the '90s, often at the expense of his solo career. This project arrived between touring with Siouxsie Sioux, writing his autobiography *What's Welsh for Zen* and composing the score to *American Psycho* starring Haverfordwest-born actor Christian Bale.

Cale's only solo album of the decade was *Walking on Locusts* from which he selected 'Some Friends' here. A song about his former Velvet Underground bandmate Sterling Morrison (who died in 1995), this interpretation featured some brilliant slide guitar from James Dean Bradfield.

His other collaboration with the Manics frontman provided the film's best performance. Despite the avid non-smoker Cale recoiling from the chain-smoker of Bradfield in rehearsal, the duo meshed together seamlessly on a beautifully haunting rendition of 'Ready for Drowning'. With Cale sat at the piano and Bradfield belting out the vocal, it's possibly even better than the *This Is My Truth* original.

Speaking of the spectral quality that pervades the song, Bradfield said:

In his book, [Cale] goes on about his upbringing and there's a lot of references to the church…I wanted to try and bring some wheezy, old church-like, chapel vibe to it where the song was creaking into life.

I think that fits the subject matter because the song deals with a town that's buried under a reservoir, and it's as if the song is having its last breath of oxygen. I wanted John to bring that old, religious, almost dead fervour.[524]

On 20 December 1999, Super Furry Animals held a huge Christmas party for 6,000 at Cardiff International Arena – their biggest gig so far.

Instead of tinsel and turkey, there were six surround sound speaker stacks with several mono points orbiting them for a mind-blowing sonic extravaganza. Inspired by The KLF, the band set about recreating the swirling wind phenomenon they had experienced at Glastonbury, albeit with Cian Ciarán manning the controls this time: 'It was like walking into a club with sounds flying around everywhere, and everyone getting the same vibe whereby people at the back would have the same buzz, sonically, as people at the front.'[525]

Mash Up the CIA wasn't only the Furries' first gig in the Welsh capital for two and a half years, but also the first time they had used such technology in a live setting. With Howard Marks as MC, the evening opened with Big Leaves and a DJ set from Massive Attack before the Furries were welcomed onstage to the sound of an alpenhorn player.

If any further proof was needed that this wasn't going to be just any gig, the band were joined by a weird and wonderful cast of characters including aliens, pandas and druids. There was even a visit from Mother Nature herself – as the droves left for the night, the tail end of El Niño blew a snowstorm through the arena's open doors!

When the Manics played Radcliff's Square Club in 1989 with only their manager and Richey's sister in attendance, not even Nostradamus would've predicted what happened a decade later.

On 31 December 1999, the Manics – who had insisted they would be the most important band of the '90s – were playing in front of 57,000 fans at the Millennium Stadium, a stone's throw away from the Square Club, and on Millennium Eve of all nights.

In January 1999, Nicky Wire said to *Select* he would be spending Millennium Eve in 'a hotel that takes dogs somewhere in west Wales'.[526] Yet, a decade on from their debut single, 'Suicide Alley', the band had plans up their sleeve for an extravaganza called Manic Millennium – the first non-rugby event to be hosted at the new Welsh national stadium.

With its retractable roof shut, this would be the largest indoor arena gig across Europe. True to their socialist roots, the Manics sold out all the tickets at a highly affordable price of £30, and it became Britain's fastest-selling millennium event.

Their early bravado was nowhere to be seen in the run-up to the event, and understandably so. Away from festivals, not only was this the Manics' biggest-ever gig, but also their only show heading into the year 2000. With a vulture-like press waiting for them to fail, they had to get this right.

In pre-show interviews, James Dean Bradfield's presence was twitchy as he expressed his fear of forgetting lyrics amid the huge scale of the show. The Manics used to think they had 'made it' when they played Newport Centre; now they were using it as a rehearsal room.

Likewise, Nicky Wire gazed into the distance as his answers lingered, his eyes hidden behind aviators. At one point, the interviewer mentioned there would be a lot of excited people in attendance. A smile crept across Wire's face: 'Pissed, you mean?'[527]

He told *Select*:

We'll be in front of 50,000 beautiful drunken people. There'll be a good 25,000 hardcore fans there, but obviously there'll also be a lot of people just out for the occasion…Once again, the Manic Street Preachers are determined to be as cheap as we can! We're not going to make any money on this gig unless we sell a million T-shirts.[528]

Aside from the Manics' nerves, Millennium Eve was laced with great excitement and tension. The news was awash with Mayan prophecies that the world was about to end. Plus, there was the dreaded 'millennium bug' where computer systems across the world would crash, planes would fall out of the sky and security systems collapse. At the University Hospital of Wales in Cardiff, concerns were so intense over life-saving equipment failing that they brought in special back-up generators.

Not long before, a section of the stadium's roof had fallen during a rugby game, so anxiety was huge amongst organisers. It was decided that seats would be left empty and structural supports installed to withstand so many fans stomping in unison. 'We're the Manic Street Guinea Pigs for sure,'[529] commented Bradfield. At a pre-gig press briefing, Nicky Wire half joked: 'All this jumping around might knock the stadium down. Try and keep calm.'

Manic Millennium kicked off with Patrick Jones and a reading of 'The Guerilla Tapestry' featuring a who's who of young Welsh acting talent including Ioan Gruffudd, Matthew Rhys, Andrew Howard and Rakie Ayola.

Next up was a bit of a curveball with Shack – one of the great, lost bands of the '90s. Fresh from supporting Red Hot Chili Peppers at Wembley Arena, Feeder followed with a set showcasing the best bits of *Polythene* and *Yesterday Went Too Soon*.

The identity of the slot immediately below the headliner was much rumoured with Catatonia and Mansun suggested, while Stereophonics were annoyed at not being invited. It was never really going to be the Cwmaman boys though, after their previous spats, and they went on to take part in a Cream event in Liverpool (of which Nicky Wire criticised the cost).

Instead, the penultimate place went to Super Furry Animals, who delivered a glorious set from the breakneck brilliance of 'Do or Die' to the maverick magnificence of 'The Man Don't Give a Fuck'.

Then it was time for the moment everyone had been waiting for.

Emerging onstage looking like Shirley Manson, Nicky Wire's grin was as wide as the River Taff. Resplendent in a sparkly tiara, pink 'Culture Slut' top matched with a mini skirt (and a Manic Millennium foam finger nicked from the merch stand), the band launched into 'You Stole the Sun from My Heart'.

An early highlight of the set was 'The Masses Against the Classes'. A stand-alone single with a Nirvana-meets-The-Stooges sound, it issued a sharp riposte to accusations that the Manics had gone soft. Whereas on 'The Everlasting' the Manics were defeated ('In the beginning, when we were winning, when our smiles were genuine'), now they were defiant ('We're tired of giving a reason why we're the only thing left to believe in'). Released on 10 January 2000, the single knocked Westlife off the top spot to become the first new entry at No. 1 of the millennium.

Like 'You Love Us', it spoke directly to fans and critics, and addressed their reaction to all the recent success. Deleted on the day of its release after securing 35,000 sales, its title derived from the nineteenth-century British prime minister William Gladstone. It also started and ended with Noam Chomsky and Albert Camus quotes. Wrapping up the whole package was artwork depicting a Cuban flag, which predated their trip to meet Fidel Castro in February 2001. At Glastonbury '99, the Manics played it safe at with a headline set that *NME* labelled 'stale, complacent and half-arsed'.[530] With 'Masses', they proved they were still raging against the dying of the light.

On its B-side was a cover of Chuck Berry's 'Rock and Roll Music', which provided a mid-set highlight alongside 'Ready for Drowning'. They even threw in 'Of Walking Abortion' off *The Holy Bible* – surely the only time it's ever been played at a New Year's Eve party! At its conclusion, a smiling Wire said: 'I bet the bar sold about 8 million pints during that one.'[531]

In 2002, Crai Records issued the *Taffia* EP by The Bard of Ely (aka Steve Andrews) fronted by a tune called 'Nicky Wire Your a Liar'[sic].

Produced by Phil Moxham of Young Marble Giants, it grumbled about the 'London prices' for a pint at Manic

Millennium, and that everyone was still sober at midnight due to waiting so long.

'I hope he [Wire] wasn't too offended by it,' laughed Rhys Mwyn.[532]

Minutes before midnight, Bradfield dedicated 'Motorcycle Emptiness' to the early disciples that came to their Cardiff University gigs. Then the band departed to enjoy the New Year celebrations privately. Thankfully, there was no sign of the apocalypse, just the usual fanfare of 'Auld Lang Syne'.

With Stereophonics' controversy at Morfa Stadium not long in the memory, *NME*'s review made for interesting reading:

The red dragons are, of course, everywhere but it's not intimidating. Wales has emerged from the post-industrial sink and tonight the kids want to celebrate this (to be offended by the fury of red and white would be ridiculously urban and isolationist). It might be their victory and vindication, but everyone's invited.[533]

Bradfield returned for an acoustic run-through of 'Can't Take My Eyes Off You'. In typically subversive Manics style, he then brought down the party vibes with a beautifully bleak solo rendition of 'Small Black Flowers That Grow in the Sky' dedicated to Richey Edwards.

'Can't Take My Eyes Off You' is a surefire singalong at any Manics gig, but when Bradfield introduced it he referenced an unhappier occasion: 'This song always reminds me of getting beaten by Romania, a very bad time.'

Andy Williams's crooner version of the song was used in BBC Wales ads for the Welsh football team's qualifiers for World Cup '94. A brilliant campaign ended in heartbreak when Paul Bodin's penalty cannoned off the crossbar against the Romanians, and Wales ended up staying home the following summer.

When they did eventually qualify for a major tournament for the first time since 1958, the Manics released the official Euro 2016 song, 'Together Stronger (C'mon Wales)', which topped the physical UK charts. Their intention initially was to rework 'Can't Take My Eyes Off You' with new lyrics, but the original song's publishers refused permission.

Perhaps feeling the effects of the midnight champers, Nicky Wire performed 'Elvis Impersonator' spreadeagled across the stage before a life-affirming triple-header of 'You Love Us', 'Stay Beautiful' and 'If You Tolerate This'. At one point, Bradfield screamed, 'Millennium consciousness means fuck all,' meaning all the over-the-top media coverage was a load of rubbish and we had all made it through to the other side.

Describing the event as one of the best nights of their lives, there was still one last hurdle to overcome – the small matter of a global audience of 2 billion via the BBC. With manager Martin Hall gesticulating wildly for the band to concentrate on the ten-second countdown, Bradfield delivered a brilliantly back-handed tribute to the Welsh capital: 'Cardiff – the most beautiful place on earth... tonight at least.' Not even a broken guitar strap during an epic finale of 'A Design for Life' phased him.

All that was left to do was for a knackered Nicky Wire to destroy his bass. 'I still haven't got over it,' he said. 'James was up till ten the next morning. I stayed up till five through nervous excitement really. We kind of said we'd do this ten years ago and everyone laughed at us then.'[534]

The Manics are still here nearly forty years on from their inception. In 1991, Steve Lamacq asked Richey Edwards if the Manics were for real. Ever since, they've confounded their critics and brushed aside pretenders to their throne.

As NME's review concluded: 'The Manics' armour is rusting, waiting for a new champion's blade to finally cut through the history and hysterics of the greatest band of the '90s and leave them to rest in peace. Until then the future somehow, incredibly, still belongs to them.'[535]

A NEW WAVE
OF CONFIDENCE

WELSH-LANGUAGE MUSIC
IN THE YEAR 2000

'This album is a celebration of Welsh culture embracing the new wave of confidence in the Welsh nation...'

So stated Plaid Cymru parliamentary leader Elfyn Llwyd MP of the Furries' fourth album, *Mwng,* which was released on 15 May 2000.

When Gruff Rhys told *Melody Maker*, 'I like the idea of creating cultural havoc,'[536] few would have guessed what he had up his sleeve: every word on the new record would be in Welsh.

It was a complete transformation from a decade before. Just months into the new millennium, politicians were glowing with praise about the feel-good factor this talented crop of Welsh musicians had created.

Llwyd continued:

> This album proves that the Welsh language is being used as a central part of Welsh popular youth culture...
>
> The confidence that Super Furry Animals have shown in releasing a Welsh album and making it so successful outside of Wales is simply amazing.

Mwng became the biggest-selling Welsh-language album of all time, and the first ever in the UK Top 20. It reached No. 11 where it rubbed shoulders with Britney Spears, Eminem and David Gray (who, incidentally, was raised in Solva, Pembrokeshire).

An early day motion is a spontaneous procedure allowing politicians to mention something of interest in the House of Commons without waiting weeks. No debate or legislation follows. It's simply noted in the official parliamentary record, *Hansard*, and the Furries were now in it – the same band who drove a tank into the Eisteddfod just four years earlier!

The anarchic band didn't necessarily crave this attention. As Gruff said: 'Ultimately, we're a band of musicians touring nightclubs… Maybe we didn't want that kind of responsibility.'[537]

This from a band who had faced cultural exile and were haunted by the ghosts of Welsh music's past. As Ric Rawlins explained:

> There's an ancient Welsh belief that anybody who makes music in the native language will be possessed by demons.
>
> Not just any old demons, however – specifically the type that make you competitive with, and jealous of, other musicians – hence the phrase *'cythraul canu'*, which means 'devil singer'.[538]

The idiom ended up inspiring 'Ymaelodi â'r Ymylon' ('Banished to the Periphery') – a harmonium-infused, sea-shanty mish-mash of The Beach Boys, Ennio Morricone and Love.

Not fearing folklore, the Furries were ready to subvert their audience in Welsh. For *Mwng*, the group emphasised simple songwriting. Out were elaborate effects pedals and sophisticated software, and in were stark, stripped-back, lo-fi pastoral folk tunes. Where *Guerrilla* took three months to record at a cost of £100,000 followed by a further month of mixing, the price of *Mwng* was just £6,000 across two weeks. Laid down on tape with a more instinctive, live-session feel, *Mwng* was shorn of studio techniques and the Furries' quality as a band became far more prominent as a result.

Returning to Bethesda following his father's death, Gruff dusted off a box of records in the attic from his formative years including Datblygu and Meic Stevens. Brainstorming whether he could combine the two, he began demoing Welsh-language songs with themes of love, loss, war, and identity crisis amid globalisation. Introducing the album to BBC Wales, Gruff said:

> *'Mwng'* means 'mane'…I suppose it's an extension of a Super Furry Animal, something that keeps you warm.
>
> It's a winter album, but we're releasing it in May, and we've been billing this album as a dark album, [but] the single's going to be 'Ysbeidiau Heulog', which means 'sunny intervals'.

[The song] is a complete contrast, and our concession to ELO. Jeff Lynne was very concerned about the weather, and he made a lot of money out of it. It's sort of throwaway pop…You've got to imagine the saxophonist from 1972 Roxy Music in a spangly red jumpsuit![539]

Aside from that anomaly, the other songs generally held a similar, rustic tone. Gruff recalled:

My four-track recorder had been stolen, so I started going up to Gorwel's…I'd throw down twenty songs. It was really basic stuff, sometimes to a drum machine, just a case of getting the song down.[540]

The album is sung in the Welsh language, but the music is a filter of everything we ever listened to – from the American underground and the Brazilian underground and the Welsh underground, and some overground influences. There was nothing to stop *Mwng* from resonating internationally. We were bringing a bit of our own selves through in it as well, but it wasn't completely alien to people's ears.[541]

The songs existed anyway and Welsh is the language we speak with each other, so in that sense it wasn't a big deal, but in reality, it was…We'd gone through quite a turbulent time of hype and TV documentaries where people followed us around the country with a stopwatch measuring the percentage of songs we sang in English.[542]

With melodies this infectious, *Mwng* was never going to take long to register. 'If I listen to a Nirvana record, I don't understand most of their lyrics cos he's just screaming away,' said Gruff. 'But I understand the frustration and the passion in his voice. I think equally people can get off on this record by connecting to the mood of the song.[543]

'If you listen to bands like Kraftwerk, if you were singing, "Motorway" [instead of "*Autobahn*"], it would sound crap, but that Germanic pronunciation *makes* the sound.'[544]

'Ysbeidiau Heulog', 'Gwreiddiau Dwfn' and 'Y Gwyneb Iau' were all recorded over one weekend in summer 1999 at Famous Studios in Cardiff. The rest was completed at Gorwel's bungalow studio between the band's festival slots. None of their previous English-language singles had landed in the Top 10, so the band jokingly put themselves on 'pop strike'. If the radio wasn't playing their English tunes, they may as well release songs in Welsh.

On Creation, the band found that their Welsh-language repertoire was tucked away on B-sides. Only 'Torra Fy Ngwallt yn Hir' made it onto an album. Daf told *Drowned in Sound*: 'We had tried putting one Welsh song on *Radiator*, but I wasn't a fan of mixing languages... You get into the sound of a song regardless of the lyrics, but you also get into the sound of a language, and you can tell if something's changed.'[545]

Many of the new Welsh songs were of a similar ilk, so rather than releasing them sporadically as token offerings, they would form a coherent album. One of the demos, 'Nythod Cacwn' ('Beehives') – featuring Gruff on drums and with lyrics made up on the spot – sounded so good, it made it onto the album intact. Only one thing stood in their way: the unlikely demise of Creation Records.

Tired and disillusioned, Alan McGee called time on the label. On his way out, he paid tribute to the Furries: 'They were the last great Creation band...There are only a few bands you could make a film out of, and the Furries are one because their story is so fucking bonkers.'

Equally cursed and blessed, the Furries may not have had the financial backing, but they were now free to release a Welsh-language album on their own label, Placid Casual. Named after the *Radiator* track, it had been set up in 1998 to release a single by Psycho VII (featuring their mates Dic Ben and Rhodri Puw). Self-releasing *Mwng* also eliminated the risk of a potential label (who didn't understand this internationalist band) doing something 'horrific' like putting a Welsh flag on the cover.

After selling the Furries as a Britpop band, Creation got it wrong again by perceiving *Mwng* as a specialist jazz album. Therefore, it was fitting that the Furries controlled its destiny. Given their history, this wasn't going to be conventional.

'We used all the worst quotes we could find from the bad reviews for the advert,' said Gruff. 'It got great reviews, but we managed to find some bad ones. Stuff like "career suicide" from the *Jewish Chronicle*. We put the advert up in the *NME*.'[546]

Mwng's desolate vibe was reflected in its austere artwork.

Renowned for his bizarre beasts and lurid landscapes, Pete Fowler took a different approach here. The music had an isolated beauty, so a monochrome and minimalist palette was befitting.

After a *Surf's Up*-inspired initial concept of a woman riding a horse was abandoned, a less obvious flowing-maned animal was chosen – a goat. The idea was multifaceted. Mirroring the rural sparseness of the recording location in Anglesey, the band loved the devilish aspect of the creature, as well as its symbolism in phrases like 'she's a tough old goat'.

Fowler, who collaborated with Cardiff artist Mark James, said:

> *Mwng*'s artwork was quite a departure. The idea for the goat was to go with something less monstrous, but also with the twist of it smoking a pipe, which gives it a human quality and a mythological edge. Almost like it was an ancient god perhaps, or a creature that has always been there throughout time in the mountains.[547]

The sleeve's simplicity was reflected in the impulsive nature of the songs, starting with the minute-and-a-half glam-rock stomp of 'Drygioni'. Its verses alternated between Good and Evil (while emphasising the listener's need for both), and demonstrated Gruff's love of wordplay harking back to Ffa Coffi Pawb. 'Drygioni' translates as 'Badness', but is phonetically close to the English word 'drug'.

That wasn't Gruff's only revisit to his old band. 'Dacw Hi' ('There She Is') was an unreleased Ffa Coffi Pawb song written in 1987: 'It's about a teacher I used to have when I was five, who claimed she had eyes in the back of her head and I took it literally…I nicked an egg, and I was going to break it on her desk when she wasn't facing me, and she caught me.'[548]

The band's trademark humour was also evident on 'Y Gwyneb Iau', which translates into the obscure insult of 'Liverface' and juxtaposes themes of war with tranquil trumpets – or as Gruff put it: 'The Velvet Underground conducting an unlikely threesome with Gladys Knight and Nick Drake.'

Although *Mwng* is internationalist, it often casts its gaze inwards with Welsh social history permeating throughout. 'Sarn Helen' revolves around the Roman road linking the two ends of Wales, while 'Pan Ddaw'r Wawr' ('When Dawn Breaks') deals with the decimation of rural communities as a result of advanced capitalism. Gruff said: 'Real estate prices are out of reach of most people, and often people have to move away and resettle, so there's a lot of displacement…It happens to a lot of rural Wales, and it does affect the language base.'[549]

Surprisingly, the Furries didn't tour *Mwng* in their homeland. It's understandable that they didn't want it to turn into a patriotic rally, nor did they, in Gruff's words, 'want to create a Hollywood, sentimental homecoming gig'. All UK fans saw of *Mwng* live was at festivals, a couple of isolated gigs and an appearance on *Jools Holland*.

Having headlined Cardiff International Arena a few months earlier, the band didn't feel the need to return so soon. 'It would've been too emotional,' Gruff told *The Observer*. 'For us, but also because people could've turned out like at rugby matches – dressed up as red dragons and leeks.'[550]

Instead, they took *Mwng* to the USA and Japan. In the latter, crowds sung back phonetically, while in America, it became the band's bestselling album accompanied by a well-attended tour. The idea was to finish in New York and begin recording the next album. That was if they hadn't been abandoned in the middle of nowhere. Gruff recalled:

> Our bus was driven by a husband-and-wife team, who were very religious from the Deep South. They were supposed to drop us at the studio, but we had fallen out with them.
>
> We ended up being dumped on the side of the road. They threw out a lot of equipment and bags; Bunf only had one shoe! We were miles from the studio by a forest and there were bears around, so that was the end of the *Mwng* tour![551]

Still widely regarded as the greatest Welsh-language album ever, *Mwng*'s legacy remains undiminished. In 2015, Band Pres Llareggub covered it in its entirety. The north Walian brass band's leader, Owain Gruffudd Roberts, said:

> You can't ignore *Mwng* in terms of the repertoire of Welsh-language pop music…Growing up, it had a big impact on me musically, and also people outside of Wales know it. It's not quite the same as covering Dafydd Iwan or Caryl Parry Jones. When

you play [Lake District music festival] Kendal Calling or a gig in London, people will generally know a few tunes off *Mwng*.[552]

In a reflection of the band's socialist values, it was also reissued on International Workers' Day in 2015. Meticulously remastered by band archivist Kliph Scurlock and engineer Donal Whelan, the process almost ended in disaster at the storage facility: 'The fire didn't affect us, it stopped at the letter "M"…M People survived,' laughed Bunf.[553]

With studio wizardry constantly evolving, *Mwng* has aged remarkably well thanks to its bare-boned production. Released to universal praise, *Mojo* described the album as a 'sensuous, sonic journey' with an 'organic, woody, mystical atmosphere'.[554] *Select* said: 'Rather than snickering behind a barrier of linguistic exclusivity, the Furries have made their warmest record yet.'[555] *Wales Arts Review* added: 'It's perhaps evidence of the normalisation of the language to the point that it's no longer seen as a weird or novelty thing – it's now something to be treasured.'[556]

The Furries certainly attained what they set out to achieve musically on *Mwng*, but Gruff's beautiful lyrics shouldn't be underappreciated. Welsh poet and playwright Menna Elfyn told *The Observer*:

> There's a lyric intensity to the songs on *Mwng*. You could almost look at them in a postcolonial way. There's so much about being on the periphery and banishment and leaving heritage, connecting with those who have been displaced.[557]

One of the most touching tributes came from the band's long-term producer, Gorwel Owen. He referenced how the band had written jokingly about the fragility of the Welsh language on their early B-side '(Nid) Hon Yw'r Gân Sy'n Mynd i Achub yr Iaith' ('This Is (Not) the Song That Will Save the Language'): 'In the song, Gruff refers to "*dim ond carreg mewn wal barhaus*", which describes the music as being a stone in a continuous wall. I think what the band created on *Mwng* was quite a significant stone in any wall.'[558]

If there was any more evidence needed that Welsh music had completed a 180-degree turn across the '90s, it was proven by *Mwng*'s most emotive track – one not even written by the band themselves. 'Y Teimlad' ('The Feeling') is the most beautiful and unlikely love song of all time. An iconic Datblygu song, it had been tucked away on *Cam o'r Tywyllwch* – Rhys Mwyn's compilation that ignited the Welsh-language music revolution in the '80s.

The endorsement of Datblygu from the likes of the Furries and Gorky's helped usher in a new generation of fandom. It was therefore apt that Ankst released the *Datblygu 1985–1995* collection at the height of Cool Cymru and recognised them as a huge inspiration for the '90s boom. No longer a rarity and now deservedly reaching a bigger audience than ever before, 'Y Teimlad' was the compilation's opening, focal track.

Originally a synth-infused heartbreaker, the Furries' straight-forward acoustic rendition was the easiest thing they ever recorded, and it was no less stunning in its simplicity. 'Y Teimlad' possessed a humanity that many of Datblygu's contemporaries lacked. Gruff acknowledged the song's unique warmth and versatility: 'It's a song about love, or it's a song about not knowing what love is or what love means. The original is a really raw, kind of an electro, dissonant song, but it could be made in a Sinatra style.'[559]

Speaking to the *Welsh Music Podcast*, Patricia Morgan recalled the first time she heard the Furries' cover: 'I was listening to John Peel and "Y Teimlad" came on, and I thought, "Hang on, this isn't us!" Their rendition is beautiful. It's such a compliment.'[560]

'Y Teimlad' was all the more poignant following David R. Edwards's death at the age of fifty-six in June 2021. Two months later, Gruff Rhys concluded his show at Clwb Ifor Bach with a special tribute.

As his bandmates exited the stage, Gruff was left alone to strum those familiar chords from four decades previously. At a time when it hadn't long felt like live music may never return, following the COVID-19 pandemic, the emotions of sadness and relief ensured there wasn't a dry eye in the house.

Y teimlad, beth yw y teimlad? / Y teimlad, sy'n cael ei alw'n gariad.

The feeling, what is the feeling? / The feeling that is called love.

Described by Gruff Rhys as 'the Welsh gospel', David R. Edwards's words resonate now more than ever – crossing cultures, languages and borders.

AFTERWORD

Cool Cymru continues to inspire today's alluring music scene in Wales like no other era.

While two of its biggest successes, Catatonia and Gorky's, split up early in the new millennium, the Welsh rock renaissance continued unabated into the next decade.

Mwng may have opened the doors for Welsh-language music, but it was English-language bands in south Wales that made the most immediate strides into the twenty-first century. These artists benefited from the infrastructure that Cool Cymru established, and they were ready to capitalise on a national media that was still hungry to discover what more Wales had to offer.

Two quick-thinking teenagers, Huw Stephens and his Glantaf schoolmate Geraint John, captured the zeitgeist by enlisting the help of Greg Haver and Ceri Collier at Big Noise to create Boobytrap Singles Club. Branded the 'best record label in the world' by *Rolling Stone*, it gave vital exposure to cult favourites like El Goodo, Keys, Zabrinski and even legendary bin basher, Ninjah.

Also released via Boobytrap were the Steve Albini-produced, post-hardcore rockers Mclusky (mclusky), who (along with Jarcrew) were the closest successors to the '90s Newport sound. Also hailing from that city was the Richard Parfitt-managed Terris, who won *NME*'s Philip Hall Award for the UK's brightest new hope in 2000. Likewise, blinged-up collective Goldie Lookin' Chain talked all things ''Portlife and stormed to No. 3 with 'Guns Don't Kill People, Rappers Do' – a satire of hip-hop culture laced with typical Welsh wit.

Elsewhere, Cowbridge band The Automatic enjoyed a 'Monster' hit, while just down the road in Bridgend, Funeral for a Friend and Bullet for My Valentine conjured a seismic sound. Along with Lostprophets, the latter two bands each won *Kerrang*'s Best British Newcomer during a four-year period when Welsh acts dominated the award (2001–5).

It's Welsh-language artists, however, who have prospered since then. In the immediate aftermath of *Mwng*, there wasn't the expected deluge of great albums in *Cymraeg* (other than notable exceptions like MC Mabon). Welsh-language artists weren't used to outside recognition so that brought additional pressure, as did replicating the success of *Mwng*.

A quarter century later, that album still endures and the Furries are the most influential band amongst contemporary Welsh artists in both languages. Their madcap melodies can be heard in the likes of Cate Le Bon, H. Hawkline, Sweet Baboo, Melin Melyn and Y Niwl.

If Damon Albarn has proven himself to be the standout talent from Britpop with Blur, Gorillaz and The Good, the Bad & the Queen, plus forays into film scores, opera and world music, then the same can be said of Gruff Rhys with Cool Cymru. An endlessly daring musical maverick, he's delved into electronica with Neon Neon, wild psychedelia with Tony Da Gatorra, collaborated with the BBC National Orchestra of Wales and National Theatre Wales, composed a BAFTA Cymru Award-winning soundtrack and released a concept album complete with accompanying documentary and book.

Since *Mwng*, Gruff has made issuing music in *Cymraeg* completely natural. His 2005 solo debut, *Yr Atal Genhedlaeth* ('The Stuttering Generation'), featured song titles based on Welsh-language puns, while on 2019's *Pang!*, he fused Welsh Americana with African pop. Gruff described the latter as 'favouring adventure over predictability' – a soundbite that has reverberated throughout a remarkable career that shows no sign of slowing down (in January 2024, he released his twenty-fifth album with *Sadness Sets Me Free*).

For the last decade, Gruff's drummer has been former Flaming Lips musician Kliph Scurlock, who has become an obsessive fan of Welsh music after moving from Kansas to Cardiff. Initially a devotee of Badfinger and Budgie, his first experience of *Cymraeg* came via Gorky's mind-bending masterpiece, 'Merched Yn Neud Gwallt Eu Gilydd' ('Girls Doing Each Other's Hair'), and he now regularly collaborates with Welsh-language electro-pop sensation Gwenno.

Likewise, Laura Nunez moved from London to Wales thanks to her love of the Furries. She has seen Gruff approximately 150 times live, while her stage name, She's Got Spies, was inspired by the *Radiator* track. Intrigued by their early B-sides like 'Dim Bendith' and 'Arnofio/Glô in the Dark', she learned Welsh and immersed herself in the bilingualism of Catatonia, Melys, Gorky's and Topper. Her 2018 debut album, *Wedi*, was written in Welsh, while its follow-up, *Isle of Dogs* in 2020, was a trilingual travelogue encapsulating Cymraeg, English and Russian.

Gwenno also writes in three languages. Born in Cardiff as the daughter of a Cornish poet and Welsh-language activist, her Welsh Music Prize-winning solo debut, *Y Dydd Olaf* ('The Last Day'), was an ode to the preservation of language. Subsequent albums *Le Kov* and the Mercury Prize-nominated *Tresor* were largely written in Cornish.

Now immortalised with a mural on the side of Clwb Ifor Bach, Gwenno has helped normalise songwriting in marginalised languages, which can now be heard on BBC Radio 1 and 6 Music. Equally inspired by her roots is Gwenno's sister, Ani Glass (her Cornish bardic name meaning 'Observer'), who won Best Album at the 2020 National Eisteddfod with *Mirores*. 'When I first started making music in Welsh, I think I was seen as a bit of a novelty act,' Ani told *NME*. 'But more than anything, I enjoyed changing people's perceptions of what Welsh-language music can be.'[561]

From London to Liverpool and Brooklyn to Budapest, Huw Stephens's *Dydd Miwsig Cymru* has flown the flag internationally for Welsh-language music every February since 2013. A day of diversity and inclusion that celebrates Welshness in all its forms, it also emphasises that there's no superior version of national identity. As Rhys Ifans said in an interview to promote the 2018 event: 'We share the Welsh language whether we speak it, or not. It's *ours*.'

The multicultural breadth of eclectic styles bursting out of Wales speaks volumes, and it is showcased each year in the nation's thriving festival scene. Previously, Welsh-language acts would've been lumped together on stages regardless of their clashing sounds because they sang in *Cymraeg*. But Welsh-language music is not a genre, and (contrary to the long-held view) it doesn't just relate to folk.

Green Man in the beautiful Brecon Beacons started out with an audience of just 300 in 2003, but has since evolved into a 25,000-capacity week-long event. From 2012–18, Festival N°6 attracted both home-grown talent and international icons to Portmeirion, while Wrexham's FOCUS Wales and Sŵn Festival in Cardiff have become our very own versions of South by Southwest (Welsh acts now often travel over to Texas to play the real thing too).

Welsh-language festivals are also proving popular. With a euphoric finale at Cardiff Castle, Tafwyl has pulled in crowds of up to 40,000 in recent years, while the National Eisteddfod continues to be the biggest celebration of one of Europe's oldest living languages. Its Maes B brand runs parallel to the main event and casts a spotlight onto the cream of the young Welsh-language crop like Candelas, Chroma, Swnami and Yws Gwynedd. Euros Childs said to *The Guardian*: 'Every year, there's 600 teenagers blind drunk and singing along, and loads of them go on to make music. That's what modern Welsh-speaking culture is like.'[562]

The success stories have been bountiful. Bethesda band 9Bach blend traditional Welsh music with electronica and world music, and in 2015 they won a BBC Radio 2 Folk Award for Best Album with *Tincian* (which aptly translates as 'Resonate'). Anglesey's Carwyn Ellis has transplanted *Cymraeg* to South America thanks to his collaborations with Rio 18, mixing Brazilian beats with sunny samba. Cardiff's Guinea-born balafonist, N'famady Kouyaté, reworks traditional West African music with words in Welsh and Malinké. Meanwhile, Mold alt-rockers The Joy Formidable have taken a page out of The Alarm's book of bilingualism. Predominantly an English-language band, they have released monthly vinyl singles in *Cymraeg* under the banner of *Aruthrol* ('Immense') and rerecorded their debut EP, *A Balloon Called Moaning*, as *Y Falŵn Drom*.

Sheffield-based quartet Sister Wives effectively use *Cymraeg* to add extra layers of magic and mystery to their concoction of spirituality and witchcraft. Plus, Merthyr Tydfil sisters Kizzy Crawford and Eädyth are of Bajan heritage, and have drawn on their childhood experiences of competing in Eisteddfodau to take bilingual modern soul into exciting new directions.

The twenty-first century has been far more focused on the music than fighting for language rights. In 1999, Tystion urged Wales to shrug off the complex of its past, and this younger generation have certainly done that. They have suffered neither clunky clichés about their Welshness, nor any insecurity over singing in *Cymraeg*.

While online streaming means that Welsh bands don't sell anywhere near as much as in their '90s heyday, the internet has transformed listeners into world consumers of music. Since streaming costs less than buying records, fans are more prepared to listen to something in a different language, lessening the Anglo-American influence. That's led to a far healthier crossover of non-Welsh speakers taking an interest in the *Cymraeg* scene. Away from major-label pressure, artists have freedom to indulge their creativity.

As Huw Stephens said in the BBC Radio 4 documentary *Art of Now: Cymru Rising*:

> What an amazing time to be making the music you really want to make – record a track in whichever style or language you like, get it online and see what happens!
>
> No more hunting down DJs in wine bars or knocking on the doors of record companies. Success comes to the most bold and creative, but overnight success isn't so important. You can let your music and sound grow and find its audience, so for any music regarded as 'niche', now is the time.[563]

In 2018, Llanrug teenagers Alffa became the first band to hit 1 million streams for a Welsh-language song on Spotify with 'Gwenwyn' ('Poison') after being placed on influential playlists by Welsh music distributor PYST. The blues-rock duo was one of twelve finalists in 2018 for Bethan Elfyn's Horizons/Gorwelion scheme. Launched by BBC Radio Cymru and the Arts Council of Wales, it showcases independent Welsh artists at festivals and secures them studio access at Rockfield and Maida Vale.

Also amongst the finalists that year were Carmarthen band Adwaith (Reaction), who have gone on to win the Welsh Music Prize with both their albums (*Melyn* and *Bato Mato*) – the only act to have landed the award twice.

Gruff Owen snapped up Adwaith for his label Libertino after seeing them at their first gig. Speaking to *NME* in 2022, he recalled another memorable show: 'Last October, the Lexington in London was packed to the brim with people singing along to lyrics that were purely in Welsh. I stood at the back of the room thinking, "Oh my God, I've been waiting my whole life for this!"'[564]

Lead vocalist Hollie Singer continued:

> We've learned to have faith in our Welshness, and not be afraid to use the language. I'm not the best Welsh speaker, but learning

has been very therapeutic and grounding because we're using the language in a different way.

We sing as we would speak naturally. In the past, a lot of Welsh music has usually been about using the language 'correctly'…We don't want to exclude less confident speakers of the language from enjoying our music.[565]

Music is an international language and by avoiding textbook Welsh, Adwaith are promoting inclusion into a blossoming ecosystem that could bring *Cymraeg* to a global audience. The Welsh government is committed to ensuring there are 1 million Welsh speakers in Wales by 2050 – that's one in three of the population, and double the current number. BBC Wales reported in 2020 that *Cymraeg* was the fastest growing language in the UK. Duolingo confirmed a 44 per cent rise in that year alone of new Welsh learners using the app (the fight isn't over though as the company confirmed in October 2023 that it would be 'pausing' updates to its *Cymraeg* course to 'channel its resources into more popular languages').

The success of the '90s Welsh bands led to a groundswell of national optimism that contributed towards the 1997 devolution victory, but it's Welsh-language artists informing politics now. In *Wales Since 1939*, Martin Johnes said: 'With astonishing speed, devolution became an accepted part of Wales and a symbol of Welsh nationhood – one that stepped into the void left by the disappearance of older symbols like coal and religion.'[566] Thanks to its handling of the COVID-19 pandemic and the prominence given to First Minister Mark Drakeford and the different choices he made to Westminster politicians, Wales was viewed UK-wide (perhaps for the first time) as its own devolved, political nation.

With supporters including Michael Sheen, Matthew Rhys and Neville Southall, there's now an upsurge in the desire for Welsh independence (*annibyniaeth*) as the next step in Wales's evolution. While still a minority movement with a membership of just under 7,000 in 2023, the likes of Gwenno, Ani Glass, Adwaith and Kizzy Crawford are passing the message onto the next generation. Welsh Music Prize-winning singer-songwriter Georgia Ruth said to Yes Is More:

> An independent Wales is a stronger Wales. We are brave, dynamic and innovative...If we are to have agency over our own language, our creative industries and – perhaps most urgently – our own environment and climate, we must be independent.[567]

Welsh football fandom has also helped perpetuate feelings of *annibyniaeth* with YesCymru stickers a regular sight at matches. Now branded by the Football Association of Wales as *'Cymru'* to a world audience at the three major tournaments since 2016, 'Y Wal Goch' ('The Red Wall') are creating a modernised, progressive and politically engaged version of Wales. Dafydd Iwan's 'Yma o Hyd' is now an alternative national anthem at home and abroad. It's a song about overcoming difficult times and fighting for a better future, much like Welsh football. In 2022, the FAW collaborated with Sage Todz – a Penygroes rapper originally from Essex and of Nigerian descent – on a drill rendition of 'Yma o Hyd'.

While the Manics have never written in *Cymraeg*, they simply couldn't have hailed from any other homeland. Along with their draping of 'Y Ddraig Goch', and softening, more respectful views of the Welsh language, a growing sense of *'hiraeth'* has permeated their work. In titanic-lunged guitar god James Dean Bradfield, they possessed the best frontman of the Cool Cymru era. In a 2006 interview with the *Belfast Telegraph*, he reflected:

> We were desperate to escape what we thought had shaped us, but disowned us...Now I'm in thrall to Wales and it's strange and befuddling to be playing catch-up.
>
> There's a place I go drinking in the valleys...One night I was leaving the bar, and this old bloke said: 'Don't forget, the mountains will never let you go.'
>
> The more I thought about it, the more I thought it was a bit true.[568]

Throughout the '90s, the Manics offered support slots to up-and-coming Welsh acts. Not only have they waxed lyrical about the old guard of Welsh music like Badfinger, John Cale and Green Gartside, but they have also endorsed, toured and collaborated with the new generation, including Gwenno, Cate Le Bon, The Anchoress,

Adwaith, The Afternoons, Georgia Ruth, The Joy Formidable and R. Seiliog. Most recently, they've gone on the road with Himalayas – a Cardiff band co-managed by Manics affiliate Terri Hall, who have racked up an astonishing 30 million Spotify streams of their 2017 single 'Thank God I'm Not You'.

Nicky Wire said to *The Guardian*:

> Since the Manics, Welsh bands are described outside Wales as Welsh. When we first went to Japan and America, people would say, 'So, what's it like living in England?' That's changed now; people know where we're from…
>
> I feel a surge of pride now when a Welsh band breaks. It's healthy for the country, and it's an easy way of conveying to the rest of world that we're really good at making music.[569]

In 2017, James Dean Bradfield guested on the Public Service Broadcasting single 'Turn No More', wherein he recited Idris Davies's Welsh-language poem 'Gwalia Deserta XXXVI'.

Recorded at Ebbw Vale Institute and featuring cameos from 9Bach's Lisa Jên Brown and Beaufort Male Choir, its parent album, *Every Valley*, chronicled the rise and fall of Wales's coal mining industry. The fact that a London band wished to tell such a story illustrates Wales's continuing resonance beyond borders.

Stereophonics proved to be the most commercial by-product of Cool Cymru. While Kelly Jones arguably never bettered *Word Gets Around* and eschewed his early storyteller songwriting (which initially seemed to be his unique selling point), he's hit upon a winning formula with fans. Eight of their twelve albums have reached No. 1 – spanning *Performance and Cocktails* in 1999 to 2022's *Oochya!*

It's not lonely at the top either. Since the '90s, Lostprophets, Duffy (a Grammy, BRIT and Ivor Novello winner), Marina and the Diamonds, Catfish and the Bottlemen, Tom Jones and Ren have all reached No. 1. Katherine Jenkins has topped the UK Classical Artist Albums Chart fourteen times, while Cardiff indie rockers

Los Campesinos! followed in Melys's footsteps by topping the BBC Radio 1 Festive Fifty. In February 2024, Skindred became the first Welsh artists to win a MOBO (Music of Black Origin) when the Newport band secured the award for Best Alternative Music Act.

The brightest young Welsh talents are also being hand-picked by huge artists for support slots – Hana Lili opened for Coldplay, Boy Azooga and Buzzard Buzzard Buzzard have supported Noel Gallagher, while James and the Cold Gun and Himalayas have warmed up crowds for Guns N' Roses and Foo Fighters respectively.

A hundred years ago, you've couldn't have foreseen what would happen to Wales with its oppressed culture and language that risked extinction. Yet, both are now thriving in the twenty-first century. Music beats at the nation's heart, and genres as diverse as indie, metal, punk, techno, DIY and hip-hop flow through its veins.

Successes are no longer anomalies. Cool Cymru created a future where Welsh artists can operate as they please, unburdened by the heavy expectations of representing their country. For the first time, Wales's rich contemporary scene can embrace its history, and ultimately craft its own.

ACKNOWLEDGEMENTS

International Velvet has been a labour of love, but it wouldn't have been possible without the undying support of my parents, Byron and Stephanie, brothers Gareth and Michael, and my much better half, Kerry-Lynne Doyle.

A massive thank you to Rhys Mwyn for providing the foreword and for his generosity in granting an extended interview. Thanks also to my *Welsh Music Podcast* co-host, James Cuff, who suggested the idea of a book when we first started the pod back in 2019.

The editorial feedback from Amy Feldman and Abbie Headon at the University of Wales Press has been invaluable and made the book so much better. Another big thank you to Caroline Goldsmith, Dave Holwill and Robert Harries for additional help on the edit; Ruth Killick, Lucy Ramsey and Maria Vassilopoulos for marketing and promotion; Georgia Winstone for social media support; Steven Goundrey and Adam Burns for the photo section; and Andy Ward for the amazing artwork.

Thanks to Helen Davies for the advice and support, Chantal Patton for a load of Catatonia archive materials, plus Nia Daniel and Dan Griffiths at the National Library of Wales for their enthusiasm for the project.

The following books are highly recommended and were vital sources of information: *Cerys, Catatonia and the Rise of Welsh Pop* – David Owens; *Everything (A Book About Manic Street Preachers)* – Simon Price; *Rise of the Super Furry Animals* – Ric Rawlins; *Stereophonics: Just Enough Evidence to Print* – Danny O'Connor; *Brittle with Relics: A History of Wales, 1962–97* – Richard King; *Wales Since 1939* – Martin Johnes; and *'Blerwytirhwng?' The Place of Welsh Pop Music* – Sarah Hill.

In addition to *NME* and *Melody Maker*, the following websites and social media accounts were particularly useful: Forever Delayed, SFA OK!, *Britpop Memories* and *Rock's Backpages*.

Last but not least, huge thanks to everyone who accepted interviews with myself or the *Welsh Music Podcast*, which have been used in the book: Greg Haver, Richard Parfitt, Huw Williams, Mike Peters, Paul Adams, Andrea Adams, Gruff Rhys, Gorwel Owen, Patricia Morgan and Mark Roberts.

Diolch yn fawr pawb.

Neil.

ENDNOTES

1. Catatonia's song 'International Velvet' was featured on the album (also called) International Velvet, WEA Records: Blanco y Negro, released 2 February 1998

2. Caroline Sullivan, 'International Velvet: Catatonia at the Brixton Academy', *The Guardian*, 23 March 1999

3. John Dingwall, 'Tomboy Jones: Catatonia Babe Cerys Matthews is the Best Thing to Come Out of Wales Since Tom Jones', *Scottish Daily Record*, 30 January 1998, *www.thefreelibrary.com/TOMBOY+JONES%3B+Catatonia+babe+Cerys+Matthews +is+the+best+thing+to+come...-a060608243*

4. Sarah Hill, *'Blerwytirhwng?' The Place of Welsh Pop Music*, Routledge, 2007

5. Brian Wright, *To Hell and Back with Catatonia*, Firefly Publishing, 2001

6. *Wales: Music Nation with Huw Stephens*, BBC 2 Wales documentary series, originally broadcast 10 September 2022

7. *Wales: Music Nation with Huw Stephens*, BBC 2 Wales documentary series, originally broadcast 10 September 2022

8. *The Story of Miwsig*, BBC Wales podcast series, Episode 1, 3 February 2021

9. David Owens, *Cerys, Catatonia and the Rise of Welsh Pop*, Ebury Press, 2000

10. Interview with the author of this book

11. Interview with the author of this book

12. David Owens, *Cerys, Catatonia and the Rise of Welsh Pop*, Ebury Press, 2000

13. David R. Edwards, *Atgofion Hen Wanc*, Y Lolfa, 2009

14. Interview with Elis James, *Welsh Music Podcast*, Episode 8, 7 February 2020

15. Sarah Hill, *'Blerwytirhwng?' The Place of Welsh Pop Music*, Routledge, 2007

16. Interview with Rhys Mwyn, *Welsh Music Podcast*, Episode 9, 21 February 2020

17. Interview with Rhys Mwyn, *Welsh Music Podcast*, Episode 9, 21 February 2020

18. Interview with Rhys Mwyn, *Welsh Music Podcast*, Episode 9, 21 February 2020

19. Interview with Rhys Mwyn, *Welsh Music Podcast*, Episode 9, 21 February 2020

20. Interview with Rhys Mwyn, *Welsh Music Podcast*, Episode 9, 21 February 2020

21. Sarah Hill, *'Blerwytirhwng?' The Place of Welsh Pop Music*, Routledge, 2007

22. '60–51 | The Greatest Welsh Albums of All Time: Datblygu – *Pyst* (54)', *Wales Arts Review*, 5 November 2021, *www.walesartsreview.org/60-51-the-greatest-welsh-albums-of-all-time/*

23. '30–21 | The Greatest Welsh Albums of All Time: Datblygu – *Libertino* (22),' *Wales Arts Review*, 5 November 2021, *www.walesartsreview.org/30-21-the-greatest-welsh-albums-of-all-time/*

24. David R. Edwards, *Atgofion Hen Wanc*, Y Lolfa, 2009

25. David R. Edwards, *Atgofion Hen Wanc*, Y Lolfa, 2009

26. Criss Sexx, 'Interview with Tigertailz', melodic.net, 13 November 2016, *www.melodic.net/ interview/tigertailz*

27. Julian Bishop, 'Out to Convert Welsh Hippies', *South Wales Echo*, 1 July 1986

28. Criss Sexx, 'Interview with Tigertailz', melodic.net, 13 November 2016, *www.melodic.net/ interview/tigertailz*

29. 'Tigertailz Biography', *Spirit of Metal* webzine, *www.spirit-of-metal.com/en/biography/ Tigertailz/6802*

ENDNOTES

30. 'Tigertailz Biography', *Spirit of Metal* webzine, *www.spirit-of-metal.com/en/biography/Tigertailz/6802*

31. 'Tigertailz Biography', *Spirit of Metal* webzine, *www.spirit-of-metal.com/en/biography/Tigertailz/6802*

32. Tigertailz biography, BBC Wales Music, November 2008, *www.bbc.co.uk/wales/music/sites/tigertailz/pages/biography.shtml*

33. Steve Beebee, *Kerrang!*, 2007

34. 'Tigertailz – *Bezerk 2.0*', BBC Wales Music, 23 June 2006, *www.bbc.co.uk/wales/music/sites/tigertailz/pages/bezerk_2.shtml*

35. Llyybr Llaethog biography, BBC Wales Music, November 2008, *www.bbc.co.uk/wales/sites/llwybr-llaethog/pages/biography.shtml*

36. Sarah Hill, '*Blerwytirhwng?' The Place of Welsh Pop Music*, Routledge, 2007

37. Llwybr Llaethog biography, BBC Wales Music, November 2008, *www.bbc.co.uk/wales/music/sites/llwybr-llaethog/pages/biography.shtml*

38. Llwybr Llaethog biography, BBC Wales Music, November 2008, *www.bbc.co.uk/wales/music/sites/llwybr-llaethog/pages/biography.shtml*

39. Sarah Hill, '*Blerwytirhwng?' The Place of Welsh Pop Music*, Routledge, 2007

40. 'Interview with Mike Peters of The Alarm', *Welsh Music Podcast*, 14 December 2020, *www.welshmusicpodcast.co.uk/interview-with-mike-peters-of-the-alarm/*

41. Rhys Mwyn, *Cam o'r Tywyllwch* (book), Y Lolfa, 2006

42. 'Interview with Mike Peters of The Alarm', *Welsh Music Podcast*, 14 December 2020, *www.welshmusicpodcast.co.uk/interview-with-mike-peters-of-the-alarm/*

43. Oliver R. Moore Howells, '"We're Hitting the Road and Living Life to the Full!" – Mike Peters Interview', *Buzz*, 26 June 2019, *www.buzzmag.co.uk/were-hitting-the-road-and-living-life-to-the-full-mike-peters-interview/*

44. Bono clip included in video trailer to promote The Alarm's fortieth anniversary concert at St David's Hall, uploaded by the band on 24 February 2020 (gig eventually took place on 15 April 2023 due to the COVID-19 pandemic). *www.youtube.com/watch?v=GFt5VeQ8_Mo&t=15s*

45. 'Interview with Mike Peters of The Alarm', *Welsh Music Podcast*, 14 December 2020, *www.welshmusicpodcast.co.uk/interview-with-mike-peters-of-the-alarm/*

46. 'Interview with Mike Peters of The Alarm', *Welsh Music Podcast*, 14 December 2020, *www.welshmusicpodcast.co.uk/interview-with-mike-peters-of-the-alarm/*

47. Helen Fitzgerald, 'Declarations of Independence', *Melody Maker*, 18 February 1984

48. David Owens, *Cerys, Catatonia and the Rise of Welsh Pop*, Ebury Press, 2000

49. Bill Harris, 'The Alarm's Mike Peters Recalls Classic Satellite Concert in '86', *Toronto Sun*, 16 September 2016, *www.torontosun.com/2016/09/16/the-alarms-mike-peters-recalls-classic-satellite-concert-in-86*

50. 'Interview with Mike Peters of The Alarm', *Welsh Music Podcast*, 14 December 2020, *www.welshmusicpodcast.co.uk/interview-with-mike-peters-of-the-alarm/*

51. Interview with Mark Roberts, *Welsh Music Podcast*, Episode 15, 11 December 2020

52. David Owens, *Cerys, Catatonia and the Rise of Welsh Pop*, Ebury Press, 2000

53. David Owens, *Cerys, Catatonia and the Rise of Welsh Pop*, Ebury Press, 2000

54. David Owens, *Cerys, Catatonia and the Rise of Welsh Pop*, Ebury Press, 2000

55. David Owens, *Cerys, Catatonia and the Rise of Welsh Pop*, Ebury Press, 2000

56. Richard King, *Brittle with Relics: A History of Wales, 1962–97*, Faber & Faber, 2023

57. David Owens, *Cerys, Catatonia and the Rise of Welsh Pop*, Ebury Press, 2000

58. David Owens, *Cerys, Catatonia and the Rise of Welsh Pop*, Ebury Press, 2000

59. David Owens, *Cerys, Catatonia and the Rise of Welsh Pop*, Ebury Press, 2000

60. David Owens, *Cerys, Catatonia and the Rise of Welsh Pop*, Ebury Press, 2000

61. Gruff Rhys interview on Jonathan Ross's Saturday morning show, BBC Radio 2, 12 January 2002, *www.youtube.com/watch?v=AFj6AQNWZAU*

62. Ffa Coffi Pawb interview, BBC Wales Music, 2004, *www.bbc.co.uk/wales/music/sites/ffa-coffi-pawb/pages/interview_02.shtml*

63. Ffa Coffi Pawb interview, BBC Wales Music, 2004, *www.bbc.co.uk/wales/music/sites/ffa-coffi-pawb/pages/interview_02.shtm*

64. Ffa Coffi Pawb interview, BBC Wales Music, 2004, *www.bbc.co.uk/wales/music/sites/ffa-coffi-pawb/pages/interview_02.shtm*

65. Alastair Campbell and Richard Stott (eds), *The Blair Years: Extracts from the Alastair Campbell Diaries*, Hutchinson, 2007 (original Neil Kinnock quote made in summer 1995)

66. Mike Parker, *Neighbours from Hell? English Attitudes to the Welsh*, Y Lolfa, 2014

67. Alwyn W. Turner, *A Classless Society: Britain in the 1990s*, Aurum, 2013

68. Simon Price, 'Street Life', *Melody Maker*, 4 January 1999

69. Simon Price, *Everything (A Book About Manic Street Preachers)*, Virgin, 1999

70. Marc Burrows, *Manic Street Preachers: Album by Album*, White Owl, 2021

71. Stuart Bailie, 'Motown Junk' single review, *NME*, 26 January 1991

72. Emily Barker, 'The 500 Greatest Songs of All Time' ('Motown Junk': 244), *NME*, 31 January 2014, *www.nme.com/photos/the-500-greatest-songs-of-all-time-300-201-1421856*

73. David Owens, *Cerys, Catatonia and the Rise of Welsh Pop*, Ebury Press, 2000

74. Richey Edwards quoted in Andrew Collins, 'The Newport Dolls', *NME*, 2 November 1991

75. Martin Power, *Nailed to History: The Story of Manic Street Preachers*, Omnibus, 2010

76. Martin Power, *Nailed to History: The Story of Manic Street Preachers*, Omnibus, 2010

77. David Owens, *Cerys, Catatonia and the Rise of Welsh Pop*, Ebury Press, 2000

78. Martin Power, *Nailed to History: The Story of Manic Street Preachers*, Omnibus, 2010

79. Martin Power, *Nailed to History: The Story of Manic Street Preachers*, Omnibus, 2010

80. Simon Price, *Everything (A Book About Manic Street Preachers)*, Virgin, 1999

81. Simon Price, *Everything (A Book About Manic Street Preachers)*, Virgin, 1999

82. Keith Cameron, 'The Mojo Interview: Nicky Wire', *Mojo: Issue 334*, September 2021, *www.nme.com/news/music/manic-street-preachers-nicky-wire-says-hed-rather-fucking-stab-his-eyes-out-than-get-an-obe-3000132*

83. Steven Wells, 'Scum On Feel The Noise', *NME*, 4 August 1990

84. Snub TV (UK) interview, BBC2, originally broadcast 21 January 1991

85. Paul Rees, 'You've Seen the Name, Heard the Buzz, But Who the Hell are Manic Street Preachers?', *Raw*, 22 January 1992

86. Martin Power, *Nailed to History: The Story of Manic Street Preachers*, Omnibus, 2010

87. A. A. Gill, *Sunday Times* column, 1997

88. Jon Wilde, 'Motorcycle Emptiness' single review, *Melody Maker*, 30 May 1992

89. Barbara Ellen, 'Rocket to Blusher', *Generation Terrorists* album review, *NME*, 8 February 1992

90. Stephen Dalton, 'Stereophonics: Cwmaman Overboard', *NME*, 10 October 1998

91. Michael Hicks, 'The Sound of the South Wales Valleys – How It Evolved', *Louder Than War*, 16 June 2013, *www.louderthanwar.com/the-sound-of-the-south-wales-valleys-how-it-evolved/*

92. Stuart Maconie, *Gold Against the Soul* album review, *Select*, August 1993

93. Stuart Bailie, 'Meek Leek Manifesto', *Gold Against the Soul* album review, *NME*, 19 June 1993

94. Paul Edwards quoted in the Angst letters page, 'Wales of Disapproval', *NME*, 10 July 1993

95. Iestyn George's response in the Angst letters page, 'Wales of Disapproval', *NME*, 10 July 1993

ENDNOTES

96. Duncan Heavisides, *Gair Rhydd*, live review of Manics' gig at Hanging Gardens (Cardiff University) on 17 February 1992

97. Jon Wilde, 'First Cuts: James Dean Bradfield', *Uncut*, July 2006

98. Alun Hamnett, 'Is Heaven a Place Where Nothing Ever Happens?', *Record Collector Presents…Manic Street Preachers*, 7 October 2021

99. Richard Rose Zoom interview with The Darling Buds, *Repeat*, 23 August 2020, *www.youtube.com/watch?v=3N2MpZJt0lM*

100. Nathan Briant, 'First Person: The Darling Buds Lead Singer and Newport Drama Teacher Andrea Lewis Jarvis', *South Wales Argus*, 23 March 2016, *www.southwalesargus.co.uk/news/14377448.first-person-the-darling-buds-lead-singer-and-newport-drama-teacher-andrea-lewis-jarvis/*

101. Nathan Briant, 'First Person: The Darling Buds Lead Singer and Newport Drama Teacher Andrea Lewis Jarvis', *South Wales Argus*, 23 March 2016, *www.southwalesargus.co.uk/news/14377448.first-person-the-darling-buds-lead-singer-and-newport-drama-teacher-andrea-lewis-jarvis/*

102. Len Brown, 'The House of Love, The Darling Buds and The Wonder Stuff: Tomorrow Belongs to Us', *NME*, 7 January 1989

103. Paul Lester, live review of The Darling Buds' gig at the Manchester International, *Melody Maker*, 28 January 1989

104. '80-71 | The Greatest Welsh Albums of All Time: The Darling Buds – *Pop Said…* (71)', *Wales Arts Review*, 22 October 2021, *www.walesartsreview.org/80-71-the-greatest-welsh-albums-of-all-time/*

105. Everett True, 'The Darling Buds: Petal Music Machine', *Melody Maker*, 26 May 1990

106. Len Brown, 'The House of Love, The Darling Buds and The Wonder Stuff: Tomorrow Belongs to Us', *NME*, 7 January 1989

107. Lockdown Session Twitter Listening Party for *Pop Said…* by The Darling Buds, *Welsh Music Podcast*, 24 April 2020, www.*x.com/welshmusicpod/status/1253590332882718720?s=20*

108. Conversation snippet at the end of 'Barbed Wire' on Gorky's Zygotic Mynci's album *Patio*, Ankst, June 1992

109. John Lawrence quoted in Stewart Lee's *Sunday Times* column, 9 June 1996, *www.stewartlee.co.uk/written_for_money/gorkys-zygotic-mynci/*

110. Elis James and John Robins, *Elis and John Present the Holy Vible: The Book the Bible Could Have Been*, Trapeze, 2018

111. Martyn Coppack, 'Wizards and Lizards', *Shindig! Issue 92*, June 2019

112. Max Ashworth, 'Great Welsh Albums: *Patio* by Gorky's Zygotic Mynci', *Wales Arts Review*, 23 November 2019, *www.walesartsreview.org/greatest-welsh-albums-patio-by-gorkys/*

113. Conversation snippet at the end of 'Sally Webster' on Gorky's Zygotic Mynci's album *Patio*, Ankst, June 1992

114. Elis James and John Robins, *Elis and John Present the Holy Vible: The Book the Bible Could Have Been*, Trapeze, 2018

115. Interview with the author of this book

116. Steve Sutherland, 'The World Is Turning On' single review, *NME*, 7 November 1992

117. Interview with the author of this book

118. David Owens, *Cerys, Catatonia and the Rise of Welsh Pop*, Ebury Press, 2000

119. Interview with the author of this book

120. David Owens, *Cerys, Catatonia and the Rise of Welsh Pop*, Ebury Press, 2000

121. Interview with the author of this book

122. Interview with the author of this book

123. Interview with the author of this book

124. Ian Fortnam, 'Helen Love Interview: Bubblegum Punk's Not Dead, Pass It On', *Classic Rock*, 25 December 2021, *www.loudersound.com/features/helen-love-interview-bubblegum-punks-not-dead-pass-it-on*

125. David Owens, 'The Story of Reluctant Indie Superstars Helen Love – Wales' Greatest Cult Band', *Nation.Cymru*, 7 March 2021, *www.nation.cymru/culture/the-story-of-reluctant-indie-superstars-helen-love-wales-greatest-cult-band/*

126. Richard Rose, 'Interview with Helen Love', *Repeat*, November 2020, *www.repeatfanzine. co.uk/interviews/Helen%20Love%202020.htm*

127. Ian Fortnam, 'Helen Love Interview: Bubblegum Punk's Not Dead, Pass It On', *Classic Rock*, 25 December 2021, *www.loudersound.com/features/helen-love-interview-bubblegum-punks-not-dead-pass-it-on*

128. 'Helen Love biography', BBC Wales Music, 17 November 2008, *www.bbc.co.uk/wales/music/sites/helen-love/pages/biography.shtml*

129. Ian Fortnam, 'Helen Love Interview: Bubblegum Punk's Not Dead, Pass It On', *Classic Rock*, 25 December 2021, *www.loudersound.com/features/helen-love-interview-bubblegum-punks-not-dead-pass-it-on*

130. Ian Fortnam, 'Helen Love Interview: Bubblegum Punk's Not Dead, Pass It On', *Classic Rock*, 25 December 2021, *www.loudersound.com/features/helen-love-interview-bubblegum-punks-not-dead-pass-it-on*

131. Ian Fortnam, 'Helen Love Interview: Bubblegum Punk's Not Dead, Pass It On', *Classic Rock*, 25 December 2021, *www.loudersound.com/features/helen-love-interview-bubblegum-punks-not-dead-pass-it-on*

132. Nathan Bevan, 'The Ramones' Love for a Cult Swansea Band', WalesOnline, 11 May 2014, *www.walesonline.co.uk/whats-on/whats-on-news/ramones-love-cult-swansea-band-7099360*

133. Mark Rees, 'Helen Loves Talks About Her Tribute to Dylan Thomas, *Where Dylan Thomas Talks to Me*', *South Wales Evening Post*, 4 November 2014

134. Nathan Bevan, 'The Ramones' Love for a Cult Swansea Band', WalesOnline, *www. walesonline.co.uk/whats-on/whats-on-news/ramones-love-cult-swansea-band-7099360*

135. Nathan Bevan, 'The Ramones' love for a cult Swansea band', WalesOnline, *www. walesonline.co.uk/whats-on/whats-on-news/ramones-love-cult-swansea-band-7099360*

136. Interview with Mark Roberts, *Welsh Music Podcast*, Episode 15, 11 December 2020

137. Interview with the author of this book

138. David Owens, *Cerys, Catatonia and the Rise of Welsh Pop*, Ebury Press, 2000

139. Steven Wells, 'Rompy Stompy Welsho Punk-Pop Sex Record of the Week', *For Tinkerbell* EP review, *NME*, September 1993

140. David Owens, *Cerys, Catatonia and the Rise of Welsh Pop*, Ebury Press, 2000

141. John Harris, sleeve notes for *Catatonia: Greatest Hits*, WEA Records: Blanco y Negro, released 15 October 2002

142. Kitty Empire, 'Welsh Rare Bits', *The Crai E.P.* review, *NME*, 1999

143. Brian Wright, *To Hell and Back with Catatonia*, Firefly Publishing, 2001

144. Ric Rawlins, *Rise of the Super Furry Animals*, The Friday Project, 2015

145. Simon Williams, 'Fur Out', *NME*, 24 June 1995

146. Simon Williams, 'Fur Out', *NME*, 24 June 1995

147. Everett True, 'Super Furry Animals: Cymru As You Are', *Melody Maker*, 5 August 1995

148. Angela Lewis, 'The Sound and the Furry', *NME*, 6 January 1996

ENDNOTES

149. Simon Williams, 'Great Balls of Fur', live review of the Furries' gig at London King's Cross Splash Club (aka Water Rats) on 19 May 1995, *NME*, 3 June 1995

150. Angela Lewis, 'The Sound and the Furry', *NME*, 6 January 1996

151. Ric Rawlins, *Rise of the Super Furry Animals*, The Friday Project, 2015

152. Elis James and John Robins, *Elis and John Present the Holy Bible: The Book the Bible Could Have Been*, Trapeze, 2018

153. Elis James and John Robins, *Elis and John Present the Holy Bible: The Book the Bible Could Have Been*, Trapeze, 2018

154. Ngaire Ruth, live review of Gorky's gig at London's Powerhaus, *Melody Maker*, 13 August 1994

155. Stewart Lee, *Sunday Times*, 9 June 1996, *www.stewartlee.co.uk/written_for_money/gorkys-zygotic-mynci/*

156. Sleeve notes for Gorky's Zygotic Mynci's album *Tatay*, Ankst, released 1 March 1994

157. James McCarthy, 'Iron Maiden, Green Day, Oasis and Samurai Swords – The Untold Stories of the World's Biggest Bands and a Small Welsh Club', WalesOnline, 26 October 2017, *www.walesonline.co.uk/lifestyle/nostalgia/iron-maiden-green-day-oasis-13816821*

158. *Sound Towns: Newport*, BBC Radio 4 music documentary series, Episode 1, 9 May 2023

159. James McCarthy, 'Iron Maiden, Green Day, Oasis and Samurai Swords – The Untold Stories of the World's Biggest Bands and a Small Welsh Club', WalesOnline, 26 October 2017, *www.walesonline.co.uk/lifestyle/nostalgia/iron-maiden-green-day-oasis-13816821*

160. James McCarthy, 'Iron Maiden, Green Day, Oasis and Samurai Swords – The Untold Stories of the World's Biggest Bands and a Small Welsh Club', WalesOnline, 26 October 2017, *www.walesonline.co.uk/lifestyle/nostalgia/iron-maiden-green-day-oasis-13816821*

161. James McCarthy, 'Iron Maiden, Green Day, Oasis and Samurai Swords – The Untold Stories of the World's Biggest Bands and a Small Welsh Club', WalesOnline, 26 October 2017, *www.walesonline.co.uk/lifestyle/nostalgia/iron-maiden-green-day-oasis-13816821*

162. *Sound Towns: Newport*, BBC Radio 4 music documentary series, Episode 1, 9 May 2023

163. *New York Times* rock critic, Neil Strauss labelled Newport 'the new Seattle' in *Spin* magazine in 1994

164. Interview with the author of this book

165. Joshua Knapman, 'How Newport Became the "New Seattle" in the 1990s', WalesOnline, 24 January 2021, *www.walesonline.co.uk/whats-on/music-nightlife-news/newport-new-seattle-tjs-dolls-19589868*

166. Matthew Davies-Kreye, 'South Wales Was the "New Seattle?" Total Bollocks!', *Vice*, 5 June 2015, *www.vice.com/en/article/6vm58y/funeral-for-a-friends-matthew-davies-kreye-dissects-the-south-wales-post-hardcore-scene-of-the-early-00s*

167. Joshua Knapman, 'How Newport Became the "New Seattle" in the 1990s', WalesOnline, 24 January 2021, *www.walesonline.co.uk/whats-on/music-nightlife-news/newport-new-seattle-tjs-dolls-19589868*

168. *Sound Towns: Newport*, BBC Radio 4 music documentary series, Episode 1, 9 May 2023

169. Roy Wilkinson, sleeve notes for the deluxe reissue of *The Big 3* by 60 Ft. Dolls, Sony: 3 Loop Music, released 2015

170. Roy Wilkinson, sleeve notes for the deluxe reissue of *The Big 3* by 60 Ft. Dolls, Sony: 3 Loop Music, released 2015

171. Interview with the author of this book

172. Interview with the author of this book

173. *Sound Towns: Newport*, BBC Radio 4 music documentary series, Episode 1, 9 May 2023

174. *Sound Towns: Newport*, BBC Radio 4 music documentary series, Episode 1, 9 May 2023

175. Roy Wilkinson, sleeve notes for the deluxe reissue of *The Big 3* by 60 Ft. Dolls, Sony: 3 Loop Music, released 2015

176. Interview with the author of this book

177. John Harris, *NME*, April 1995

178. Interview with the author of this book

179. Everett True, 'Happy Shopper' reissued single review, *Melody Maker*, 1996

180. Johnny Cigarettes, 'Trio Grand!', *The Big 3* album review, *NME*, May 1996

181. Simon Williams, 'Sindy Incidentally', *NME*, 1994

182. The Stud Brothers, 'Fucking Great!', *Melody Maker*, October 1995

183. David Owens, 'Britpop, bullets and break-ups – hellraising rockers 60 Ft. Dolls remembered', WalesOnline, 11 December 2015, *www.walesonline.co.uk/whats-on/music-nightlife-news/britpop-bullets-break-ups-hellraising-9680107*

184. Interview with Richard Parfitt and Carl Bevan, 'The Making Of…*The Big 3* by 60 Ft. Dolls', *Wales Arts Review*, 12 April 2022, *www.walesartsreview.org/the-making-of-the-big-3-by-60-ft-dolls/*

185. Johnny Cigarettes, 'Trio Grand!', *The Big 3* album review, *NME*, May 1996

186. Victoria Segal, 'Mannequin Street Nietzsches', *The Big 3* album review, *Melody Maker*, May 1996

187. '20–11 | The Greatest Welsh Albums of All Time: 60 Ft. Dolls – *The Big 3* (12)', *Wales Arts Review*, 3 December 2021, *www.walesartsreview.org/20-11-the-greatest-welsh-albums-of-all-time/*

188. Interview with the author of this book

189. Interview with the author of this book

190. Interview with the author of this book

191. Interview with the author of this book

192. Dom Lawson, 'Dub War's *Pain*: Ragga-Metal and Revolution on a Lost '90s Classic', *Metal Hammer*, 20 July 2020, *www.loudersound.com/features/dub-war-pain-story-behind-album*

193. Dom Lawson, 'Dub War's *Pain*: Ragga-Metal and Revolution on a Lost '90s Classic', *Metal Hammer*, 20 July 2020, *www.loudersound.com/features/dub-war-pain-story-behind-album*

194. '90–81 | The Greatest Welsh Albums of All Time: Dub War – *Pain* (83)', *Wales Arts Review*, 15 October 2021, *www.walesartsreview.org/90-81-the-greatest-welsh-albums-of-all-time/*

195. Dom Lawson, 'Dub War's *Pain*: Ragga-Metal and Revolution on a Lost '90s Classic', *Metal Hammer*, 20 July 2020, *www.loudersound.com/features/dub-war-pain-story-behind-album*

196. *Sound Towns: Newport*, BBC Radio 4 music documentary series, Episode 1, 9 May 2023

197. Interview with the author of this book

198. Interview with the author of this book

199. Interview with the author of this book

200. Interview with the author of this book

201. Ben Thompson, *Seven Years of Plenty: A Handbook of Irrefutable Pop Greatness, 1991–1998*, Victor Gollancz, 1998

202. Ben Thompson, *Seven Years of Plenty: A Handbook of Irrefutable Pop Greatness, 1991–1998*, Victor Gollancz, 1998

203. *NME* review of *S4C Makes Me Want to Smoke Crack*, January 1995

204. Ric Rawlins, *Rise of the Super Furry Animals*, The Friday Project, 2015

205. Ben Thompson, *Seven Years of Plenty: A Handbook of Irrefutable Pop Greatness, 1991–1998*, Victor Gollancz, 1998

ENDNOTES

206. Ben Thompson, *Seven Years of Plenty: Handbook of Irrefutable Pop Greatness, 1991-98*, Phoenix, 1999

207. Interview with Richard King, *Welsh Music Podcast*, Episode 22, 1 April 2022

208. Interview with Richard King, *Welsh Music Podcast*, Episode 22, 1 April 2022

209. Interview with Richard King, *Welsh Music Podcast*, Episode 22, 1 April 2022

210. Interview with Richard King, *Welsh Music Podcast*, Episode 22, 1 April 2022

211. Ben Thompson, *Seven Years of Plenty: A Handbook of Irrefutable Pop Greatness, 1991–1998*, Victor Gollancz, 1998

212. Jennifer Nine, 'Prime Simian Cuts: A Gorky's Guide', *Melody Maker*, 22 March 1997

213. 'Gorky's Zygotic Mynci: Turning Over a New Leaf', *Exclaim Magazine*, 1 February 2000

214. Stuart Maconie, 'Who Do You Think You Are Kidding, Mr Cobain?', *Select*, April 1993

215. Interview with Noel and Liam Gallagher, Oasis: *Stop the Clocks* DVD, Big Brother, 2006

216. John Harris, 'A Shite Sports Car and a Punk Reincarnation', *NME*, 10 April 1993

217. David Cavanagh, 'A Hard Day's Night', *Mojo*, November 2000

218. Jon Savage interview in John Dower's docufilm *Live Forever: The Rise and Fall of Brit Pop*, BBC, 21 March 2003

219. Interview with the author of this book

220. Interview with Rhys Mwyn, *Welsh Music Podcast*, Episode 9, 21 February 2020

221. Oasis's debut single 'Supersonic', Creation Records, released 11 April 1994

222. Simon Williams, 'Revelations Terrorists', *The Holy Bible* album review, *NME*, 27 August 1994

223. Stuart Bailie, 'Manic's Depressive', *NME*, 1 October 1994

224. Stuart Maconie, 'We Shall Overcome', *Select*, July 1996

225. Emily Mackay, 'The Record that Changed Our Lives', *NME*, 16 August 2014

226. Nicky Wire's outburst from the stage at Glastonbury on 24 June 1994, which was televised by Channel 4

227. Jon Wilde, 'Pork Life', *Loaded: Issue 5*, September 1994, *www.damonalbarnunofficial. wordpress.com/2015/03/28/loaded-magazine-february-2015/*

228. Danny Wallace, 'Icon of the Year: Noel Gallagher', *GQ*, 16 October 2013, *www.gq-magazine. co.uk/article/icon-noel-gallagher*

229. A double-page ad including *The Holy Bible*'s lyrics was included in NME on 27 August 1994 along with a free four-track album sampler flexi disc. The lyric 'analyse, despise and scrutinise' appeared in the song 'Mausoleum'

230. Emily Mackay, 'Baker's Dozen: Reinventions of the Near Future: James Dean Bradfield's Favourite LPs', *The Quietus*, 23 September 2014, *www.thequietus.com/articles/16303-james-dean-bradfield-manic-street-preachers-favourite-albums-interview*

231. Dorian Lynskey, '"Who's Responsible? You Fucking Are!" Manic Street Preachers: Of Walking Abortion: The Protest Song Eats Itself' chapter in *33 Revolutions Per Minute: A History of Protest Songs*, Faber & Faber, 2010

232. *Later…with Jools Holland*, BBC2, Series 12: Episode 1, 16 October 1998

233. David Evans, *33 ⅓: Manic Street Preachers – The Holy Bible*, Bloomsbury, 2019

234. Noel Gallagher's onstage introduction at the second night of Knebworth, 11 August 1996

235. Nicky Wire's onstage introduction at the Manics' gig at Wembley Arena supporting The Stone Roses, 29 December 1995

236. Mark Goodier interview with James Dean Bradfield on *Classic Album Club* podcast, 'Manic Street Preachers: *Everything Must Go*', Series 1: Episode 5, 5 December 2018

237. Simon Price, *Everything (A Book About Manic Street Preachers)*, Virgin, 1999

238. Mark Goodier interview with James Dean Bradfield on *Classic Album Club* podcast, 'Manic Street Preachers: *Everything Must Go*', Series 1: Episode 5, 5 December 2018

239. *Manic Street Preachers: Escape from History* directed by Kieran Evans, 2017

240. Taylor Parkes, 'Escape from Our History', *Melody Maker*, 1 June 1996

241. *Manic Street Preachers: Escape from History* directed by Kieran Evans, 2017

242. Simon Price, 'And If You Need an Explanation: Manic Street Preachers Interviewed', *The Quietus*, 2 June 2016, *www.thequietus.com/articles/20332-manic-street-preachers-everything-must-go-interview-simon-price*

243. Simon Price, *Everything (A Book About Manic Street Preachers)*, Virgin, 1999

244. *Carling Homecoming: Manic Street Preachers*, Series 1: Episode 3, Channel 4, originally broadcast 18 November 2002

245. Michael Sheen's foreword in Kevin Cummins's *Assassinated Beauty: Photographs of Manic Street Preachers*, Faber & Faber, 2014

246. *Inheritance Tracks: Michael Sheen*, BBC Radio 4, 13 July 2019

247. Mark Goodier interview with James Dean Bradfield on *Classic Album Club* podcast, 'Manic Street Preachers: *Everything Must Go*', Series 1: Episode 5, 5 December 2018

248. Simon Price, *Everything (A Book About Manic Street Preachers)*, Virgin, 1999

249. Neil Collins, 'Preaching to the Converted', *Buzz*, May 2016

250. *Manic Street Preachers: Escape from History* directed by Kieran Evans, 2017

251. Simon Williams, 'You Have Ways of Making Them Talk: The Manic Street Preachers Answer Your Questions', *NME*, 18 August 1998, *www.nme.com/news/music/manic-street-preachers-323-1385979*

252. Marc Burrows, *Manic Street Preachers: Album by Album*, White Owl, 2021

253. Nicky Wire's onstage remark from the Manics' gig at Cardiff International Arena on 12 December 1996

254. Alun Hamnett, 'Is Heaven a Place Where Nothing Ever Happens?', *Record Collector Presents…Manic Street Preachers*, 7 October 2021

255. Interview with the author of this book

256. Richard King, *Brittle with Relics: A History of Wales, 1962–97*, Faber & Faber, 2023

257. Interview with the author of this book

258. Interview with the author of this book

259. Twentieth anniversary special episode for *Mwng* by Super Furry Animals, *Welsh Music Podcast*, 15 May 2020

260. Tom Cox, 'Super Furry Animals: A Furry Good Year', *The Guardian*, 22 May 1998

261. K. Ross Hoffman, 'Magnet Classics: The Making of Super Furry Animals' *Rings Around the World*', *Magnet*, 10 October 2016, *www.magnetmagazine.com/2016/10/10/magnet-classics-the-making-of-super-furry-animals-rings-around-the-world/*

262. Ric Rawlins, *Rise of the Super Furry Animals*, The Friday Project, 2015

263. Sylvia Patterson, 'Despair. Inspiration. Happiness. Despair. Sport. That's the Crux of It', *NME*, 1 August 1998

264. Mick Middles, *Manic Street Preachers: A Biography*, Omnibus, 1999

265. Ric Rawlins, *Rise of the Super Furry Animals*, The Friday Project, 2015

266. Tom Cox, 'Super Furry Animals: A Furry Good Year', *The Guardian*, 22 May 1998

267. Cam Lindsay, 'Drug Smuggler: Super Furry Animals Revisit Making Their Debut', *Vice*, 6 December 2016, *www.vice.com/en/article/ppa4z8/an-armored-tank-and-a-drug-smuggler-super-furry-animals-revisit-making-their-debut-fuzzy-logic*

268. Cam Lindsay, 'Drug Smuggler: Super Furry Animals Revisit Making Their Debut', *Vice*, 6 December 2016, *www.vice.com/en/article/ppa4z8/an-armored-tank-and-a-drug-smuggler-super-furry-animals-revisit-making-their-debut-fuzzy-logic*

269. Cam Lindsay, 'Drug Smuggler: Super Furry Animals Revisit Making Their Debut', *Vice*, 6 December 2016, *www.vice.com/en/article/ppa4z8/an-armored-tank-and-a-drug-smuggler-super-furry-animals-revisit-making-their-debut-fuzzy-logic*

270. Ric Rawlins, *Rise of the Super Furry Animals*, The Friday Project, 2015

271. Simon Price, sleeve notes for the compilation album *Zoom! The Best of Super Furry Animals (1995–2016)*, BMG, released 2016

272. Ric Rawlins, *Rise of the Super Furry Animals*, The Friday Project, 2015

273. Alex Wisgard, 'Gathering Moss' by Super Furry Animals selected in 'Nine Songs: James Dean Bradfield', *The Line of Best Fit*, 14 August 2020, *www.thelineofbestfit.com/features/interviews/james-dean-bradfield-manic-street-preachers-nine-favourite-songs*

274. Simon Price, 'Everything Must Go!', *Melody Maker*, 21 December 1996

275. Ric Rawlins, *Rise of the Super Furry Animals*, The Friday Project, 2015

276. David Owens, *Cerys, Catatonia and the Rise of Welsh Pop*, Ebury Press, 2000

277. Cam Lindsay, 'An Armoured Tank and a Drug Smuggler: Super Furry Animals Revisit Making Their Debut *Fuzzy Logic*', *Vice*, 6 December 2016, *www.vice.com/en/article/ppa4z8/an-armored-tank-and-a-drug-smuggler-super-furry-animals-revisit-making-their-debut-fuzzy-logic*

278. David Bennun, 'Fur Out!', *Fuzzy Logic* album review, *Melody Maker*, 11 May 1996

279. Simon Williams, 'Caught By the Fuzzy', *Fuzzy Logic* album review, *NME*, 18 May 1996

280. Paula Shutkever, 'Song of the Month: "The Man Don't Give a Fuck" by Super Furry Animals', *Vox*, 7 December 1996

281. David Owens, 'The True Story Behind Super Furry Animals' "The Man Don't Give a Fuck"', *Nation.Cymru*, 2 December 2021, *www.nation.cymru/culture/the-true-story-behind-super-furry-animals-the-man-dont-give-a-fck/*

282. 'The Man Don't Give a Fuck' single review, *NME*, 1996

283. Ric Rawlins, *Rise of the Super Furry Animals*, The Friday Project, 2015

284. John Harris, 'Sleep Smell of Success', *NME*, 24 September 1994

285. John Harris, 'Sleep Smell of Success', *NME*, 24 September 1994

286. John Harris, sleeve notes for *Catatonia: Greatest Hits*, WEA Records: Blanco y Negro, released 15 October 2002

287. Liz Catermole, live review for Catatonia's gig at London King Cross' Splash Club (aka Water Rats) on 25 February 1995, *Heaven Up Here* fanzine, 1995

288. David Owens, *Cerys, Catatonia and the Rise of Welsh Pop*, Ebury Press, 2000

289. David Owens, *Cerys, Catatonia and the Rise of Welsh Pop*, Ebury Press, 2000

290. Stephen Dalton, *Way Beyond Blue* album review, *NME*, 1996

291. Stephen Dalton, *Way Beyond Blue* album review, *NME*, 1996

292. Stephen Dalton, *Way Beyond Blue* album review, *NME*, 1996

293. Mark Jenkins, 'Welsh Band Catatonia: Internationalists Abroad', *The Washington Post*, 9 August 1998 *www.washingtonpost.com/archive/lifestyle/style/1998/08/09/welsh-band-catatonia-internationalists-abroad/92125089-54b7-4064-b831-50168766bf79/*

294. Stephen Dalton, *Way Beyond Blue* album review, *NME*, 1996

295. John Harris, sleeve notes for *Catatonia: Greatest Hits*, WEA Records: Blanco y Negro, released 15 October 2002

296. Karl Hyde, *I Am Dogboy: The Underworld Diaries*, Faber & Faber, 2016

297. Hugh Montgomery, 'How We Met: Rick Smith and Karl Hyde', *The Independent*, 14 November 2010, *www.independent.co.uk/news/people/profiles/how-we-met-rick-smith-amp-karl-hyde-2130458.html*

298. David Owens, 'The Welsh Rooftop Gig by the Band That Would Become Underworld', *Nation.Cymru*, 20 February 2022, *www.nation.cymru/culture/the-welsh-rooftop-gig-by-the-band-that-would-become-underworld/*

299. 'The Modern Heartbeat that Pulses Through *T2 Trainspotting*', ABC Australia, 21 February 2021, *www.abc.net.au/listen/doublej/music-reads/features/the-modern-heartbeat-that-pulses-through-t2-trainspotting/10268506*

300. Dorian Lynskey and Dave Simpson, "Born Slippy" Was a Greyhound We Bet On, *The Guardian*, 24 February 2006, *www.theguardian.com/music/2006/feb/24/popandrock2*

301. Dorian Lynskey and Dave Simpson, "Born Slippy" Was a Greyhound We Bet On, *The Guardian*, 24 February 2006, *www.theguardian.com/music/2006/feb/24/popandrock2*

302. '60–51 | The Greatest Welsh Albums of All Time: Underworld – *Second Toughest In the Infants* (60)', *Wales Arts Review*, 5 November 2021, *www.walesartsreview.org/60-51-the-greatest-welsh-albums-of-all-time/*

303. David Owens, 'The Welsh Rooftop Gig by the Band That Would Become Underworld', *Nation.Cymru*, 20 February 2022, *www.nation.cymru/culture/the-welsh-rooftop-gig-by-the-band-that-would-become-underworld/*

304. James McLaren, 'Donna Lewis Reflects on 15 Years Since "I Love You Always Forever"', BBC Wales Music, 13 September 2011, *www.bbc.co.uk/blogs/walesmusic/2011/09/donna-lewis-interview.shtml*

305. James McLaren, 'Donna Lewis Reflects on 15 Years Since "I Love You Always Forever"', BBC Wales Music, 13 September 2011, *www.bbc.co.uk/blogs/walesmusic/2011/09/donna-lewis-interview.shtml*

306. James McLaren, 'Donna Lewis Reflects on 15 Years Since "I Love You Always Forever"', BBC Wales Music, 13 September 2011, *www.bbc.co.uk/blogs/walesmusic/2011/09/donna-lewis-interview.shtml*

307. 'Sharp End: The Night Wales Changed', *Sharp End*, ITV Wales, originally broadcast 9 November 2022, *www.itv.com/walesprogrammes/articles/sharp-end-the-night-wales-changed*

308. 'Sharp End: The Night Wales Changed', *Sharp End*, ITV Wales, originally broadcast 9 November 2022, *www.itv.com/walesprogrammes/articles/sharp-end-the-night-wales-changed*

309. 'Sharp End: The Night Wales Changed', *Sharp End*, ITV Wales, originally broadcast 9 November 2022, *www.itv.com/walesprogrammes/articles/sharp-end-the-night-wales-changed*

310. 'Sharp End: The Night Wales Changed', *Sharp End*, ITV Wales, originally broadcast 9 November 2022, *www.itv.com/walesprogrammes/articles/sharp-end-the-night-wales-changed*

311. 'Sharp End: The Night Wales Changed', *Sharp End*, ITV Wales, originally broadcast 9 November 2022, *www.itv.com/walesprogrammes/articles/sharp-end-the-night-wales-changed*

312. Richard King, *Brittle with Relics: A History of Wales, 1962–97*, Faber & Faber, 2022

313. Neil Mason, 'Catatonia: New Adventures in Sci-Fi', *Melody Maker*, 24 January 1998

314. David Owens, *Cerys, Catatonia and the Rise of Welsh Pop*, Ebury Press, 2000

315. Interview with the author of this book

316. Martin Johnes, *Wales Since 1939*, Manchester University Press, 2012

317. *NME* quote included in Link2Wales biography, *www.link2wales.co.uk/south-wales-a-m/south-wales-d/*

318. Mark Sutherland, *Dial M for Merthyr* album review, *NME*, 1997

319. Mark Sutherland, *Dial M for Merthyr* album review, *NME*, 1997

ENDNOTES

320. Dylan Moore, 'Dial M for Merthyr: Classic Welsh Albums', *Wales Arts Review*, 11 January 2013, *www.walesartsreview.org/classic-albums-dial-m-for-merthyr-2/*

321. Danny O'Connor, *Stereophonics: Just Enough Evidence to Print*, Virgin, 2001

322. Brian Wright, *To Hell and Back with Catatonia*, Firefly Publishing, 2001

323. 'Tystion Biography', BBC Wales Music, *www.bbc.co.uk/wales/music/sites/tystion/pages/biography.shtml*

324. Sarah Hill, *'Blerwytirhwng?' The Place of Welsh Pop Music*, Routledge, 2007

325. 'Tystion Biography', BBC Wales Music, *www.bbc.co.uk/wales/music/sites/tystion/pages/biography.shtml*

326. Sarah Hill, *'Blerwytirhwng?' The Place of Welsh Pop Music*, Routledge, 2007

327. 'Y Byd Hip Hop vs Y Byd Cymraeg' was featured on Tystion's album *Hen Gelwydd Prydain Newydd*, Ankstmusik, 2000

328. 'Tystion Biography', BBC Wales Music, *www.bbc.co.uk/wales/music/sites/tystion/pages/biography.shtml*

329. Sarah Hill, *'Blerwytirhwng?' The Place of Welsh Pop Music*, Routledge, 2007

330. Stuart Bailie, 'Feeder: Sixth Form Poetry? We Didn't Even Get to the Sixth Form!' *NME*, 9 October 1999

331. Stuart Bailie, 'Feeder: Sixth Form Poetry? We Didn't Even Get to the Sixth Form!' NME, 9 October 1999

332. Stuart Bailie, 'Feeder: Sixth Form Poetry? We Didn't Even Get to the Sixth Form!' NME, 9 October 1999

333. Gary Ryan, 'Does Rock'n'Roll Kill Braincells?!: Grant Nicholas, Feeder', NME.com, 16 September 2019, *www.nme.com/features/music-interviews/rock-n-roll-kill-braincells-grant-nicholas-feeder-2547580*

334. Stephen Hill, 'Feeder's *Polythene* at 25: How "The British Smashing Pumpkins" made *Metal Hammer's* Album of 1997', *Metal Hammer*, *www.loudersound.com/features/feeders-polythene-at-25-how-the-british-smashing-pumpkins-made-metal-hammers-album-of-1997*

335. Stephen Hill, 'Feeder's *Polythene* at 25: How "The British Smashing Pumpkins" made *Metal Hammer's* Album of 1997', *Metal Hammer*, *www.loudersound.com/features/feeders-polythene-at-25-how-the-british-smashing-pumpkins-made-metal-hammers-album-of-1997*

336. Interview with Grant Nicholas, *Kerrang!*, 21 June 2008

337. *Amber Gambler* EP review, *Melody Maker*, 1996

338. Martyn Coppack, 'Wizards and Lizards: Gorky's Zygotic Mynci – Welsh Pop's Other Great Explorers,' *Shindig! Issue 92*, June 2019

339. Stewart Lee, *Sunday Times*, 9 June 1996, *www.stewartlee.co.uk/written_for_money/gorkys-zygotic-mynci/*

340. Elis James and John Robins, *Elis and John Present the Holy Vible: The Book the Bible Could Have Been*, Trapeze, 2018

341. Jake Kennedy, '*Patio/Tatay/Bwyd Time*: Gorky's Zygotic Mynci', review of Gorky's first three albums reissued, *Record Collector*, 28 August 2007, *www.recordcollectormag.com/reviews/album/patio-tatay-bwyd-time*

342. John Robinson, 'Simian Says!', *NME*, 22 March 1997

343. Joel Dear, 'From the Crate: Gorky's Zygotic Mynci – *Barafundle*', *God Is in the TV*, 17 April 2017, *www.godisinthetvzine.co.uk/2017/04/17/crate-gorkys-zygotic-mynci-barafundle/*

344. Victoria Segal, 'Barafundle of Joy', *Melody Maker*, 22 March 1997

345. '20–11 | The Greatest Welsh Albums of All Time': Gorky's Zygotic Mynci – *Barafundle* (11)', *Wales Arts Review,* 3 December 2021, *www.walesartsreview.org/20-11-the-greatest-*

welsh-albums-of-all-time/

346. Ric Rawlins, *Rise of the Super Furry Animals*, The Friday Project, 2015

347. Ric Rawlins, *Rise of the Super Furry Animals*, The Friday Project, 2015

348. Ben Thompson, 'Super Furry Animals', *Mojo*, August 1997

349. Ric Rawlins, *Rise of the Super Furry Animals*, The Friday Project, 2015

350. Tom Cox, 'Super Furry Animals: A Furry Good Year', *The Guardian*, 22 May 1998

351. Tom Cox, 'Super Furry Animals: A Furry Good Year', *The Guardian*, 22 May 1998

352. Dave Simpson, 'Valley Cats!', *Melody Maker*, 10 May 1997

353. Sarah Hill, *'Blerwytirhwng?' The Place of Welsh Pop Music*, Routledge, 2007

354. Tom Doyle, 'The Men Do Give a Fuck', *Select*, December 1998

355. John Lavin, 'Great Welsh Albums: *Radiator* by Super Furry Animals', *Wales Arts Review*, 14 April 2019, *www.walesartsreview.org/classic-welsh-albums-radiator-by-super-furry-animals/*

356. Simon Price, sleeve notes for the compilation album *Zoom! The Best of Super Furry Animals (1995–2016)*, BMG, released 2016

357. Dave Simpson, 'Valley Cats!', *Melody Maker*, 10 May 1997

358. Louis Pattison, 'Waxing Lyrical: Gruff Rhys, Super Furry Animals', *The Guardian*, 24 February 2011

359. Marc Burrows, 'Anger Through Grace: Nicky Wire's Favourite Albums', *The Quietus*, 26 September 2013, *www.thequietus.com/articles/13448-nicky-wire-manic-street-preachers-favourite-albums?page=3*

360. Simon Price, sleeve notes for the compilation album *Zoom! The Best of Super Furry Animals (1995–2016)*, BMG, released 2016

361. Everett True, 'Radiator: Every Bedroom Should Have One!', *Melody Maker*, 1997

362. Kevin E. G. Perry, 'Stereophonics' Kelly Jones: "I Stand By What We Did"', *The Independent*, 18 February 2022, *www.independent.co.uk/arts-entertainment/music/features/sterephonics-interview-kelly-jones-b2017275.html*

363. An anecdote Kelly Jones related each night of his *Don't Let the Devil Take Another Day* solo tour in 2019

364. Brian Wright, *To Hell and Back with Catatonia*, Firefly Publishing, 2001

365. Kelly Jones interview with Chris Moyles, Radio X, originally broadcast 12 October 2017, *www.x.com/RadioX/status/918400396925767680*

366. Danny O'Connor, *Stereophonics: Just Enough Evidence to Print*, Virgin, 2001

367. Danny O'Connor, *Stereophonics: Just Enough Evidence to Print*, Virgin, 2001

368. Danny O'Connor, *Stereophonics: Just Enough Evidence to Print*, Virgin, 2001

369. Neil Mason, 'Stereophonics: Be Herr Now!', *Melody Maker*, 14 February 1998

370. Paul Elliott, 'Stereophonics: Under Pressure', *Q*, August 2003

371. *Stereophonics: The Road Up Is the Worst* documentary, BBC2 Wales, 1998

372. Danny O'Connor, *Stereophonics: Just Enough Evidence to Print*, Virgin, 2001

373. Danny O'Connor, *Stereophonics: Just Enough Evidence to Print*, Virgin, 2001

374. Catatonia's song 'International Velvet' was featured on the album (also called) *International Velvet*, WEA Records: Blanco y Negro, released 2 February 1998

375. David Quantick, 'Catatonia: Bubbling Under', live review of Catatonia's gig at Tenby's De Valence Pavilion on 7 January 1998, *Q*, March 1998

376. David Quantick, 'Catatonia: Bubbling Under', live review of Catatonia's gig at Tenby's De Valence Pavilion on 7 January 1998, *Q*, March 1998

377. Album review of Catatonia's *International Velvet*, *Welsh Bands Weekly*, 1998

378. Barbara Ellen, 'Catatonia: Welsh Rabbit', *The Observer*, 22 March 1998

ENDNOTES

379. Steven Wells, 'Catatonia: Feds and Rockers!', *NME*, 7 February 1998

380. Barbara Ellen, 'Catatonia: Welsh Rabbit', *The Observer*, 22 March 1998

381. Caroline Sullivan, 'Cerys and the Cool Cymru Catablokes: Catatonia, Brixton Academy', *The Guardian*, 23 March 1999

382. 'I Am the Mob' single, WEA Records: Blanco y Negro, released 6 October 1997

383. Brian Wright, *To Hell and Back with Catatonia*, Firefly Publishing, 2001

384. Robin Bresnark, 'Catatonia: The Hit-Man and Her', *Melody Maker*, 11 October 1997

385. David Owens, *Cerys, Catatonia and the Rise of Welsh Pop*, Ebury, 2000

386. Brian Wright, *To Hell and Back with Catatonia*, Firefly Publishing, 2001

387. Brian Wright, *To Hell and Back with Catatonia*, Firefly Publishing, 2001

388. Brian Wright, *To Hell and Back with Catatonia*, Firefly Publishing, 2001

389. Brian Wright, *To Hell and Back with Catatonia*, Firefly Publishing, 2001

390. 'Lee's Parents Attack Road Rage Song', *The Birmingham Post*, 6 April 1998

391. Maureen Harvey, *Pure Evil: How Tracie Andrews Murdered My Son, Deceived the Nation and Sentenced Me to a Life of Pain and Misery*, John Blake, 2008

392. John Harris, sleeve notes for *Catatonia: Greatest Hits*, WEA Records: Blanco y Negro, released 15 October 2002

393. Interview with the author of this book

394. Everett True, *Rumours and Curses* album review, *Melody Maker*, 1998

395. 'Achilles Heel' was featured on Melys's album *Rumours and Curses*, Pinnacle, released 15 June 1998

396. Lockdown Session Twitter Listening Party for Melys's *Rumours and Curses*, *Welsh Music Podcast*, 26 April 2020, *www.x.com/welshmusicpod/status/1254485391039696896?s=20*

397. Lockdown Session Twitter Listening Party for Melys's *Rumours and Curses*, *Welsh Music Podcast*, 26 April 2020, *www.x.com/welshmusicpod/status/1254485391039696896?s=20*

398. Interview with the author of this book

399. Steven Wells, 'Catatonia: Feds and Rockers!', *NME*, 7 February 1998

400. Interview with the author of this book

401. *The Slate: Stereophonics – The Great Escape*, BBC Wales, 1997

402. *The Slate: Stereophonics – The Great Escape*, BBC Wales, 1997

403. 'Kelly's Zeroes', *NME*, 9 March 1999, *www.nme.com/news/music/stereophonics-221-1391434*

404. Ted Kessler, 'We Do Give a Puck!', *NME*, 16 May 1998

405. Ted Kessler, 'We Do Give a Puck!', *NME*, 16 May 1998

406. Stevie Chick, 'Creature Comforts', live review of Super Furry Animals' gig at Manchester Academy on 16 May 1998, *Melody Maker*, 23 May 1998

407. Ted Kessler, 'We Do Give a Puck!', *NME*, 16 May 1998

408. Tom Cox, 'Super Furry Animals: A Furry Good Year', *The Guardian*, 22 May 1998

409. Ted Kessler, 'We Do Give a Puck!', *NME*, 16 May 1998

410. Ric Rawlins, *Rise of the Super Furry Animals*, The Friday Project, 2015

411. Ric Rawlins, *Rise of the Super Furry Animals*, The Friday Project, 2015

412. Ric Rawlins, *Rise of the Super Furry Animals*, The Friday Project, 2015

413. Sarah Hill, *'Blerwytirhwng?' The Place of Welsh Pop Music*, Routledge, *2007*

414. David Owens, 'Wales' Rock'n'Roll Dairy Farm Where Queen, Oasis, Bowie Coldplay and Led Zeppelin Came to Play', WalesOnline, 18 July 2020, *www.walesonline.co.uk/whats-on/music-nightlife-news/wales-rock-roll-dairy-farm-18606578*

415. Simon Price, 'The Super Furry Animals: When Paul McCartney Played the Celery', *The*

Independent, 23 July 2001, *www.independent.co.uk/arts-entertainment/music/features/the-super-furry-animals-when-paul-mccartney-played-the-celery-9273739.html*

416. Elis James and John Robins, *Elis and John Present the Holy Vible: The Book the Bible Could Have Been*, Trapeze, 2018

417. Martyn Coppack, 'Wizards and Lizards: Gorky's Zygotic Mynci – Welsh Pop's Other Great Explorers', *Shindig!* June 2019, *Issue 92*, June 2019

418.'My Favourite Record: Bill Ryder-Jones on *Gorky 5* by Gorky's Zygotic Mynci', *Nothing But Hope and Passion*, 19 November 2015, *www.nbhap.com/sounds/bill-ryder-jones-gorky-5-gorkys-zygotic-mynci*

419. Phil Sutcliffe, live review of the Manics' gig at Chester's Northgate Arena on 16 September 1998, *Q*, 1998

420. *A Design for Life: The Story of Manic Street Preachers*, BBC Radio 2 documentary, originally broadcast 12 October 2002

421. Andrew Trendell, 'Manic Street Preachers Look Back on "If You Tolerate This Your Children Will Be Next" on its 20th Anniversary', 24 August 2018, *www.nme.com/news/music/manic-street-preachers-if-you-tolerate-this-your-children-will-be-next-lyrics-meaning-video-song-stories-interview-2370143*

422. Philip Wilding, 'The Manic Street Preachers: Their Best Songs in Their Own Words', loudersound.com, 23 March 2022, *www.loudersound.com/features/the-manic-street-preachers-their-best-songs-in-their-own-words#:~:text=I%20can%20remember%20our%20producer,off.%E2%80%9D%20And%20I%20did*

423. *A Design for Life: The Story of Manic Street Preachers*, BBC Radio 2 documentary, originally broadcast 12 October 2002

424. *A Design for Life: The Story of Manic Street Preachers*, BBC Radio 2 documentary, originally broadcast 12 October 2002

425. *Carling Homecoming: Manic Street Preachers*, Series 1: Episode 3, Channel 4, originally broadcast 18 November 2002

426. Sam Jones, 'Manics' Tribute to International Brigades Crops Up on BNP Website', *The Guardian*, 28 March 2009, *www.theguardian.com/music/2009/mar/28/manic-street-preachers-bnp-website#:~:text=Simon%20Darby%2C%20a%20spokesman%20for,by%20BNP%20leaders%2C%20he%20said*

427. Interview with *The Quietus* Editor John Doran on *British Masters*, Noisey, Series 1: Episode 9, 10 September 2013, *www.thequietus.com/articles/13313-nicky-wire-manic-street-preachers-on-noisey-british-masters*

428. Sylvia Patterson, 'Despair. Inspiration. Happiness. Despair. Sport. That's the Crux of It', *NME*, 1 August 1998

429. Keith Cameron, 'Sooth Park', *This Is My Truth Tell Me Yours* album review, *NME*, 12 September 1998

430. David Bennun, 'All that Glitters…', *Melody Maker*, 29 January 1994

431. Caroline Sullivan, 'Nicky Wire Reflects on the Musical Tradition of His Home Country: Wales', *The Guardian*, 15 February 2015, *www.theguardian.com/music/2008/feb/15/popandrock4*

432. David Evans, *33 ⅓: Manic Street Preachers – The Holy Bible*, Bloomsbury, 2019

433. *Remembering Tryweryn*, BBC Radio 4 documentary, originally broadcast 6 February 2020

434. Martin Power, *Nailed to History: The Story of Manic Street Preachers*, Omnibus Press, 2010

435. Henry Yates, 'James Dean Bradfield: The Manic Street Preachers Frontman on Fame, Hecklers and Getting Beaten to UK No. 1 by the "fucking *Greatest Showman*…"', *Classic Rock*, December 2018

436. Keith Cameron, 'Sooth Park', *This Is My Truth Tell Me Yours* album review, *NME*, 12 September 1998

437. David Stubbs, *This Is My Truth Tell Me Yours* album review, *Uncut*, October 1998

438. Simon Price, *Everything (A Book About Manic Street Preachers)*, Virgin, 1999

439. David Stubbs, *This Is My Truth Tell Me Yours* album review, *Uncut*, October 1998

440. *Carling Homecoming: Manic Street Preachers*, Series 1: Episode 3, Channel 4, originally broadcast 18 November 2002

441. Alun Hamnett, 'Is Heaven a Place Where Nothing Ever Happens?', *Record Collector Presents…Manic Street Preachers*, 7 October 2021

442. 'The Top 10 Welsh Horror Films', *Darklands* (10), WalesOnline, 30 October 2010, www.walesonline.co.uk/lifestyle/showbiz/the-top10-welsh-horror-films-1894188

443. Caroline Sullivan, 'Catatonia: Glowing in the Dark', Margam Park live review, *The Guardian*, 31 May 1999

444. John Harris, sleeve notes for *Catatonia: Greatest Hits*, WEA Records: Blanco y Negro, released 15 October 2002

445. Brian Wright, *To Hell and Back with Catatonia*, Firefly Publishing, 2001

446. Brian Wright, *To Hell and Back with Catatonia*, Firefly Publishing, 2001

447. Live review of Catatonia's gig at Margam Park on 29 May 1999, *Select*, 1999

448. David Owens, Cerys, *Catatonia and the Rise of Welsh Pop*, Ebury Press, 2000

449. Katharine Viner, 'Alive Outside the M25', *The Guardian*, 5 March 1999

450. Live review of Catatonia's gig at Margam Park on 29 May 1999, *Select*, 1999

451. *The Edge* fanzine quoted in *David Owens, Cerys, Catatonia and the Rise of Welsh Pop*, Ebury, 2000

452. Cayte Williams, 'Just Call Me Duchess', *The Independent*, 17 May 1998, *www.independent.co.uk/life-style/just-call-me-duchess-1159492.html*

453. Steven Wells, 'Feds and Rockers!' *NME*, 7 February 1998

454. David Owens, Cerys, *Catatonia and the Rise of Welsh Pop*, Ebury Press, 2000

455. Mark Beaumont, 'Strings Attached', *Equally Cursed and Blessed* album review, *NME*, 8 April 1999

456. *Melody Maker* quoted in *Brian Wright, To Hell and Back with Catatonia*, Firefly Publishing, 2001

457. *Maxim* quoted in *Brian Wright, To Hell and Back with Catatonia*, Firefly Publishing, 2001

458. Danny O'Connor, *Stereophonics: Just Enough Evidence to Print*, Virgin, 2001

459. Danny O'Connor, *Stereophonics: Just Enough Evidence to Print*, Virgin, 2001

460. Danny O'Connor, *Stereophonics: Just Enough Evidence to Print*, Virgin, 2001

461. Dan Gennoe, 'The Stereophonics Interview', *Making Music*, 1998

462. Danny O'Connor, *Stereophonics: Just Enough Evidence to Print*, Virgin, 2001

463. Danny O'Connor, *Stereophonics: Just Enough Evidence to Print*, Virgin, 2001

464. Barry Walters, *Performance and Cocktails* album review, *Rolling Stone: Issue 822*, 30 September 1999, *https://web.archive.org/web/20090807064417/http://www.rollingstone.com/artists/stereophonics/albums/album/237354/review/5942086/performance__cocktails*

465. Johnny Cigarettes, 'OK Composers: Stereophonics – *Performance and Cocktails*', *NME*, 6 March 1999

466. Neil Mason, 'Stereophonics: Be Herr Now!', *Melody Maker*, 14 February 1998

467. Danny O'Connor, *Stereophonics: Just Enough Evidence to Print*, Virgin, 2001

468. Danny O'Connor, *Stereophonics: Just Enough Evidence to Print*, Virgin, 2001

469. Nathan Bevan, 'Stereophonics' Iconic Gig at Morfa Stadium Remembered', WalesOnline,

11 December 2018, *www.walesonline.co.uk/whats-on/whats-on-news/stereophonics-iconic-gig-morfa-stadium-15534311*

470. Nathan Bevan, 'Stereophonics' Iconic Gig at Morfa Stadium Remembered', WalesOnline, 11 December 2018, *www.walesonline.co.uk/whats-on/whats-on-news/stereophonics-iconic-gig-morfa-stadium-15534311*

471. Angst letters page, *NME*, 21 August 1999

472. Angst letters page, *NME*, 21 August 1999

473. Danny O'Connor, *Stereophonics: Just Enough Evidence to Print*, Virgin, 2001

474. Danny O'Connor, *Stereophonics: Just Enough Evidence to Print*, Virgin, 2001

475. James Oldham quoted in Angst letters page, *NME*, 21 August 1999

476. Danny O'Connor, *Stereophonics: Just Enough Evidence to Print*, Virgin, 2001

477. *Western Mail*, 28 August 1999

478. 'Welsh Pride or Fascism?', *NME*, 11 September 1999

479. Ric Rawlins, *Rise of the Super Furry Animals*, The Friday Project, 2015

480. Ric Rawlins, *Rise of the Super Furry Animals*, The Friday Project, 2015

481. Marc Hogan, '*Fuzzy Logic/Radiator/Out Spaced/Guerilla/Mwng*', review of reissued albums, *Pitchfork*, 6 June 2005, *www.pitchfork.com/reviews/albums/11835-fuzzy-logic-radiator-out-spaced-guerilla-mwng/*

482. Erik Himmelsbach, *Guerrilla* album review, *Spin*, September 1999, *https://books.google.co.uk/books?id=bGjsvmNt8UgC&pg=PA187&redir_esc=y#v=onepage&q&f=false*

483. Ric Rawlins, *Rise of the Super Furry Animals*, The Friday Project, 2015

484. Gruff Rhys interview with Shane Brown and Kari Winn, Excellent Online, 1 September 1999, *https://web.archive.org/web/20110710211502/http://www.excellentonline.com/story/super-furry-animals-interview-468*

485. Sylvia Patterson, 'Tripping the Lite Fantastic!', *NME*, 22 May 1999

486. Gruff Rhys interview with Shane Brown and Kari Winn, Excellent Online, 1 September 1999, *https://web.archive.org/web/20110710211502/http://www.excellentonline.com/story/super-furry-animals-interview-468*

487. Ric Rawlins, *Rise of the Super Furry Animals*, The Friday Project, 2015

488. 'Fire in My Heart' single review, *Melody Maker*, 7 August 1999

489. Robin Bresnark, 'Super Furry Animals: I Like the Idea of Creating Cultural Havoc', *Melody Maker*, 19 January 2000

490. Robin Bresnark, 'Super Furry Animals: I Like the Idea of Creating Cultural Havoc', *Melody Maker*, 19 January 2000

491. Mark Beaumont, 'Underground Control', *Melody Maker*, 12 June 1999

492. Andrew Male, 'The Wind of Strange', *Select*, June 1999

493. Neil Kulkarni, 'Guerrilla: A Maximum High', *Melody Maker*, 5 June 1999

494. 'Super Furry Animals Strike Kit Deal', BBC Wales, 9 September 1999, *http://news.bbc.co.uk/1/hi/wales/443338.stm*

495. 'SFA: CCFC', NME.com, 13 September 1999, *www.nme.com/news/music/super-furry-animals-168-1397124*

496. Kate Hodges, 'Life Thru a Lens', *Kerrang!*, 31 August 1999

497. Stuart Bailie, 'Feeder: Sixth Form Poetry? We Didn't Even Get to the Sixth Form!' *NME*, 9 October 1999

498. Kate Hodges, 'Life Thru a Lens', *Kerrang!*, 31 August 1999

499. Kate Hodges, 'Life Thru a Lens', *Kerrang!*, 31 August 1999

500. Kate Hodges, 'Life Thru a Lens', *Kerrang!*, 31 August 1999

ENDNOTES

501. 'Gorky's Zygotic Mynci: Turning Over a New Leaf', *Exclaim Magazine*, 1 February 2000

502. Martyn Coppack, 'Wizards and Lizards: Gorky's Zygotic Mynci – Welsh Pop's Other Great Explorers,' *Shindig! Issue 92*, June 2019

503. Martyn Coppack, 'Wizards and Lizards: Gorky's Zygotic Mynci – Welsh Pop's Other Great Explorers,' *Shindig! Issue 92*, June 2019

504. Mark Jenkins, 'Gorky's Relaxed Vibe', *The Washington Post*, 9 December 1999, *www. washingtonpost.com/archive/lifestyle/1999/12/10/gorkys-relaxed-vibe/ce3b7adf-2789-4243-aff1-2e6ad0a23a39/*

505. Jim Wirth, *Spanish Dance Troupe* album review, *NME*, 27 November 1999, *https://web. archive.org/web/19991127224831/http://www.nme.com/reviews/reviews/19991007121836.html*

506. 'Charlotte Church: Biography', BBC Wales Music, 3 July 2009, *https://www.bbc.co.uk/wales/music/sites/charlotte-church/*

507. 'Charlotte Church: Biography', BBC Wales Music, 3 July 2009, *www.bbc.co.uk/wales/music/sites/charlotte-church/pages/biography.shtml*

508. 'The Words Are Coming', Nicky Wire foreword to Patrick Jones's *Fuse: Selected Works*, Parthian, 2001

509. Mick Middles, *Manic Street Preachers: A Biography*, Omnibus, 1999

510. Caroline Sullivan, 'Everyone Must Go,' *The Guardian*, 25 February 1999, *www.theguardian. com/theguardian/1999/feb/25/features11.g2*

511. Martin Chapman, *Socialist Review*, April 1999, *www.repeatfanzine.co.uk/archive/everything%20must%20go%201999.htm*

512. Martin Chapman, *Socialist Review*, April 1999, *www.repeatfanzine.co.uk/archive/everything%20must%20go%201999.htm*

513. Richard King, *Brittle with Relics: A History of Wales, 1962–97*, Faber & Faber, 2022

514. Caroline Sullivan, 'Everyone Must Go,' *The Guardian*, 25 February 1999, *www.theguardian. com/theguardian/1999/feb/25/features11.g2*

515. John Robb, *The Nineties: What the F**k Was That All About?*, Ebury, 1999

516. Tom Jones, *Over the Top and Back: The Autobiography*, Penguin, 2016

517. *Do You Love Us? A Podcast About Manic Street Preachers*, Series 1: Episode 39, 23 November 2020

518. *Tom Jones at 70*, BBC1 Wales, originally broadcast 4 July 2010

519. Tom Jones, *Over the Top and Back: The Autobiography*, Penguin, 2016

520. Tom Jones, *Over the Top and Back: The Autobiography*, Penguin, 2016

521. Peter Doggett, sleeve notes for *The Definitive Tom Jones 1964–2002*, Universal & Decca, 2003

522. Tim Mitchell, *Sedition and Alchemy: A Biography of John Cale*, Peter Owen, 2001

523. Tim Mitchell, *Sedition and Alchemy: A Biography of John Cale*, Peter Owen, 2001

524. *The Making of Camgymeriad Gwych*, S4C, originally broadcast in 2000

525. Ric Rawlins, *Rise of the Super Furry Animals*, The Friday Project, 2015

526. John Harris, 'Nicky Wire: British Music's Moral Conscience', *Select*, January 1999

527. *Leaving the 20th Century: Manic Street Preachers at Cardiff Millenium Stadium 1999/2000*, Sony Music, 2000

528. Pat Long, 'We Only Want to Get Drunk,' *Select*, December 1999

529. *Leaving the 20th Century: Manic Street Preachers at Cardiff Millenium Stadium 1999/2000*, Sony Music, 2000

530. Steven Wells, 'Banging on About the Manics in the Millennium', *NME*, 23 October 1999

531. Nicky Wire's onstage remark following 'Of Walking Abortion', Manic Millennium gig, Millennium Stadium, 31 December 1999

532. Interview with Rhys Mwyn, *Welsh Music Podcast*, Episode 9, 21 February 2020

533. Neil Thomson, 'Boss Hogmanay', live review of Manic Millennium at Cardiff's Millennium Stadium on 31 December 1999/1 January 2000, *NME*, 15 January 2000

534. Martin Power, *Nailed to History: The Story of Manic Street Preachers*, Omnibus, 2010

535. Neil Thomson, 'Boss Hogmanay', live review of Manic Millennium at Cardiff's Millennium Stadium on 31 December 1999/1 January 2000, *NME*, 15 January 2000

536. Robin Bresnark, *Melody Maker*, 19 January 2000

537. Ric Rawlins, *Rise of the Super Furry Animals*, The Friday Project, 2015

538. Ric Rawlins, *Rise of the Super Furry Animals*, The Friday Project, 2015

539. 'Super Furry Animals – *Mwng*: Track by Track', BBC Wales Music, 2000, *www.bbc.co.uk/wales/music/sites/super-furry-animals/pages/mwng.shtml*

540. Ric Rawlins, *Rise of the Super Furry Animals*, The Friday Project, 2015

541. Twentieth anniversary special episode for *Mwng* by Super Furry Animals, *Welsh Music Podcast*, 15 May 2020

542. Ric Rawlins, *Rise of the Super Furry Animals*, The Friday Project, 2015

543. 'Super Furry Animals – *Mwng*: Track by Track', BBC Wales Music, 2000, *www.bbc.co.uk/wales/music/sites/super-furry-animals/pages/mwng.shtml*

544. Twentieth anniversary special episode for *Mwng* by Super Furry Animals, *Welsh Music Podcast*, 15 May 2020

545. Ric Rawlins, 'Super Furry Animals: The Making of *Mwng*', *Drowned in Sound*, 7 May 2015, *www.drownedinsound.com/in_depth/4148964-super-furry-animals--the-making-of-mwng*

546. Ric Rawlins, *Rise of the Super Furry Animals*, The Friday Project, 2015

547. Twentieth anniversary special episode for *Mwng* by Super Furry Animals, *Welsh Music Podcast*, 15 May 2020

548. 'Super Furry Animals – *Mwng*: Track by Track', BBC Wales Music, 2000, *www.bbc.co.uk/wales/music/sites/super-furry-animals/pages/mwng.shtml*

549. Gemma Samways, 'Vote Furry: Gruff Rhys on Politics, *Mwng* and the Future', *Drowned in Sound*, 6 May 2015, *www.drownedinsound.com/in_depth/4148963-vote-furry--gruff-rhys-on-politics-mwng-and-the-future*

550. Laura Barton, 'Super Furry Animals: "Any More Years for the Conservative Party and It's Going to Be Disastrous"', *The Observer*, 26 April 2015, *www.theguardian.com/music/2015/apr/26/super-furry-animals-any-more-years-for-conservative-party-disastrous*

551. Twentieth anniversary special episode for *Mwng* by Super Furry Animals, *Welsh Music Podcast*, 15 May 2020

552. 2Twentieth anniversary special episode for *Mwng* by Super Furry Animals, *Welsh Music Podcast*, 15 May 2020

553. Sarah Lay, 'Super Furry Animals: Guitarist Huw Bunford Talks *Fuzzy Logic* and More', *Louder Than War*, 4 November 2016, *www.louderthanwar.com/super-furry-animals-interview/*

554. Pat Gilbert, *Mojo: Issue 79*, June 2000

555. Toby Manning, *Select: Issue 120*, June 2000

556. Craig Austin, 'Super Furry Animals Interview', *Wales Arts Review*, 3 December 2016, *www.walesartsreview.org/interview-super-furry-animals/*

557. Laura Barton, 'Super Furry Animals: "Any More Years for the Conservative Party and It's Going to Be Disastrous"', *The Observer*, 26 April 2015, *www.theguardian.com/music/2015/apr/26/super-furry-animals-any-more-years-for-conservative-party-disastrous*

558. Twentieth anniversary special episode for *Mwng* by Super Furry Animals, *Welsh Music Podcast*, 15 May 2020

559. 'Super Furry Animals – *Mwng*: Track by Track', BBC Wales Music, 2000, *www.bbc.co.uk/wales/music/sites/super-furry-animals/pages/mwng.shtml*

560. Interview with Patricia Morgan, *Welsh Music Podcast*, Episode 19, 4 February 2022

561. Sophie Williams, 'Cool Cymru 2.0? Meet the New Bands Reviving the Welsh Language', *NME*, 4 February 2022, *www.nme.com/blogs/nme-radar/cool-cymru-new-welsh-language-bands-dydd-miwsig-3152904*

562. Jude Rogers, 'The Year of the Dragon', *The Guardian*, 24 August 2007, *www.theguardian.com/music/2007/aug/24/popandrock.folk*

563. *Art of Now: Cymru Rising*, BBC Radio Wales, 13 October 2019

564. Sophie Williams, 'Cool Cymru 2.0? Meet the New Bands Reviving the Welsh Language', *NME*, 4 February 2022, *www.nme.com/blogs/nme-radar/cool-cymru-new-welsh-language-bands-dydd-miwsig-3152904*

565. Sophie Williams, 'Cool Cymru 2.0? Meet the New Bands Reviving the Welsh Language', *NME*, 4 February 2022, *www.nme.com/blogs/nme-radar/cool-cymru-new-welsh-language-bands-dydd-miwsig-3152904*

566. Martin Johnes, *Wales Since 1939*, Manchester University Press, 2012

567. Georgia Ruth, Yes Is More, *www.yesismore.cymru/artists/georgia-ruth/*

568. James McNair, 'James Dean Bradfield: Everything Must Go', *Belfast Telegraph*, 28 July 2006, *www.belfasttelegraph.co.uk/news/james-dean-bradfield-everything-must-go/28102207.html*

569. Caroline Sullivan, 'Manic Street Preachers: Nicky Wire Reflects on the Musical Tradition of His Home Country', *The Guardian*, 15 February 2008, *www.theguardian.com/music/2008/feb/15/popandrock4*